THE
STRUGGLE
FOR
ACADEMIC
DEMOCRACY

THE STRUGGLE FOR ACADEMIC DEMOCRACY

Lessons from the 1938 "Revolution" in New York's City Colleges

ABRAHAM EDEL

TEMPLE UNIVERSITY PRESS

PHILADELPHIA

Temple University Press, Philadelphia 19122
Copyright © 1990 by Temple University. All rights reserved
Published 1990
Printed in the United States of America

The paper used in this publication meets the minimum
requirements of American National Standard for Information
Sciences—Permanence of Paper for Printed Library Materials,
ANSI Z39.48-1984

Library of Congress Cataloging-in-Publication Data
Edel, Abraham, 1908–
The struggle for academic democracy : lessons from the 1938
"revolution" in New York City's colleges / Abraham Edel.
        p.   cm.
Includes bibliographical references.
ISBN 0-87722-691-1 (alk. paper)
1. Universities and colleges—United States—Administration—Case
studies. 2. Universities and colleges—New York (N.Y.)—
Administration. 3. University autonomy—United States—Case
studies. 4. University autonomy—New York (N.Y.) I. Title.
LB2341.E34 1990
378.747'1—dc20   89-27741
CIP

Contents

v

Contents

APPENDICES

Preface

THE SEEDS OF THIS BOOK were planted in 1939 when the American Federation of Teachers' national Committee on Democracy in Higher Education suggested that I prepare an account of the experiment in democratic governance at the New York city colleges. This work, scarcely begun, was interrupted by the beginning of World War II. But the materials gathered lingered deep in my files. In the 1980s, while writing *Interpreting Education*, I came of course to the problem of governance.[1] It seemed, however, too large a topic, and too connected in my mind with the concrete experiences at the city colleges during the 1930s, to be disposed of in one chapter. Moreover, I began to feel that the topic was heating up again, with the rising general concern about the state of American education. Occasional items appeared in the press about crises and problems of governance, as well as general formulations by foundations concerned with teaching. Soon it was "*déjà vu* all over again." I dug up the old files (the Appendices are documents from the 1930s) and continued the work. The interlacing of case study and theory, it is hoped, will be more illuminating than either separately. It is refreshing to be able to discuss theory with a thick slice of practice rather than work out philosophical problems at two removes from practice.

I am deeply indebted to the many who worked with me in the 1930s on the events described, particularly the members of the Educational Policies Committee of the New York College Teachers Union, a group coming from such diverse fields as philosophy, psychology, classics, religion, social theory, and others. (I do not recall any member from political science, to tell us—in the 1930s' emphasis in that discipline on power— that democracy was an idle dream.) In the recent preparation of the book, I have special thanks to friends, colleagues, and relatives who discussed the work with me and offered not only suggestions about detail but important structural ideas and vigorous criticism. My special thanks to Bernard Bellush, Jewel Bellush, Matthew Edel, Elizabeth Flower, Irving Horowitz, Naphtali Lewis, Martha Montgomery, Finbarr O'Connor, and Ralph Sleeper.

THE
STRUGGLE
FOR
ACADEMIC
DEMOCRACY

CHAPTER I

Introduction

THIS BOOK CONCERNS the philosophy of governance in higher education: the nature of governance and some forms it may take; the meaning of democracy in university governance and criteria for assessing governance systems; the underlying relevant assumptions about aims and efforts. It goes about this task in a special way. First it tells a story, set in the New York of the 1930s, where under special conditions the staffs of the city colleges became conscious of governance as a problem; it relates what they did about it, and what happened to them. The narrative is from the point of view of their growing awareness at that time and that place, and so it is set in the background of the world of the 1930s and the state of the colleges in that period. Then the account skips a half century to the present, to extract the lessons of that experience as we now can probe it. The growth of experience already moves into and better equips us for the outline of a philosophy of governance and its significance in the higher education of the contemporary world. By this procedure the outcome is not only more vivid, but gains in clarity.

The narrative itself tells of a "revolution"—for that is how it appeared at the time—which reached a climax about fifty years ago. To be exact, it was June 20, 1938, when the trustees of New York's city colleges (now the expanded City University of New York) changed the bylaws on the governance of the colleges.

3

They abolished what one member of the board had called a system of "Mussolinis and teeny-weeny Mussolinis," referring to the powers of presidents and department heads. They replaced it with a "democratic" organization. Now behind this formal act lay several years of intense and bitter struggle by the staffs and students of the colleges. It included the growth of a union, which at its height had about a thousand members from institutions of higher education in the New York area; a sit-down strike carried out by students, just as the CIO was startling the country with such tactics in the mass industries; controversy, agitation, pamphleteering, organizing. The teaching staffs were awakened and hurdled headlong into political action. Was it a successful revolution? A measure of counter-revolution followed, as such things usually go, although some gains in teacher power were lasting. In any case, with the beginning of World War II both revolution and counter-revolution became smaller episodes in the face of world-shaking events, overshadowed also by later upheavals in the educational world. The revolution in New York's city colleges could not compare to the wave of uprisings from Berkeley to Paris in the 1960s. The Rapp–Coudert investigation of the city college teachers in the New York area in the early 1940s was local compared to the nationwide McCarthyism of the 1950s. The agitation by a college teachers union was restrained compared to the teachers' strike that in a later decade established a new and very successful union of teachers in New York. With the passing of time and the crowding of the later scene, the passionate drama enacted in Manhattan and Brooklyn and Queens may even be overlooked.

Yet it is worth retelling and rethinking, for its intrinsic interest and for its pioneering significance. It was an experiment in the governance of a large-scale system of higher education. It was done as a whole, and at one blow, not in bits. It was carried through as an experiment in democracy at a time when democracy itself was being challenged by fascism, branded as inefficient, while dictatorship "got things done." It was also novel in carrying democracy beyond the general political scene into a particular social institution. And it was offered as a prescription for dealing with social, economic, and political turmoil. Much is therefore to be learned from the story: lessons about piecemeal and systematic reform, about the relation of ideas and social movements, about what is utopian and what is realistic, about human responses to institutional change. This continues to be important.

The philosophy of governance goes beyond a descriptive study of governance (a bit of which enters into our history) and the advocacy of one or another type of pattern (though my preference for the democratic will be clear enough). It involves going back of both descriptive and normative inquiries to explore the terms in which the questions are to be asked and the answers sought. It has to clarify the idea of governance itself, which is likely to be taken for granted because of familiarity with political governing. The governing system of an enterprise or an institution is usually understood as the way in which designated people set its policies and they or other designated people carry them out, that is, "administer" the institution. It is associated with a notion of authority resident in the policymakers and passed on to administrators. In the background is an assumption of definite aims or purposes that "govern" the decisions of the policymakers. A philosophy of governance has to reflect on many aspects of these complex processes. It may ask how systematic the structure of a governance system really is, where it depends on the definiteness of the aims and purposes, where the aims of education are fixed or in a process of change in the contemporary world, and what degree of conflict there is in their directions. Again, it may raise doubts about the firmness of the distinction between policy formation and administration, comparable to the many controversies that are found in moral philosophy about the separation or interrelation of ends and means. (An immediately practical consequence involved is whether a separate administrative staff involves educational dangers.) It has the task of assessing the present status of the notion of authority—the familiar inquiry in political theory concerning how authority differs from power. Even more, it raises the far-reaching question whether the notion of authority belongs to authoritarian systems before the advent of democracy, and might perhaps be overshadowed today by ideas of participation and responsibility.

On a more general level (a meta-level), a philosophy of governance has the task of suggesting how governance systems should be studied. Thus the frequent approach to governance in higher education as if it were a problem in the science of management, with competing complex models of management, needs a prior consideration of the conditions under which given models may or may not be invoked. Perhaps the model of management is applicable only under certain conditions—institutions whose aims are fairly specific and separable from means, and where there can be a fairly sharp division of powers and functions. Higher education may be more complexly interrelated, more pluralistic and less unified. Its aims may need constant refinement and clarification in the process of working with means and conditions. In brief, management models may be too bureaucratic, too simplistic and static, for higher education.

Even the political conception of governance in terms of designated rulers setting policies, and executives or administrators carrying them out, may prove too narrow for higher education. In New York, budgetary control by municipal authorities certainly had a "governing" role in the colleges, while not formally part of governance. And the establishment of a policy of open admissions (or something like it) was as good as dictated by the students and those from the Harlem community who had taken over the City College and held it (it was rumored) with the tacit threat that if they were attacked in force the college would be burned to the ground. Of course a philosophy of governance will distinguish between political rule, public pressure, and judicious compromise. In general, however, it is clear that we need sociological as well as political categories for understanding governance. To take a simple historical parallel, not much is gained for political science itself by insisting that Tammany did not govern New York, it only "bossed" the governing personnel.

The tasks of a philosophy of governance, then, are many, broad, and fundamental. This book does not attempt to present a systematic analysis for higher education. It is offered rather in the belief that the philosophical aspects have not been sufficiently treated and that the concern with governance in less than philosophical scope begs too many questions and enshrines too many local biases, social and cultural. To work toward a philosophy of governance it seemed best to present its issues and tasks in the concrete chronicle of a definite period in the history of the New York colleges, during which they went through a basic change in the system of governance. The general lessons from the analysis of that experience are presented in the last three chapters of the book.

With respect to the sources for the story of the revolution, I write as a participant, not merely as an observer. I began teaching at the City College in 1931, and so shared the experiences described. They entered deeply into the life of department and faculty, staff associations, relations with colleagues at the other municipal colleges. More directly, I was chairman of the

Educational Policies Committee of the New York College Teachers Union, which initially formulated the central program for the reorganization of governance. My sources and perspective on these events come in large measure from that work and from the records of the union. Moreover, in 1939, the American Federation of Teachers, impressed by what happened in the New York city colleges, set up a national Committee on Democracy in Higher Education, with its first task to draw the lessons of that episode for the country at large. For the first two years of that committee I also was its chairman, corresponding with active union teachers in locals throughout the country and gathering materials for the study of the New York events. The entry of the United States into World War II, as well as conflicts within the federation itself, interrupted all such plans.

A comment on the role of the union. It came to have very wide support within the colleges during the years from 1936 to 1939. It served most effectively to get the support of labor in New York for securing tenure and democratic reorganization, as well as on important grievance cases that set patterns of regulation within the colleges. The struggle for tenure, in which the union took part, had of course much wider support among the staff. Leadership in formulating the program on tenure was focused in a cross-college conference—the "Legislative Conference"—that dealt with legislative matters affecting the colleges in New York and Albany. With respect to governance, I think that the initiative of the union in formulating the program pointed the way. Given the growing dissatisfaction of the staffs and the political changes we shall examine on the New York scene, there would have been important reforms in administration at the colleges. But, after reviewing the story, I believe that without the initial union program the change would have consisted largely in replacing autocratic politically appointed presidents with more benign educationally oriented administration. (In public elementary and high schools at that time, teachers colleges were stressing better-educated and wiser administration, structured along the lines of efficient business management.) That the reforms in the New York colleges were tied to the democratic idea was the consequence of the union's campaign. What needs explaining is why it so readily caught on, not merely among the staffs but even among the majority of the trustees, and why it was on the whole accepted for a time in the community, except for the extreme political right.

In presenting the narrative, a choice had to be made between two perspectives. It could have been an account interlaced with a half century's later lessons, adjudicating at every point the significance of what was going on, the mistakes made and bold steps that brought unforeseen consequences. Or it might stay with the growing consciousness of the time, the world as people then saw it, not as later decades revised it. As indicated, I followed the second course, with perhaps occasional trespass. (This, incidentally, explains why the reader will still find gender-laden language in the first few chapters and the appendices. In the 1930s, even after the revolution, a woman would be chairman of a department.) The narrative is then the past recalled or reconstructed as of that time, postponing consideration of what might have been done instead and what was properly learned.

Separating later from then contemporary awareness is not without some difficulties. For example, the events of the 1930s were then clearly felt as revolutionary. (The dictionary includes under "revolution" not only a political upheaval, but "a radical change of circumstances or of systems.") But from a half century's later perspective it may be felt that with the vast growth of higher education some greater participation of teachers in one way or another would have been inevitable. The radical changes of 1938 thus become viewed as simply turbulent reform. (The quotation marks around *revolution* in the subtitle accommodate either view.)

To the historian such perspectival shifts with the lapse of time are an old story. Take so straightforward an episode as Caesar crossing the Rubicon, saying, "Let the die be cast." His utterance makes it a momentous event: Crossing the boundary of his province with his army was equivalent to declaring war against the Senate, a move that brought the Roman Republic to an end and created the Roman Empire. Since then, any fateful irreversible step with momentous consequences is a "crossing of the Rubicon." Historical questions, however, muddle the simple picture of Caesar's crossing. Had he already exceeded the time limits of his proconsulship? Had the Senate ended his office early, in a possibly illegal action? Thus a detailed study of a several-year period is required to assess the significance, if any, of Caesar's crossing of what today is at least often a rather small and insignificant stream. Only then can we decide whether Caesar's crossing the Rubicon was in fact what we now mean by a real "crossing of the Rubicon." Was the 1938 episode of changing governance systems in New York's city colleges a revolution? The question simply raises the curtain for the drama.

CHAPTER 2

The Temper of the Thirties

WHAT HAPPENED IN 1938 in the New York city colleges has to be understood in the light of the way people of the 1930s viewed their country and their world. The chief obstacle to our understanding is that we may read back into this earlier period much that is taken for granted today. For example, labor unionism, however presently viewed, is commonplace; in the United States of the thirties it was struggling for recognition, emerging from times when it had been regarded as a conspiracy in restraint of trade or else as anarchism or communism. Again, scientists and intellectuals were then acceptable in their own fields—scientific freedom and academic freedom were recognized as the proper outcome of a long historical enlightenment—but practical matters were better left to politicians and businessmen, who worked from experience, not theory. Even as late as the 1950s intellectuals were called "egg-heads." For teachers in the 1930s to ask for a place in the governance of their institutions was, to say the least, startling.

The 1930s have been much written about by those who lived through them, and different interpretations and evaluations have issued from the varieties of subsequent positions and reflections. They run the gamut from fond recollection to recantation. But there can be no disagreement that the root phenomena of the time were the Great Depression and the rise of fascism.

Less extensive depressions may be, to a large part of the population, a matter of statistics plus an occasional encounter with those affected. In the Great Depression there was complete and constant visibility. Farmers lost their land, and city folk suffered foreclosure on their mortgages or were evicted from their apartments when they could no longer pay the rent. In New York, on parts of Riverside Drive, one could see the roughly constructed shacks along the Hudson in which people took refuge; they were called "Hooverville." Meanwhile, on Broadway, the unemployed sold apples at street corners. Childs restaurant posted a notice, "All you can eat for 60 cents," but this was beyond the reach of a goodly part of the public. Turbulence was in the air. Farmers tried to block the auctioning of confiscated land, and in the cities neighbors would carry back into the apartments of the evicted the furniture that had been put out on the street. At New York's Union Square on May Day, time for marching was strictly rationed so that veterans, socialists, communists each had their hour, with mounted police sternly guarding against scuffles turning into riots. In Washington, when the veterans of World War I organized a "Bonus March" calling for aid, they were fired upon.

Labor organization in the early 1930s was still concentrated on skilled or craft labor. The mass industries were largely unorganized, and below both were the unemployed, who got attention only from the most radical political movements. However, the two years after the Wagner Act (1935) legitimized union organization and set up the National Labor Relations Board to enforce labor rights witnessed the rise of the Congress of Industrial Organizations, which broke away from the craft-oriented American Federation of Labor and adopted industrial organization; in 1937 it met with major successes, employing the sit-down strike as a technique. The novelty of the technique added to its effectiveness. Force could not be used against the strikers without endangering the machinery in the plant; court injunctions interpreted it as trespass, though workers claimed they were simply staying overtime. (In one injunction it was argued that labor was running a restaurant without a license!) In most instances injunctions were ignored, and the matter settled in the resolution of the strike. Unionization, with this spur, spread into white-collar fields and with growing strength into public employment.

Roosevelt's New Deal restored economic life in the United States, aided agriculture, reformed the financial system of the country, initiated massive public works, provided for increased employment in all fields from hospitals to the arts, and created systems of unemployment insurance and social security. These are familiar enough, yet it is less their specific character than their intellectual impact that entered into the temper of the thirties. The 1920s were a period of the triumph of capitalism and the belief that security and prosperity required government to stay out of business; collapse in the Great Depression and the rescue of American life through the agency of the federal government shook the hitherto unquestioning faith in the self-sufficiency of capitalism. At the very least it meant that government intervention was needed for those segments of society that business operations would not reach, and to provide for countervailing powers to control business excesses. But more was involved. It opened the possibility of considering other modes of economic organization. The Russian revolution had raised the spectre of communism; now in intellectual circles an interest arose in seeing what Marxism had to say, which might throw light on the Great Depression. Books like John Strachey's *Coming Struggle for Power* (1933) restated Marxian ideas in language less ponderous than that of dialectical materialism. Again, the British Labour Party had been gaining strength under a banner of socialism, and the writings of Harold Laski, directed to a democratic socialism as the outcome of the economic and social history of liberalism, had wide influence.[1] Many sought some intermediate social form between capitalism and socialism; Marquis Childs's popular work was called *Sweden: The Middle Way* (1936). In California, which had established the legislative mechanism of the referendum, plans for revision of the economy came in rapid succession: the Townsend plan, to distribute two hundred dollars to everyone at the beginning of the month in the form of dated money that had to be spent during the month; Upton Sinclair's EPIC (End Poverty in California) plan, for utilizing unused equipment with state aid. Significant were the large support these plans gathered and the threat of their winning a referendum if something broadly effective were not done. Even the corporate ideas of Mussolini's fascism won some attention, at least in the view that economic interests—capital, labor, consumer—might be the basis of organization, with the state as a kind of umpire. A work like Adolf Berle's and Gardiner C. Means's *Modern Corporation and Private Property* (1932) showed the changing character of capitalism itself, and toward the end of the decade the congressional study of monopoly, carried out by the Temporary National Economic Committee, showed the powers and dangers of monopoly in American life. In sum, the 1930s produced an intellectual ferment around the idea of capitalism.

The Great Depression of the 1930s was felt in its national immediacy. One knew of course that there was a depression in Europe as well; indeed, Herbert Hoover, speaking once over that fairly new instrument, the radio, explained the cause of the depression by saying that everything had been going perfectly well in America but trouble began in Europe and it spread to America! Fascism too was an international phenomenon, if not when it was localized in Mussolini's Italy, then certainly when Hitler's Nazism took power in Germany.

His aggressive intentions were stated at the outset—he had set them forth in his *Mein Kampf*—and it was impossible not to see them operative in the rapid expansion of Germany from 1933 to the beginning of World War II in 1939. Moreover, fascism was felt during the 1930s as the central threatening problem of that age. It would be a complete misunderstanding of the temper of the 1930s in the United States to miss this fact and read back into that period the view of world politics that became dominant after World War II with the cold war, after fascism was defeated. There were, it is true, both intellectual and political conceptions in the 1930s that linked communism with fascism as basic enemies of Western liberal outlooks. Some intellectual formulations combined the two into a homogenized "totalitarianism" whose essential characteristic was the fact that the state controlled the whole of the life of its people. The political view took practical form in the first of the investigative committees on un-American activities (the Dies Committee) that was set up by Congress under anti-fascist stimulation but soon devoted most of its energies to investigating communists and socialists and left-wing liberals, especially in the labor movement. It was only after the Hitler–Stalin pact of 1939 and the Russian–Finnish war that communism became tied in one bundle with fascism, and even then it was untied when America and Russia became allies in the war against the Nazis.

Doubtless the chief property of fascism that made it so central in the mind of the 1930s was its brutal irrationality. Difference of theory about economics and human nature and desirable patterns of social institutions was one thing: Such difference could be argued and made the subject of a search for evidence. A liberal and a conservative and a Marxist could carry on an argument; they could appeal to history and psychology and the evidence of the social sciences, though they might dif-

15

fer at points on how the evidence should be sought and what it pointed to, or how a synthetic view could be constructed. But the irrationality of Nazism lay beyond intellectual bounds; its racial theory violated all scientific standards, and its attacks on reason and the intellect glorified sheer action and "thinking with the blood." The remark of the Nazi youth leader Baldur von Schirach was often quoted: "When I hear the word 'culture' I reach for my gun." Communism was thus regarded as part of the Western tradition, but Nazism was outside it.[2] It was something that required sociological or historical explanation, not a viable theory of society.

Two sociological theories of fascism were current in the 1930s. One regarded it as a revolt of the lower middle class, suffering increasingly from monopoly capitalism above and organized labor below. Now both of these offered rationalistic ideologies. Capitalism justified itself by a complex intellectual system of economics, and organized labor (largely socialist in Europe) by an intellectual–historical analysis of the direction of capitalist development. With no justifying theory to support itself, the lower middle class in Germany turned against the intellect itself; it found irrationalist appeals tempting, with their adulation of action over thought. Psychologists later puzzled over this growth of irrationalism. During World War II, Erich Fromm published *Escape from Freedom* (1941), expounding the psychological basis of such an outlook; and later, Theodor Adorno and others, in their *Authoritarian Personality* (1950), explored the role of paternal authoritarianism in the traditional German family. Sigmund Freud had called attention to the unusually stringent superego in German culture with the jest that whereas in Italy a sign to warn people of a third rail would say simply "If you touch, you die," a corresponding sign in Germany would read "It is forbidden by the state to touch this rail" and then add why. In one direction or another, scholars looked for leads that would explain the retreat from reason and the acceptance of irrationality that had so startled the Western world.

The second theory of fascism, advanced by Marxian writers, stressed its economic basis. Capitalism, it was said, had grown in association with a liberal political theory, using the support of the working class to overcome the older landed classes. An intellectual liberalism, with its individualistic outlook, was congenial to small-scale enterprise so long as it had scope for development. With the growing difficulties of capitalism (due, according to Marxian theory, to its inner contradictions), it could no longer carry out its reasonable liberal promises. Growing socialism in the laboring class thus became the guardian of rationality and social welfare. The emerging monopoly–finance capitalism began instead to exploit ideas of corporate identity and corporate loyalty. This took an especially distorted form in Germany because its powerful economy came late on the imperialist scene and had lost its World War I attempt at expansion, with intense consequent suffering in the pressure of reparations and in inflation during the 1920s. Moreover, Germany still had strong pre-capitalist feudal elements in the Junkers, where liberalism had had no hold at all.

Whatever the complex socioeconomic and psychological bases of fascism, its rapid growth cast a shadow over social and political theory in liberal-democratic countries. Books appeared about the decline of democracy, the impasse of democracy, with recommendations of retrenchment to survive and recover its dynamism. For example, Walter Lippmann published a brief book in the mid-thirties, *The Method of Freedom* (1934), in which he criticized the American Congress for an inability to act, for getting tied up in dispersive pressures and counterpressures. He went so far as to toy with the idea that the executive branch alone should be able to offer legislation, and Congress be limited to accepting or rejecting it. In general, the underlying assumption of all these critiques was that dictatorship is efficient, it gets things done, while democracy is inefficient, and the question is how much democracy we can tolerate in a world of dictatorships.

Actually, the legislative branch in the 1930s faced fairly readily problems of social change. If at times there was a welter of proposals in different directions, the Roosevelt administration on the whole worked out its compromises and succeeded in getting them accepted by the legislature. The judicial branch interposed more serious obstacles. Americans today are long accustomed to a Supreme Court that breaks fresh ground—in the interpretation of equality (as in integrating the schools and extending the rights of women and minorities) or of privacy (as in legalizing contraception and permitting abortion). It requires a change of focus to think back to the Court of the 1930s, which exerted major energies to block welfare measures, seeing them as violations of the constitutional rights of property and freedom of contract. The Supreme Court yielded unwillingly, under strong executive pressure and even the threat of enlarging the Court's membership. Further, within the executive department itself, the expansion of regulative agencies raised constitutional issues of the delegation of powers in administrative law—whether, for example, the rule making of regulative agencies did not trespass on legislative powers. In due course a balance was worked out on what could and what could not be appealed to the courts.

In all these controversies and struggles of the 1930s—some of which, as about the nature of the Supreme Court's interpretive function, still go on today—the basic conflicts concerned social policy. They would not have disappeared in any retrenchment of democracy, but simply would have moved to a different arena. Still, in the 1930s the focus in popular political science was on democracy as a whole, and dictatorship as a whole, and it was democracy that was on the defensive.

A more global philosophical gloom was found in the occasional appeal to Oswald Spengler's *Decline of the West*, with its cyclical theory of history: A people rose to power in the early spring of its appearance on the world scene, a time of culture with energy and spontaneity. In its summer it reached its height of conquest and contribution. In its autumn urban civilization replaced the vigor of rural culture, and the decline began. In its winter that people fell before some fresh and energetic barbarian people, with a different culture. (Democracy appeared in the autumn of a people, with a dessicating rationalism; dictatorship, with sheer force, spread in the winter.) Spengler tried to list the succession of such peoples in the history of human kind, and to find the marks of each stage in such fields as morals and mathematics and architecture, as well as politics. Writing during World War I, he named the Russians as the next triumphant barbarians.

In the marketplace of national politics, the most striking phenomenon was the conflict going on in all political parties and social outlooks. It was least characteristic of the Democratic party, for it had gained power in the New Deal and fashioned a unified and coherent program. It did have the cleavage between the solid democratic South and the urban Northeast, and in New York there was also a conflict between the old-line Tammany Democrats, who were in power at the opening of the 1930s, and the Roosevelt Democrats, who opposed Tammany. (It was this latter conflict that enabled Fiorello La Guardia to win election as mayor on a Republican–Fusion ticket, an incident of some importance for what happened in the city colleges.) In the Republican party the chief conflict was between those who advocated American isolationism and those who took an international perspective and wanted the United States to help and even to participate with Britain and France in the war against Nazi Germany. This came to a head in the early 1940s when Wendell Willkie won the Republican nomination over the isolationist Taft, thus ensuring that whether he or Roosevelt won (which of course Roosevelt did) the internationalist perspective would dominate.

The minor parties, influential in New York's labor and social movements, though this was rarely reflected in political results, were even more sharply split. The socialists broke apart on the issue of cooperation with Roosevelt and his program. The hard-line or pure socialists (whose candidate against Roosevelt was Norman Thomas) took the view that the New Deal operated only as a temporary expedient that saved capitalism, that it could bring no satisfactory long-range solution for economic problems and only an outright socialist platform was an honest way to treat the working people. The Social–Democratic Federation was ready to cooperate with the Roosevelt program, arguing that it constituted a step forward, helped the contemporary situation, and experience would show its inadequacies and make possible further progressive steps. The conflict was bitter and the separation permanent. The Social Democrats were later to be the moving spirits in the founding of the Liberal Party in New York.

Communism had a checkered career in the 1930s. On the international scene a split hardened between supporters of Stalin and those of Trotsky. The former maintained that socialism could be built up in one country and need not wait for world revolution; the latter saw this as a betrayal of socialism by a Stalinist dictatorship. (The differences were to be important in many countries, particularly in Spain during the civil war of the mid-thirties.) Within the United States the influence that communists had during the 1930s came not from their international positions so much as from their intensive efforts and militancy in the then current struggles of workers in both labor and middle-class circles. They were among the first to attempt organization of the unemployed in the Depression, and they widely raised the question of justice for Blacks against entrenched discrimination. Many communists played an active part in the CIO organization of the mass industries and in the mobilization of intellectuals against fascism.

Sharp changes in communist policy stemmed from close adherence to the Soviet Union as the leading socialist state, and more concretely from the Soviet domination of the central communist International, which set down fundamental policy. By 1934 it was clear that the split in the German working class between socialists and communists had helped Hitler come to power; communists now therefore sought a United Front to secure united worker action against fascism. The rapidity of Germany's rearmament and the strength of the aggression were quickly perceived as a serious danger to the Soviet Union. This, combined with the general threat of fascism, led to the policy of the Popular Front, addressed beyond workers to the middle class. The influence communists gained through their militant social action in the years of the Popular Front was broken by their sharp turn with the Hitler–Stalin pact, when they went on to brand the early part of the war against Hitler (1939–41) as an imperialist war. They recovered somewhat during the period of the alliance between America, Britain, and Russia, after Hitler invaded Russia in 1941 and America was at war with both Germany and Japan. They lost all influence when the cold war came to dominate American policy after World War II. This checkered career of communism in America is important, for its role in events cannot be understood in general terms but has to be referred to particular periods of policy and program. In this respect the thirties were distinctive.

The thirties were also critical for liberalism generally, particularly in its relation to conservatism. In its historical origins, liberalism, with its emphases on individualism and liberty, had been tied to economic freedom or what came to be called "free enterprise." In the 1930s, however, with the questioning of free enterprise in the light of the Great Depression, the center of gravity in liberalism had shifted to social provision for the basic well-being of people, in short, toward what was generally called thereafter a "welfare state." This was seen by its advocates not as the abandonment of liberty but as the ensuring of concrete liberties. Thus during World War II, in which social programs became of practical importance for maintaining morale, Roosevelt proposed an Economic Bill of Rights, and his Four Freedoms included freedom from want. A neoconservative like James Burnham might protest that the notion of freedom from want was meaningless, that man is a wanting being and to be free from want is to be free from desire, hence to be dead.[3] But people living in poverty or on the edge of poverty knew quite well what freedom from want meant. For example, the British electorate, after the privations of World War II and in spite of their gratitude for Winston Churchill's recognized services, put the Labour party in power at the end of the war to set up a welfare state. In the United States, New Deal welfare policies expanded in the two decades after the war. They reached an imposing level, after President Kennedy's assassination, in President Johnson's measures for the Great Society. This experiment was made possible by the tremendous economic growth of the United States after World War II. The important point in all this, which there has been some tendency to ignore in subsequent conservative trends, is that in the 1930s and from then into the 1960s a social-welfare program was not socialism, but a liberalism providing a broader interpretation of freedom. In later years this was sometimes labeled "left liberalism."

What this meant can be strikingly illustrated from government literature in the period of World War II. For example, the Economic Bill of Rights, included in Roosevelt's message to Congress in 1944, specified "the right of every family to a decent home" and "the right to a good education." And a publication expounding the Four Freedoms included under freedom of speech not only protection against interference in one's public speech (as against restrictive ordinances directed at labor organization or radical political agitation), but also the positive opportunity to acquire knowledge for more informed speech, illustrated by public support of libraries throughout the country.

The centrality of free enterprise thus put into the background by the dominant liberalism of the thirties was picked up by conservatism after the war. For a moment there was a blossoming of elitist conservatism that looked to the older categories of tradition and a Burkean veneration of custom and feeling over abstract thought,[4] but such a plant could not thrive in the practical soil of America. Mainline conservatism simply took over the component of free enterprise that had been loosened from liberalism in the thirties, so that the conservatism of America in the twentieth century incorporated the liberalism of the nineteenth century. This is clearly seen in the writings of Herbert Hoover. In *The Challenge to Liberty* (1934) he finds the American people faced for the first time with "the primary issue of humanity and all government—the issue of human liberty."[5] Liberty is not a catalogue of political rights, but a spirit of freedom that lets the individual choose his own calling, develop talents, earn and spend and save and accumulate property. In *The Problems of Lasting Peace* (1942) by Hoover and Hugh Gibson, free enterprise is called the "fifth freedom," conceived as basic to the Four Freedoms enunciated by Roosevelt as war aims.[6] Since the aim of the war had been the restoration of liberty throughout the world, we are left with the clear implication that the war was fought to restore free enterprise everywhere. Now free enterprise is distinguished from laissez-faire by controlling some of the latter's excesses; but it is also contrasted with the whole range of alternative systems competing throughout the world—fascism, Nazism, communism, socialism, and even the regimented or managed economy. Here the detailed discussion of economic steps leaves no doubt that the New Deal is following the path of the managed economy. Somewhere along the way of these discussions in that period the concept of *statism* was coined to embrace all the enemies of free enterprise. Broader than *totalitarianism* and a powerful intellectual weapon, its strength became evident in the conservatism of the Reagan administration.[7]

Meanwhile, however, the wing of liberalism that could not accept left liberalism had to find another focus than the economic, and it did this by incorporating as almost its essence the anti-communist stance of the cold war.[8] Such liberalism—we may call it right, as against left, liberalism—is today a major referent in the public domain. That is one reason why it is difficult to understand the liberalism of the 1930s.

Perhaps because of the tendency in cold-war ideology to bunch every approach left of center into a uniform radicalism that is either "pro-communist" or "soft on communism," it is necessary, if one is to understand the liberalism of the 1930s, to distinguish the variety of attitudes within left liberalism to communists and communism in the conditions of that decade. They were by no means uniform, nor reducible to a simple formula. Common to all these attitudes was the interpretation already noted that liberty or freedom, the central ideas of liberalism, should include the elements of social security and social well-being as a public responsibility. Some had lost faith in free enterprise and were looking for new developments within the parameters of liberty; to many of them the Russian experiment then seemed to hold some promise, but any movement in that direction should be nonviolent and any new form developed should firmly retain liberal ideals of freedom. Others thought of communism as but one form in which the peoples of various countries were experimenting to break out of the backwardness or repressions of the past; the whole world was stirring against the continuing imperialisms, and we might expect an age of social change and a variety of social organization. Still others thought that communism in its Russian form would be the natural object of attack in the advance of fascism and could therefore be a proper ally in resisting fascism. All of these had no objection to the Popular Front and the active role of communists in social battles in the United States. Communists themselves might look to the Soviet Union for guidance and even dictation, but liberals could simply welcome their participation in specific movements when their policies coincided, confident that when any communist policies went counter to mainstream liberalism, communist influence would simply disappear. (This seemed to be confirmed in 1939 when American communists supported the Nazi–Soviet pact, and became completely isolated.) Finally, there were many among the liberals accepting the Popular Front who saw a major threat in the growth of an ideology of anti-communism. This had been used as a weapon by Hitler in winning his way to power, and they saw the beginnings of such use of the slogan in America. They treated communists as simply a political party whose support on specific organizations or policies might be accepted or rejected piecemeal. They looked on the applications of "soft on communism," "fellow traveler," or omnibus terms like "totalitarianism" and "statism" as ideological instruments of the far political right.

Finally, only a glance here at the idea of democracy for its fuller meaning will concern us throughout. Democracy, retrospectively, went through many phases: first, the face-to-face democracy of ancient Greece or the Vermont town meeting; second, the representative democracy of elected representatives; third, the idea of participatory democracy that became widespread as a result of the youth revolts of the 1960s. Today, the idea of participation as central to democracy is so widespread that even politics is often carried on with an apprehensive look at the most recent polls. In the 1930s the idea of rule by the people as against rule by the elected representatives of the people was a matter of serious debate. The official view was that rule was best carried out by leaders who, however, should be judged by their public in periodic elections, since temptation and corruption are inherent in human weakness. For that public to take part in ruling was to invite "mobocracy."

Such a view carried over into suspicion of the very concept of democracy. Meetings of a learned society might debate whether America was to be described as a democracy at all, rather than as a republic. Occasionally in the political forum—in spite of the familiar seesaw of Republicans and Democrats—a too ready invocation of the label of democracy invited suspicion of subversion! For example, after World War II an organization that sought to distinguish itself from the American Legion called itself "Veterans for Democracy." According to a story in the *New York Times*, it received a letter from the counsel of an official investigating committee in which he wrote that they were doubtless aware that America was not a democracy but a republic. Hence they were proposing to change its form of government. Would they please let him know whether they were ready to do so by violence!

In the chapters that follow, the different theories of democracy or models in which it was cast will concern us in detail. For in the period we are exploring these ideas were being worked out and given institutional shaping, rather than ready-made ideas applied. In that process many of the differences and conflicts we have looked at in this chapter had an impact.

CHAPTER 3

New York and Its City Colleges

IN THE LATE 1840S, when uprisings were sweeping the great cities of Europe, agitation grew in New York for the establishment of a college that would open opportunities for the children of working people. It succeeded, helped in part by a middle-class desire that immigrants be appropriately Americanized. In the latter part of the century the general movement for the public school spread throughout the country. Its history and motivations have been much discussed, and its achievements debated. In the case of the New York city colleges the record in the twentieth century is an open book—indeed many books.[1]

City College (often called just CCNY) for men and Hunter College for women were both in Manhattan, both founded in the last century. Brooklyn College, coeducational, was established at the beginning of the 1930s; there was some worry about having both sexes in one place. In the middle of that decade Queens College, also coeducational, was founded. City College had long had Townsend Harris High School attached to it, from the time before academic high schools had developed in the city; it had an accelerated program. Hunter College had Hunter High, which in due course became a magnet for promising young people.

Significantly, the city colleges in the 1930s were free. The costs involved in attending were largely transportation (the subway fare was still five cents, not then a negligible amount), lunches (which could be brought from home), and student activity fees. Of course there was also loss to the family of the earning power of the young, when they could find a job. Students, however, could find part-time work, and did.

Admission to the colleges was not a complicated affair in the 1930s. The applicant did not have to have special individual qualifications or activities, nor pass a college entrance examination. No director of admissions was required. It was a straightforward matter of scholastic high-school average. At that point the filtering of applicants was a function of the city budget for the colleges. A calculation of the number of students that the budget could carry was used to set an entrance grade average; it could be lowered in good financial years and raised in bad years. The entrance grade stayed mostly over eighty, and sometimes over eighty-five. The result was that the city colleges always had outstanding students. Of course the few who could afford it—fewer in the depression—might go to Columbia or New York University, or even out of town. The general low income, at least up to the mid-century, ensured the quality of the student body.

The composition of the student body reflected the ethnic composition of the city modified by the tradition of interest in college education found in different groups. At different times over the century, the Irish, Jews, Germans, Italians, Ukrainians, Blacks, Chinese, and others were found in different proportions; the study of shifting proportions would be an interesting topic for community research. Besides the variable of financial ability and that of interest in college education, religion played some part; many Catholic students turned to the Catholic colleges in the city, such as Fordham, Manhattan, St.

Johns, though here the matter of fees was sometimes relevant. In any case, in the 1930s the preponderant group in the city colleges was Jewish, largely Russian Jewish.

Before World War II, that is, in the period including the 1930s, the city colleges felt insecure. Both faculty and trustees thought that the colleges existed by the good graces of the city, and that they had to behave properly if that support was to continue. In any episode accompanied by notoriety, opinions were usually expressed in the community that it would be better to abolish the city colleges and use the money for scholarships to other colleges. While universities like Columbia and New York University found the city colleges advantageous for placing their graduate students in teaching jobs, occasionally they competed with the city colleges for funds from New York State. Again in some quarters the city colleges were still suspect as secular institutions—a matter over which there had been serious strife on the American scene in earlier decades and which still lingered in more conservative quarters. (A notable case had been the founding of Cornell University, as a nonsectarian institution.[2]) Catholic attitudes in New York, particularly in Brooklyn, still reflected this in the 1930s; but the situation changed after Pope John XXIII's Vatican II, when Catholic thought fully entered the mainstream of American academic life. In many respects this history is now being repeated in its earlier phase in other parts of the country where conservative forms of Protestantism struggle against "secular humanism."

The feeling of insecurity about the city colleges in the 1930s was probably even then exaggerated. They had firm support in the aspirations of the laboring part of the New York population as the avenue of upward mobility for their children. They also served a variety of practical functions. For example, Hunter College furnished a continuing stream of women teachers for the New York public schools. Perhaps some part of the feeling of precariousness was contributed by the state of college education generally; higher education was not yet seen as necessary for the life of the community. This happened only after World War II.

New York City at the opening of the 1930s was politically still controlled for the most part by Tammany Hall, which acted in many respects as a social-service system for the lower economic strata of the city. A jest had it that people would not object if the machine took 15 percent through its irregular channels, but more was exorbitant and called for reform. In the early 1930s the machine was challenged by a Republican–Fusion movement that elected Fiorello La Guardia as mayor. This impinged on the city colleges, for the board of trustees (the Board of Higher Education) was appointed by the mayor, and the board had complete powers of governance over the colleges. The individual members had staggered nine-year terms, so the transition on the board to appointees of the new regime was a gradual matter.

The governance system itself in the 1930s was straightforward. The board appointed the president of a college, and the president had full authority within the college. He submitted his recommendations to the board for acceptance, and he served as executive agent of the board to carry out its policies. He was, in short, the empowered manager of the college. The board divided itself into administrative committees, one for each college; while in practice each exercised the powers of the board for that college, formally everything went through the whole board. In effect, then, each college operated independently, tied to its own borough, and political influences had a shorter route than would have been the case in a thoroughly unified system. For the most part the Administrative Committee left governance to the president of the college with which it was concerned. In the early 1930s the presidents were Frederick B. Robinson at City, Eugene A. Colligan at Hunter, William A. Boylan at Brooklyn. Power was personal and fairly complete. (City had in its past a military president, who set the pattern of discipline in running the college.) The president appointed department heads, who ran the department with full authority. The president might interfere on occasion: One department head told the story of the president calling him in and introducing him to a new member of his department! It was rumored that sometimes the path to faculty appointment (or at least the recommendation thereto) ran through the office of the precinct captain; but it could go through personal channels as readily.

The Great Depression brought a fundamental change. Since there were no jobs to be found, students flocked to the colleges in greater numbers. Once there they sometimes stayed as long as possible; a favorite device was to postpone a required course so that they had to come for an extra term to take it, and meanwhile took other courses as well. The faculty grew rapidly, adding young and energetic teachers, generally of quality, to the lower ranks. But the character of a department, the selection of faculty, the educational policies adopted, the detail of curriculum, depended on the attitudes of the department head.

With respect to students, the faculty were taken to be *in loco parentis*. Student clubs had to have faculty advisors, but if their advice was not for the most part followed, they were expected to resign. A club unable to secure a faculty advisor—and taking such a post for a club the president did not approve of made it a risky business for the advisor—could not function officially. On the whole, at the City College, the students had in the late twenties developed an adversarial attitude toward the president. The focus was on military training (ROTC) on the campus. Students agitated against it on the ground that training for war had no place in an academic program. When they carried out public demonstrations, usually some disorder arose, and sizeable numbers of students were suspended or even expelled.

In the 1930s student clubs flourished, differentiated by political views covering the detailed spectrum. The issues of prominence were ones that brought them together. Thus, on the question of fascism, when President Robinson invited a touring student delegation from Italy to visit the college, the students objected because it was an official group, representing Mussolini. The reception was held in the Great Hall. The Great Hall is an imposing setting with seating for several thousand; flags of the great universities of the Western world fly impressively down both aisles. The representative of the student body, in his required official greeting to the visitors before the vast throng, began: "I bring the greetings of the City College students to the tricked and deluded students of Italy." At that point President Robinson tried to stop him, a scuffle ensued, and eventually another batch of City College students was expelled. These incidents were reported in the press, and the administration feared the effects of what was regarded as radicalism.

Graduates of the City College who have achieved eminence in intellectual, professional, and political fields have written about their experience in the college "alcoves" that acted as headquarters for different student clubs. These were cubbyholes along the walls in the large basement of the main building. In the center of the basement there was a counter at which food was served, and students carried it to the alcove of their interest. For example, Alcove 2 was the favorite of communist students; Alcove 1 of Trotskyites, socialists, and other radicals opposed to communists. There was constant crossfire over international affairs and national policy, drawing lines so fine that at the time they seemed talmudic, but in later perspective they can be seen to mark an important divide in political action. They competed for student allegiance, for editorship of the campus student newspaper, and they produced sizeable political-pamphlet literature. At the end of the 1930s an astute president of the student council invited the New York City Council to lunch at the college, and instead of taking them to the faculty dining room had them stand up at the counter. The lesson was obvious, and the City Council voted money for a lunch room in the basement, with tables. The alcoves, however, remained in this more ample atmosphere, destined for historical symbolism.

On the whole, the public causes that students pursued in the 1930s, and for which many made sacrifices, were general programs of peace, anti-fascism, anti-racism, and greater measure of student control over their own affairs. Such programs at that time were regarded at highly radical, and in this sense the term later used—"premature anti-fascists"—characterized the students well. They met with sympathy among a part of the faculty. Most prominent among these in the late 1920s and early 1930s was the eminent professor of philosophy Morris Raphael Cohen, whose Socratic method of teaching marked him as an intellectual influence in generations of students. When the administration set up a discipline committee consisting of three students and three professors, who would then elect a fourth professor to chair the committee, the three students voted for no one other than Cohen; they held out until the president yielded and allowed the faculty members to accept Cohen. The students, counting on Cohen to vote with them to make a majority, would thus be able to prevent the committee from being used as an automatic device for expelling students. This incident showed that the students, rightly or wrongly, regarded the faculty generally as coercible by the administration.

The character of the student body of the 1930s provided the

33

dynamic background of events; without student support at crucial moments, little would have happened. Of course its intellectual quality was well known. The City College produced more than its share of eminent scientists and scholars and future Nobel Prize winners. For a long period it competed with the University of California at Berkeley for the largest numbers of graduates to go on to the Ph.D. In graduate schools its students were said to be recognizable in class by their readiness to ask questions and offer answers, and engage in consequent argument. Relevant here, however, is rather the unique relation of theory and practice that marked the students of those critical decades. They were deeply concerned about theory and the justification of their beliefs, and there was little gap between their acceptance of theory and their embarking on individual and social practice. Among those who were most active, the sense of principle was often very strong. On one occasion students from a club of which I was then faculty advisor were being tried for demonstrating. Feeling my role to be in some sense defender–advocate for my (though nominal) charges, I suggested they may have simply misunderstood an ambiguous regulation. They interrupted to reject this: They were definitely violating the rule on principle, and would not accept a legalistic escape route. They were, as a matter of course, expelled.

Perhaps one or two recollections from classroom experiences far from such contexts may convey the character I have in mind. In an ethics class one term in the early years of American entry into World War II, a class delegation approached me at the beginning of the term. They said that they faced practical problems, for example of the draft. Would I agree to spend the whole term on practical problems? I explained that the point of an ethics course way to understand the resources of theory for practice; this required historical and analytic study. They offered to do the theoretical reading outside of the classroom. So we worked out a stringent arrangement by which, far beyond the call of usual assignment, they would hand in every week essays on the theoretical readings of the week, and hand them in on time for my reading and comment, but the actual class meetings would deal with problems. (I never had a more hard-working class, nor one more responsible in its assignments.) I recall most vividly the discussion about conscientious objection. Four students presented position papers, two on each side. The first student stressed the importance of the war against fascism and found it to override all personal considerations or competing principles; his view had overwhelming support. Interestingly, no one defended an uncritical patriotism of the "my country right or wrong" type; they inclined rather to the usually forgotten qualification, "to defend it when right, to correct it when wrong." (Incidentally, the student who presented this position later became an outstanding legal authority on civil liberties.) The second student was an extreme advocate of conscientious objection; he would not even admit alternative service of a humanitarian sort. He held to his position in spite of vigorous class criticism, and did indeed choose prison when he was drafted. The third student had begun from the same position as the second but became convinced by the class discussion that such intransigence was not justified; he thereafter served in the ambulance corps in Italy under extremely dangerous conditions. The fourth student openly stated his Trotskyite convictions. He would accept the draft, he said, to become a trained soldier who could in due course turn his skills against his "imperialist bosses." At a particularly critical point in his argument for accepting the discipline of a system he theoretically rejected, the third student interrupted in an emotional tone: "You have just been ordered by your commander to shoot me for refusing an order I thought wrong. Will you shoot?" The class waited breathless, almost as if the scene

were being enacted. After a pause, the fourth student said slowly: "I would—regretfully." The fourth student did enter the
army; his experience must have altered many of his views, for I
next heard of him years later as a political scientist and a dean
at a well-known private college.

A quite different example from an ethics class in a later decade when the Black liberation movement was just beginning to
get under way shows that the relation of theory and action continued unabated. Two students—a young man and a young
woman (for City College by then admitted women)—came to
ask me before class if they could have the class's advice on a
personal moral problem. They were about to be married. The
girl's mother was planning a reception for them, but when they
included a Black friend in their list of college friends to be invited, the mother objected intransigently. What should they do
in this conflict of family loyalty and social principle? With
class consent, the question was discussed, from points of view
that ranged from stoic resignation to utilitarian institutional
conflict to militant principle. The class overwhelmingly held
that the girl should not yield to her mother, but should refuse
to go to the reception unless the most critical moral issue of
the day—the growing principle of Black equality—was re-
spected. The climax of the class's discussion was the argument
of an older woman who had returned to college to finish the
degree. She said she knew from experience the practical function of such receptions. The mother was not operating on principle, but was worried about what her husband's business
friends invited to the reception would think. The bride was
thus being treated not as an end, but as a means. Would she
allow this to happen after her study of Kant's ethics, with its
fundamental position of respect for person?

The bride and groom felt morally supported by the class's
advice. Actually, an innovative solution was worked out. There
were two receptions—one held by the bride's brother for the

couple's friends, to which her parents did not come, and one by her parents, to a list of their own choosing to which the couple invited no one.

Students were generally ready to act in terms of their ideas, and when they argued about ideas they were arguing about potential actions. On the whole, the student body was not split between political extremes. The number of socially active students, as is usual, constituted only a small part of the whole student body, but it was larger than usual and more widely supported. There was little opposition to their progressive stands among students—only an occasional complaint at City College from engineering students that a reputation for radicalism might stand in their way in the competition for jobs. But in questions of racism or of academic freedom the students showed both immediate understanding and trigger reactions. Much later, in the McCarthy period, a committee in New York investigating subversive activities asked a student about what a professor had said in the classroom. She made it public immediately, and leaflets were circulated within a few hours. The threat of academic inquisition was so vigorously and publicly condemned that the committee did not venture along such lines again.

The teaching staff in the early 1930s was only beginning to find an organized voice. The formal governance of the college gave it no such scope. The situation was aptly summarized for the country at large by Professor A. J. Carlson, in a presidential address before the annual dinner of the American Association of University Professors on December 31, 1937:

I, for one, am puzzled by the vagaries in social evolution in our American democracy that have led to development and retention of an autocratic or dictatorial type of organization in the field devoted to higher learning, where we would expect to meet only those individuals best equipped by nature and training for democratic control and self-orientation.[3]

As suggested earlier, administrative power was delegated from trustees to presidents, and from presidents to deans and department heads. In the department, the head was usually supreme; where he was not, it was because of control by officials higher up, rather than through any responsibility to members of the department. The official "faculties," usually limited to the professorial ranks from assistant to full professor, had little actual power and were effectively under presidential control. A surviving copy of the old bylaws of the faculty at the City College from the first decades of the twentieth century even said that the president's permission had to be secured for a faculty member to leave a faculty meeting; moreover, the rules dictated that every faculty member in every class meeting had to ask a question of every member of the class! (To have followed this rule literally as the classes grew larger would have provided an ideal union tactic of slowdown in a dispute with the administration—were the administration to have noticed it.) In the 1930s teachers not only had to keep strict attendance records but to hand in attendance books to the registrar's office on Fridays for checking and return on Monday mornings.

It was this entire situation that John T. Flynn, leader of the reform group in the Board of Higher Education, was later to describe as one in which "the president becomes a little tyrant and his faculty becomes yes-men dummies. If a man's career is at the mercy of one person, all intellectual energy is crushed! This situation is intolerable" (*New York Times*, April 1938).

The growth of the city colleges and the faculties in the period of the Great Depression had serious economic consequences. To save money, teachers were employed in the very lowest ranks. If they had doctorates, they could be instructors, the rank below assistant professor. If they had not completed the doctorate, they were appointed as tutors. Full-time tutors carried a full-time schedule (fifteen hours of classes per week); they were not, as in many other institutions, simply graduate discussion assistants. They thus did regular jobs at substandard salaries. Indeed, below tutors was the rank of fellows, also doing regular teaching. The net result was that about two-thirds of the faculty consisted of teachers in the rank of instructor and below. One could find, in the science departments especially, teachers who were tutors after seven years on the teaching staff, getting a salary of sixteen hundred dollars. To compensate for the low salaries in the tutorial rank, teachers were offered the opportunity of extra teaching in the evening session at hourly wages that amounted to about a third of their day session wages for comparable hours of work. (The evening session was for extension students, often older people or else those employed during the day, or for students who had not made the required high-school average for day session entrance. Evening session students paid fees, but could transfer to the free day session if they maintained a "B" average.) The total result was to allow such teachers no time or energy to complete their doctorates, and therefore no opportunity to move up to the instructorship. There was no genuine tenure, although the term was used to mean simply that one did not receive a fresh contract every year; it gave no rights of permanence or protection against non-reappointment. The great fear in pressing for better conditions was—and events showed it to be real—that tutors would simply be dropped in large numbers, with newcomers starting at lower wages. "Rotation"—circulating a proportion of appointments out of the system—would be a budget-cutting device.

At this time too, the rise of fascism affected many of the staffs. Especially from 1933 on, intellectuals began to feel they should play some part in meeting the menace. Political scientists should be heard on the dangers of state absolutism, sociologists on what happens where freedoms are repressed, anthropologists on the falsity and dangers of the myth of race superiority, philosophers on the havoc that would be wrought by the attacks on reason. At the colleges, many teachers organized into anti-fascist associations. They grew rapidly, met with some frequency, and had little disagreement about goals. But it soon appeared that there were differences of opinion about means and methods, whether to think chiefly in terms of research and education or of active public campaigning.

These different ideas of method touched more seriously staff organizations that dealt with economic issues and problems of tenure. City College had a chapter of the American Association of University Professors (AAUP), as did Brooklyn and Hunter. City College also had an Instructional Staff Association; Brooklyn College, an Association of Instructors, Tutors, and Fellows; and Hunter College, a separate Assistant Professors' Association and an Association of Instructors and Fellows. Cooperation among these associations had secured, during the earlier part of 1935, a state law (the Feld–McGrath Law) giving employees of the city colleges the kind of tenure enjoyed by teachers in the elementary and high schools. This meant tenure after three years of service, upon reappointment for a fourth year. (This law was later declared unconstitutional on the ground that it established tenure by "reference" rather than by explicit provision.) Among the instructional associations, the controversies about modes of action to secure improvement of conditions became intense. The more traditional view was that results could best be achieved by education about needs and principles and by political influence of well-placed persons through quiet negotiation. This was challenged by the view that aims could best be furthered by social action and that

40

especially individual grievance cases should be fought in public, not by private negotiation. In short, it was a call for the methods of labor unions. It was not surprising therefore that in the fall of 1935 a college section was founded in the Teachers Union, Local 5, of the American Federation of Teachers, a union covering elementary and high schools of New York. College teachers in the New York city colleges were soon caught up in the surge of union organization that was getting under way throughout the country.

It was not too early for the pace of events. Within a few months the City College administration took steps that threatened the security of tutors. On April 23, 1936, it notified a man who had been a tutor for eight years in the English department that his "efficiency was not sufficiently notable" to warrant his reappointment. This alarmed the large number of tutors, for it suggested that a policy of rotation was in the offing. The particular tutor, Morris U. Schappes, was not only popular among the students but was well known for his efforts to organize the staff in seeking better conditions. Colleagues and students alike recognized that academic freedom was at stake. The dismissal was immediately opposed by the instructional Staff Association and the union.

A wide public campaign was initiated by the college section of the union. It sought support from progressive public opinion and New York labor unions. The Board of Higher Education was flooded with protests. One member of the board expressed his puzzlement: What connection was there, he said, between meatcutters and academic freedom? A spontaneous student sit-down strike began outside President Robinson's office and continued days on end. The Board of Higher Education was not prepared for such an outpouring, and it yielded. On May 7, 1936, barely more than a fortnight from the time Schappes was notified of his dismissal, the City College Administrative

Committee of the board passed a resolution notifying department heads that "it was a wise and proper policy to continue in
their position tutors classed as probationary or temporary who
had served more than three years unless there exist strong
compelling reasons based on teacher-qualifications, for their
separation from the service." This not only led to the dropping
of the action against Schappes but saved the jobs of eleven
other men who were to be dismissed as part of a move toward
retrenchment by a policy of rotation. Tenure so rapidly won in
principle for the lower ranks with this three-year provision still
had to be worked out in detail for board bylaw, and eventually
(given the fate of the Feld–McGrath law) for a state law.

This signal victory considerably strengthened the college
union, and staff members turned to it in increasing numbers as
a channel for protecting their interests. In the two years that
followed, the union had many other cases involving large-scale
activity. Both where it won and where it lost there was a widespread feeling that the vigilant energy of its Grievance Committee was a constant hindrance to autocratic administrative
tendencies.

The growing strength of the union is seen in the stand taken
within a few months by the chairman of the Board of Higher
Education. A story in the *World-Telegram* of February 19, 1937,
read:

HIGHER EDUCATION HEAD FAVORS TEACHERS' UNIONS

*Mark Eisner Also Advocates Passage of Tenure Laws as
Safeguard Against Violation of Academic Freedom in
Speech Before City College Chapter*

Mr. Eisner said that for teachers who are discharged for
their beliefs "their only recourse is in organizations such as
yours here."

"I am a firm believer in militancy at a time like this, when various insidious pressure groups operate freely to intimidate and terrorize our legislators and administrators of colleges."

The strength of the union that won such acknowledgment from the chairman of the board came not only from the support of teachers and students, but from the readiness with which organized labor in the city gave assistance. Even more lay behind this. Eisner was the representative of the older Democratic group on the board whose members were slowly ending their term and being replaced by La Guardia appointees. The balance had not yet been tipped on the board. The new appointees welcomed what they recognized as broad staff support through so vocal an organization as the union. Among the older members, some were not unready to extend an olive branch. Others were adamantly opposed to change. When three hundred college teachers and members of Local 5 picketed the full session of the board on June 15, 1937, in connection with a grievance case, board member Seelman stated, "I'm against having teachers sink to the level of trade union tactics" (Local 5's *Teacher News*, June 21, 1937). Many of the moves made by board members during 1937 can be seen as jockeying for position or preparing programs while waiting for the outcome of the mayoralty election of November 1937. Much depended on whether La Guardia would win reelection.

The union did not immediately think in terms of large-scale reorganization of the colleges. It recognized that educational issues were involved in the grievance cases it handled. In its own organization, the union had set up an Educational Policies Committee. When that committee held its first meeting (November 11, 1936), it found a request from the Grievance Com-

43

mittee. Since serious grievance cases centered on probationers whose positions were being threatened, and grounds for termination invariably made reference to competence, what should be the criteria for teacher competence? (A probationer was, technically, any member of the staff of any rank who would be considered for tenure after a given period.) This was no abstract theoretical issue but a very concrete one. For example, would satisfactory service for three years be sufficient for tenure, or could the demand be for excellence? What if a department took a "shopping attitude" and wanted to find someone even better, through the probationer was satisfactory or even good?

The Educational Policies Committee set to work on this investigation. In the next few weeks department heads were questioned about the criteria actually used, teachers of college teaching were interviewed, civil-service procedure studied, relevant literature examined. The survey revealed little agreement and less precision. A good teacher was one who "fired the imagination of his students" or "was recognized as good by the experienced judgment of his superior." The search for general criteria of competence was accordingly postponed. Perhaps criteria of competence varied in different fields, and a general account would be only the ability to achieve the objectives of the specific field. Accordingly trans-college divisions were set up in the physical sciences, social sciences, languages, humanities, and other areas to track down possibly special criteria. Now this involved discussion of curricular content, methods, and objectives, and the experience of cooperative discussion was carried beyond the question of competence into larger ares of educational policy. Both the special researches and the general inquiry showed the tremendous need for wider participation of teachers in formulating policy.

Meanwhile, the general question of criteria of competence was transformed into the practical question of necessary conditions for a fair judgment of a teacher within a department. It was surprising how rudimentary might be mistakes made in the absence of cooperative teacher participation. In one case the department head had reported that all senior members were agreed that the work of a teacher was unsatisfactory. It was found, however, that each had a different complaint and disagreed about the complaints of the others. A mutual discussion cleared the ground, and the teacher was retained. In another case, the objection to a teacher of physics was found to be that he did not engage in research. In fact he was a superior teacher, yet admittedly without interest in research. The complex issue was thus whether the department had room for a nonresearch physicist with ability and special interest in teaching, a question of policy rather than of individual competence. Interestingly, he was continued.

At this point, the Educational Policies Committee issued a report on "some minimum conditions necessary for a fair judgment of competence in the case of a person against whom there have been complaints." It roused so much interest that it was decided to survey all phases of departmental and faculty procedure.

The programmatic aspect of the revolution at the city colleges was now under way. It no longer existed just in the deliberations of a committee, but it existed in the ferment of the teaching staffs as well.

CHAPTER 4

Revolution in Governance

THE REVOLUTION IN ACADEMIC GOVERNANCE matured over about two years: from the time when the Board of Higher Education passed the resolution granting effectual tenure to tutors who had three years of satisfactory service (May 7, 1936) to the actual revision of governance bylaws (June 20, 1938). For the staffs it was a time of agitating about grievances, piecemeal experimenting, program formulating, and consolidating of lessons learned in practice.

During 1937 members of the staffs began to petition collectively for redress of grievances. For example, in the chemistry department at City College (numbering well over a hundred members) there were fellows and tutors qualified for the instructorship, yet paid only twelve hundred to seventeen hundred dollars a year after three and a half to seven years of service. They now petitioned their department head for recommendation to the instructorship. This collective bargaining procedure, mild when looked at from a distance, though then novel, was successful in winning largely favorable recommendations. Significant at the time, however, was that the younger men united to formulate their own salary recommendations, and were compelled to press them directly before the trustees with the aid of the union. The justice of the case was recognized by the trustees, who granted many of their requests. Waging this campaign produced a spirit of cooperation; long-standing cliques and intrigues gave way to a sense of departmental responsibility. The constructive character of these moves was soon recognized by the older men as well. In a short time a formal departmental structure was established. The head of the department decided to confer with his staff and to be guided by the opinions of men assigned to study intensively the various departmental problems. The department took the stand that every member of the staff shared in the responsibility for its smooth and efficient functioning, and that experience and judgment should be fostered in all members through active participation in staff deliberations. They decided on the following procedural principles: stated meetings of the entire department and special meetings on request of a sufficient number; balloting by the entire staff, including laboratory technicians; rotation of committee memberships; a majority of each committee to be replaced each year by new members; indication by members of committee preferences; committee meetings announced and open to all department members; committee minutes and reports posted on the department's bulletin board. Officially, committees were appointed by the head, who alone had legal power, but the duties, composition, and membership of committees were in fact suggested to him by the Committee on Committees, which was named by the head after nominations by balloting of the entire staff. Other committees included Budget, Building Facilities, Curriculum, Finance, Library, Non-teaching Services, New Appointments and Probationers, Public Relations, Safety, Salary and Promotion, and Stock. The committee on Salary and Promotion consisted of three members of professorial rank, three teachers of subprofessorial rank, and one member engaged solely in laboratory work; it was appointed by the head after balloting of the entire staff, every staff member voting on all of the seven memberships of the committee. The memberships of the other com-

48

mittees were selected by the Committee on Committees without regard to rank or salary, but chiefly with regard to special qualifications of the men to perform their duties.

Such democratic organization operated even in a short time to intensify the interest of department members in all phases of educational policy. It generated more critical consideration of qualifications, standards, and curriculum, and resulted in such changes as a remodeling of the department's basic course. The department as a whole began to concern itself with the problems facing its students. It took steps toward establishing relations with groups in the community that were important for its graduates. It held an open house, at which industrial and educational leaders and public officials discussed problems of training and employment, and where the work of the department was exhibited.

Another interesting case was that of a smaller department— the Department of Philosophy and Psychology, with about fifteen members. For several years it had determined the character of its required courses by cooperative discussion and decision. As the movement toward democracy grew, this department became one of the first to adopt democratic procedures, although formally within the college such procedures had no official status under the existing bylaws. Both the department head and the majority of the department welcomed the experiment, recognizing the need for patience in a transitional period while the habits of democracy were being consciously cultivated. The whole department met on questions of general concern, while the separate divisions (of philosophy and psychology) dealt with matters peculiar to them. Thus an appointment to an important post in the department was discussed and voted upon by the whole; on the other hand, where the appointment did not affect the whole department, the candidates were canvassed and recommendation made by one division.

Committees reported to the assembly or division. The department voted on recommendations for promotion. There were appointment committees in each division, and the divisions each acted as curriculum committees. The organization was not very formal, although meetings were conducted according to regular democratic procedure, and minutes were taken. With the growth of this cooperative spirit there came large-scale revisions in curriculum and organization of classes; a greater latitude for experimentation in some of the required courses; more frequent consultation among those teaching the same subject; a wider distribution of elective courses; and more satisfactory teaching schedules.

Another remarkable example of democratic reorganization was found in a noninstructional group—the registrar's office. They held regular meetings and set up committees to deal with planning and distribution of work, personnel, adjustment of members' interests (such as schedule of vacations), and so forth. They approached problems with a definite conception of their integral relations to the teaching staffs. Instead of regarding nonteachers as appointed merely to perform routine clerical or manual tasks, they looked to the development of the work as a career and set as its objective an administrative staff fully studied in the operations of the college and keenly interested in its problems.

Experiences like these were repeated in some measure throughout all the colleges. They were amplified by what was learned from particular grievance cases during the spring of 1937. A number were cases of attempted dismissal. Others involved whole categories of employees—such as hygiene departments or noninstructional staffs whose character would be affected seriously by being divided into a professional upper group and a merely servicing but larger lower group at considerably lower pay. This proposal, for example in a hygiene department, meant that physical activity would be reduced to merely exercising and would not be part of a continuous educational process. Whatever the merits or demerits of such plans, they were put forward as budget-saving devices, without raising for general departmental consideration the educational shifts they would involve. Similar dividing lines were proposed for the library, and to some extent in science departments with respect to laboratory maintenance workers, though these were skilled labor. In various areas, then, the union brought the educational assumptions into the analysis and tended on the whole to favor an integrated educational labor force rather than a divided departmental staff.

Grievance cases served especially to reveal the autocratic character of the current administrative structure. Questions of salary schedules, standards for promotion, grounds and procedures of dismissal, petty tyrannies, and restrictions on curricular renovation were intertwined in a ferment of questioning. By the end of May the Educational Policies Committee of the union had formulated a program on the democratic organization of departments, and had recommended to the union that "the task of democratizing departments and faculties should be one of the major endeavors of the College Section next fall since this alone will check many current abuses." The proposed program was widely circulated, discussed, and revised in the light of experience.

At this time plans were being made for the opening of Queens College, the fourth of the city colleges. The question of its organizational structure could thus be approached as a general problem in an integrated way. On June 3, 1937, the union wrote to President Paul Klapper and to John T. Flynn (chairman of the board's Administrative Committee for Queens) recommending:

1. That no permanent heads of departments be appointed at present in order that the Administrative Committee may be free to consider more democratic methods of depart-

mental administration, e.g., electing rotating chair-
manships, department committees, etc.

2. That matters of departmental jurisdiction be settled democratically within departments.

3. That the faculty include administrative officers and everyone on the staff who teaches or has educational or guidance contact with students, and any others who may be
admitted by the faculty so constituted.

4. That, subject to the jurisdiction of the Board of Higher
Education, the faculty be the ultimate source of all authority on matters of policy within the college. That, accordingly, it be empowered to set up and elect any
committees it may think best, and that all committees be
responsible to it.

Dr. Klapper and Mr. Flynn replied with an encouraging as-
surance that Queens College would be organized democratically. Klapper was himself an educator, having been dean of
the School of Education at City College. Flynn was one of the
leaders of the La Guardia reform group on the board. It became
clear that appeal to democracy could play an important part in
the reconstruction of the colleges. What "democracy" would
mean and what it would stand for were more complicated
questions. The next academic year was to be a time for programs, discussion, and agitation, and eventually decision.

In addressing the Queens administrative committee on the
matter of faculty as well as department structure, the union
was moving to the issue of governance of the institution as a
whole, not merely to greater participation in departments by
department members. To broaden the membership of the faculty and assign it ultimate authority on policy within the college would make of it in effect a parliamentary or congressional
body for the college. Presidents would no longer be able to
make educational changes on their own, such as eliminating

programs or establishing new ones; nor could they appoint professors without educational evaluation by the faculty. Moreover, "matters of policy within the college" might well include budgetary, not merely educational, policy. The president's role would be one of leadership, not of autocratic rule.

In October of 1937 the union made the first move by requesting that all instructors in all the colleges be admitted to the faculty. Queens College already included everyone in its faculty. At Hunter College, the faculty still excluded assistant professors as a group, and it now requested the inclusion of all assistant professors and one out of every twelve instructors. The fear among the upper faculty was that they would be swamped if the lower ranks were admitted in their entirety. The union, refining the proposals it had made to Queens, adopted the following principles concerning faculties:

1. *Composition of the faculty:* The Faculty should include all members of the teaching staff, together with all others on the staff who have educational relationships or guidance contact with students.

2. *Organization of the faculty:* The Faculty should organize itself in any way it deems suitable, elect its own officers, draw up the agenda for its meetings, and establish its own bylaws and rules of procedure. The full Faculty should meet at least once each term, and a special meeting of the full Faculty should be called upon the petition of 10% of the members.

3. *Powers of the faculty:* Subject to law and the Board of Higher Education the Faculty should be the supreme governing authority of the college. The Faculty should set up and elect any committees it may deem fit, and all committees within the college should be responsible to it. The Faculty should have the power, through its secretary or representatives selected by it, to communicate with or

appear before the Board of Higher Education on any matter pertaining to the college.

The City College Instructional Staff Association and the Hunter Association of Instructors passed resolutions embodying fundamentally similar sets of principles. Union bulletins widely publicized these steps.

In November of 1937 came the critical mayoralty election. A broad coalition of labor, progressive groups, Republican and independent voters swept La Guardia into office for a second time. The election was a clear mandate for reform. The Board of Higher Education now had a clear majority of La Guardia appointees. They acted immediately. On November 16, in an attempt to remove existing irritations from the municipal system, the board set up a Committee of Five. Flynn was chairman; Ordway Tead, a member of the committee who had written on questions of structure in higher education, undertook the task of investigating programs of personnel administration. It was at a dinner held in honor of President Klapper of Queens that Flynn pointed out that the colleges could dispense with Mussolinis at their head and "teeny-weeny Mussolinis" in each department.

It was now time for the union campaign to move into high gear. The union wanted first to secure a maximum of staff unity on the actual changes to be proposed. Accordingly it called an informal conference of representatives of staff organizations to correlate and unify proposals in a common staff program. AAUP chapters at the colleges and instructors' and other associations sent observers, unofficial representatives, and in some cases official delegates. Meetings were held on November 3, on November 20, and finally on December 4. The last was an eight-hour meeting, spurred by the union's declaration that it could no longer wait to launch its all-out campaign. A proposed set of bylaws was drawn up for consideration by the various

groups that had participated (Appendix I). It largely followed
the principles that had been offered by the union on composition, organization, and powers of the faculty, but went into
much greater detail. It included the faculty's right to communicate directly with the Board of Higher Education, thus revers-
ing the existing regulation that all communication be through
the president. And it added a faculty committee with one representative from each rank (including instructors) to attend
board meetings with voice but not vote. It went on to consider
the role of presidents, deans, and directors. Presidents were to
be the chief executive agents of the board, and subject to the
jurisdiction of the faculty on matters of faculty authority. Some
matters were left to their entire responsibility, and others (such
as budget) to their cooperative action with faculty committees.
Faculties were given a role in the selection of presidents, deans,
and directors. If the role of the president seemed to be reduced,
it was only in power, not in the tasks of leadership. It was, in
effect, a shift from monarchy to presidency. Ample room remained for initiative—but with responsibility—in both policy
and executive administration as agent of the board and the faculty. Indeed, in the spirit of the proposals, the mark of a good
president would be the character and ability to exercise cooperative leadership and to maintain support through farsighted educational understanding.

These proposals were immediately adopted by the union as
consonant with what it had been advocating and in the firm
belief that they had widespread staff agreement. They were the
proposals from which the union assessed the board's own proposed bylaw revisions when these were later announced, and
which the union subsequently refined in the light of experience after the democratic reorganization was carried through.
A delegation of the union's Educational Policies Committee
immediately presented them to Mr. Tead on December 14,

1937—ten days after they had been worked out as a common program. In the months that followed, this program was approved by the instructional staffs at the colleges.

This program, it will be noted, did not cover the structure of departments. It dealt with the major faculty organization and administrative organization of the college as a whole. It touched departmental structure only in giving the faculty governing authority over "principles of organization and administration in and between departments and the assignment of work therein." The desirable character of democratic organization within a department was thus still to be considered, whether it would be determined by faculty or in basic principles by board bylaw. Now throughout the colleges, it was in departments that the most effective democratic movement had been taking place. Faculty and administrative bodies were still under firm presidential control. The initial union investigations of structure had begun with problems of departmental operation, with initial recommendations and their criteria, with curricular policy and appointment policy. The various experiments in democracy recounted were all tried out in departments, and their degree of success was used to revise and refine the proposals that had been made for departmental structure. It was now time for the union to adopt an official program in this basic area. In January 1938 the detailed program on departmental structure came before the membership for final ratification. The New York College Teachers Union (recently separated from Local 5 and established as Local 537 of the American Federation of Teachers) officially approved the program after two hours' careful consideration, with only one dissenting vote, in a meeting of several hundred. The program was formulated in such a way as to be a model for smaller as well as larger departments (Appendix II). It should be noted that in the city colleges larger departments, such as English, chemistry, and economics, sometimes approached and sometimes even exceeded a hundred members.

The program set up departmental assemblies that for matters of personnel included all permanent members, and for other matters all members. In the latter, what the voting membership would be for what kinds of matters was left for the assembly to decide. Provision was made for committee responsibility, for policy determination by assembly vote, for interdepartmental relations. Elected department chairmen, subject to the approval of the faculty, were to replace presidential appointment of department heads. The chairmen were given no additional remuneration, but instead a reduced teaching load and adequate clerical help. There were to be elective committees with adequate representation on them of different interests. Broad participation was ensured for determining what kind of appointments were needed and procedures for appointment. Procedures for the treatment of probationers emphasized guidance and security against peremptory judgment, openness of discussion, and opportunities for remedying faults. Conditions were set for dealing with charges of incompetence, as well as for recommendations on salary increments and promotions. The area of participation in curricular revision was broadened and the freedom of teachers to experiment within the curriculum ensured, while cooperative determination of standards was maintained on required courses.

During December 1937 and the early months of 1938, the union pressed its overall program in conferences with members of the board and publicized it among the staffs. It made analyses of the basic problems at the colleges and sent evidence to the board. It prepared briefs, comparative studies, and analyses of current writings on governance. Staff members were urged to establish the maximum of informal democracy feasible within the existing bylaws. In some departments the campaign bore fruit rapidly, and first steps toward democratization were taken—in some, large; in others, hesitant. In one department, a committee of senior professors was appointed by the head, who announced his intention of consulting with it on all major questions. In a number of departments meetings of all members were held—a most unusual event—but attempts to provide for regular participation by department members in determining policy were turned aside. Many made a genuine attempt to test the possibilities of wider participation. In three departments the head requested the election of an appointments committee. In another, the members forced the setting up of a committee to determine standards for promotion. In one department a curriculum committee was established—for the first time. Others asked the head to regularize informal democratic procedures hitherto existing. Two departments asked for the right to fill vacant headships by election. On a widely scattered front, teachers began to realize that the problems of education were *their* problems.

On January 17, 1938, the board turned to removing irritations that had characterized administration–student relations. They passed the "McGoldrick resolution" concerning extracurricular activities. It permitted any group of students to form an organization, association, club, or chapter by filing with a designated faculty officer the name and purpose of the organization and the names and addresses of its president and secretary. Organizations with a program against religion in general or the religion of a particular group, or against any race, were specifically forbidden; military or semi-military organizations required special faculty and board authorization.

Students accustomed to constant friction with the college administrations (often terminating in mass expulsions at City College) hailed the new step as a fundamental reform. Nevertheless, looking back, it was a shortcoming in the program of democratic governance not to propose ways for integrating participation of students. The union, mindful of past administrative autocracy in the treatment of students, rested content with a proposed shift of general regulation from administration to faculties, and with the greater freedom of students in their own affairs. Anything more was not yet envisaged on "the agenda of history."

In these early months of 1938, the disadvantages of autocratic administrative forms were carefully assessed in the many meetings, conferences, and bulletins that centered on the proposed changes. It was argued that the evils were a consequence of the dictatorial type of structure, not of personalities; that possibly creative contributions of the staffs had been thwarted; that standards were absent; that arbitrariness was common; that the curriculum reflected personal inclination and not wide educational deliberation; that department rivalries were aggravated. Objections currently offered to democratic governance were also discussed. Would democratic organization be an empty formalism, or would it encourage initiative and responsibility? Might it not overburden teachers and distract from scholarly work? Were teachers really interested in it, or was it simply attractive because of existent grievances that could be otherwise remedied? Indeed, was discussion of such matters as salary unprofessional? Were younger members of the staff mature enough? Would democracy lead to anarchy and stagnation? (A summary of the arguments offered in the campaign for democratic governance at that time is given in Appendix III.)

The question of tenure had remained in the background since the board's agreement to the three-year probationary period. Now it suddenly moved to the center. On March 8, 1938, the New York Court of Appeals declared the Feld–McGrath tenure law to be unconstitutional. Alarmed, the staffs of the

59

colleges rapidly organized for a legislative drive to replace it. This was spearheaded by the Legislative Conference of the City Colleges, the cross-college committee that kept an eye on legislation affecting the colleges. The union secured two guarantees in the draft of the bill. One was protection against discrimination by a provision that "conduct unbecoming a teacher," listed as a ground for dismissal, should not be interpreted in such a way as to interfere with academic freedom. The other was to prevent a situation of unavoidable academic retrenchment from being used as an occasion for dismissing militant teachers: Any departure from strict seniority was limited to special educational reasons not discriminatory against person or persons.

Within six days the bill had been drawn up, agreed upon, and presented to the Board of Higher Education for support. But on March 14 the board unanimously refused the request that it present this bill in the then current session of the legislature, although it indicated general approval of the provisions and promised a tenure bylaw. From this point on, though democratic reorganization was the more disputed item, tenure and reorganization were joined in one campaign. The board's postponement of the tenure question rested in part on its view that tenure and reorganization were related and should be dealt with together.

On April 12, 1938, the board's Committee of Five, which had drafted a proposed bylaw revision concerning both tenure and governance, held a hearing so that the staffs might comment on the proposals. Two hundred members of the staff crowded into the meeting room, and the meeting lasted from 3 P.M. to 12:30 A.M., with an hour's break for dinner. The afternoon was devoted to tenure discussion. The proposals on tenure, which followed largely the measures agreed on in the bill constructed by the staffs, were favorably received. Union spokesmen pointed to the omission of the noninstructional staffs and the lack of safeguards for probationers. The board members indicated that the question of noninstructional staffs was to be considered separately at a subsequent time. Strong pressure came from administrative sources for tenure for administrators in their administrative posts, not merely in their college departmental posts, but this did not prevail. In the evening attention turned to the proposed bylaw on governance. Strong pressure was exerted for postponing consideration until the fall: whole departments had sent in petitions to this effect, with everyone's name faithfully following the department head's. Twenty or more heads at City College in a single petition urged postponement. Of the whole-department petitions, Mr. Flynn, recognizing the coercive atmosphere that produced such a lineup, commented: "Almost as good as Hitler's 99 per cent Ja!"[1] The move for postponement was denied by the Committee of Five on the ground that the committee could not recommend tenure provisions without knowing how appointments would be made, and tenure bylaws had been promised the staffs without delay.

The report of the discussion in the union's *College Newsletter* states the argument of the opposition to democratic reorganization:

> Professors Moore of Hunter College and Stair of C.C.N.Y. argued in favor of a sort of "benevolent despotism" within departments as a better guarantee of the rights of young teachers than their own participation in departmental decisions would be. Professor Stair went on to warn the committee against the danger of allowing instructors to occupy places on the faculty, indicating his suspicion that radicalism might be particularly strong in this rank. Mr. Flynn intimated that the principle of democracy granted even such persons a voice in deciding their own interests, and Professor Stair replied that perhaps a "limited" form of democracy might be preferable to the full application of a

principle that he thought was sometimes very thoughtlessly invoked. Professor Stair concluded that the college did not suffer so much from lack of democracy as it did from "factionalism" and insufficient "turnover" in the lower ranks.[2]

In the tense silence that followed this expression of opposition, Professor H. A. Overstreet, of the Department of Philosophy and Psychology at City College, arose. He was one of the few department heads at City College who had refused to sign the petition for delay, and his department was one of those that had been self-consciously developing democratic procedures. He traced what his department was trying to do; he saw it as an appropriate time to extend the participation of staff members in the government of the colleges; if democracy was trustworthy in other fields, it could be no less so in education. He was followed by the present writer as union spokesman, who expressed the union's conviction concerning the momentous character of the steps being taken, urged no retreat, and for the greater part of an hour examined the proposals in detail, recommending numerous changes in the direction of still more complete democratization. Representatives of other staff organizations followed: departments, special groups, individuals. Opinion for the most part reinforced the case for democratization.

This meeting, the first of its kind in the history of the colleges, itself marked the inauguration of a democratic approach to the board by the staffs of the colleges. The Committee of Five promised to consider all criticisms and prepare a draft to present to the board's Committee on Curriculum and By-Laws. That committee in turn held a second open hearing on that draft, on May 9, and again about two hundred members of the staff attended. It was clear that by this time everyone within the colleges was using the language of democracy, and opposition to the program began to find ready objections from the standpoint of a "true" or "higher" or "reasonable" democracy. For example, it was suggested that departments should themselves decide whether they wanted to elect their chairman or continue the present system.

The board at its meeting of May 16 postponed action on bylaw revision. It elected Ordway Tead as its chairman; the reform group thus took over formal control. Final action came on June 20. From the first hearing to the final action, there were two whole months in which agitation by all sides was carried on. The union mobilized the sentiment of the staffs and appealed to trade unions and progressive groups in the city to counter pressures against proposed changes. The response was ready, public, and strong. On May 7 the union held its first annual educational forum, focusing attention on Democracy and Higher Education. It raised the problems that the staffs would turn to in a democratized institution. Among its panels were Democracy in College Administration, College Curriculum in a Democratic Society, the Student in a Democratic College, Standards of Competence for the College Teacher, Labor and Higher Education.

In those years, no progressive campaign in New York could be carried on without encountering a Red Scare technique. In May a letter from a Brooklyn College professor appeared in the Brooklyn *Daily Eagle*, under the headline "REDS BACK PLAN TO REORGANIZE COLLEGES." It said: "It is my opinion that the hue and cry that has been raised about dictatorial department heads and other administrative authorities has back of it radical propaganda, the object of which is to cause the disintegration of our present organization." This was used by a New York councilman in an attack on Mayor La Guardia.

On June 20 the board finally acted to adopt the bylaws on tenure and faculty reorganization recommended by its Committee of Five. (A condensed summary of major changes is given in Appendix IV.) In the provisions on tenure it followed for the most part the proposals of the staffs. It insisted on an affirmative act by college authorities in placing a person on the permanent staff. However, no statement of reasons was required in failing to recommend probationers for reappointment conferring tenure. (The union had urged as a very minimum that there should be review of an appeal where a probationer believed that there had been some special discrimination against him on grounds of race, religion, or political belief.) The provisions on democratic reorganization of governance structure had in major respects the broad sweep that the staffs had urged. The educational role of faculties in matters of policy was augmented by giving them through committees a budgetary role, rather than by a direct assignment of ultimate authority on all matters of policy. The president of the college retained considerable power as executive agent of the board, but access of faculty to board became direct. Some of the mechanisms established were felt to have troublesome potential. For example, the Personnel and Budget Committee of the faculty was to be composed of the elected department chairmen; this might generate a club spirit in which they would be reluctant to decide appeals against a fellow member. Again, since this committee was not responsible to the faculty or faculty council (the latter a representative body where the faculty exceeded a hundred in number), it would have insufficient incentive to develop standards consciously in its judgments about personnel. However, the reorganization of departmental structure was thought to be quite thorough, starting with the election of chairmen, and utilizing a committee system for appointments (though without a return responsibility to the department as a whole), and a vote by all members of professorial ranks above for recommending promotion to a professorial rank.

Criticism slipped into the background in the initial rejoicing at the new freedom. The revolution seemed complete, and its outcome to justify the two years of tension, of ferment, of creative thought and discussion and agitation. Even board members exulted in the event. The report in the *New York Times* (June 21, 1938) went to the heart of the matter:

> The plan was described as the most significant step taken by the Board of Higher Education in the last five years by John T. Flynn, chairman of the committee that framed the new proposal. The essence of the plan, according to Mr. Flynn, is the taking of the autocratic powers from the presidents of the colleges and lodging the government of the colleges in faculties and departments. The plan, Mr. Flynn said, introduces democratic rule into the colleges.

In the *Herald Tribune* of the same day, Flynn and Tead were quoted as saying that "the decision would place the city's colleges in the front ranks with only a handful of other institutions in this country in placing democracy in operation in college administration."

CHAPTER 5

Progress, Reaction, and Counter-Revolution

ON OCTOBER 1, 1938, the "democratic experiment" got under way. A story in the *College Newsletter* of the union gives Tead's view of the situation:

Foreseeing the development of a community of scholars who would be "able to do better together what they agree they want to do," Mr. Ordway Tead, Chairman of the Board of Higher Education, last week urged members of the city college staffs to regard the new Faculty Reorganization by-laws as a minimum basis for cooperative activity in the colleges . . .

The by-laws, said Mr. Tead, were intended by the Board to effect improvement in the quality of higher education by developing direct responsibility for the conduct of the colleges among the Faculty itself . . .

The widest possible basis for the deliberation of college policy was recommended to the staffs by Mr. Tead, who suggested that the meetings of the Faculty Council be open and that action of authoritative bodies be widely and quickly publicized. The department chairman, said Mr. Tead, should be "a leader among equals," a most important part of whose work must be the careful supervision of the work of probationers. Although tutors do not have a vote in the department, they should, said Mr. Tead, be allowed the fullest participation in their colleagues' deliberations . . .

Among the other problems recommended by Mr. Tead to the careful deliberation of the staffs was the question: "What are the objectives of the college?" Mr. Tead suggested that the faculties devote part of the next few years to careful formulation of collegiate aims, both for the entire college curriculum and at the level of the individual departments. In addition, Mr. Tead presented the following questions to the staff for consideration: 1. the problem of the relationship of the Faculty to the Board; 2. the problem of Faculty–student relationships in an "organized way"; 3. the problem of developing techniques for the appraisal of the work of probationers; 4. the problem of integrating and unifying the work of the Evening Session with that of the day.[1]

In the three older colleges (Queens was excluded from the bylaws for its first three years) forty-five incumbent department chairmen were reelected out of a total of approximately sixty. Departments had, thereafter, to make recommendations on reappointments, budget, and promotions within a very short time.

Within the colleges the reorganization had been supported by the large majority, who felt the pressure of existing grievances. It had been opposed only by a minority, who felt it overturned the existing order in which authority over teachers was safely entrusted to administrators and authority over students safely entrusted to the wisdom of teachers. Once the reorganization was carried out, the basis on which unity had been achieved was removed. Within a large group objections had been less to the power system that existed than to the fashion in which that power had been exercised. As members of this group moved into leadership positions, especially those who had a sounder conception of educational policy and a sounder attitude to human relations, full democratization became less imperative in their eyes. They tended to pin hopes on the good administrator rather than on a good system; and at times the good administrator began to view democratic organization as a curb to sweeping changes he might want to make. The weight of such a group (which came to occupy a prominent position in the colleges) was thrown toward making democracy a method of selecting the best persons to whom power could be entrusted rather than toward making it a constantly operative deliberative decision system.

Again, older habits of authority and acceptance did not disappear overnight: elitist attitudes of professors toward instructors, of teachers toward nonteachers (laboratory assistants, library and clerical staff, etc.), of day teachers toward evening or extension teachers. Thus often the limited group of voting members of a department threatened to become an oligarchy, ruling without even consultation over the affairs of a considerably larger departmental group. Sometimes appointments committees made recommendations without even consulting the voting members of the department. Often a supervisory attitude was substituted for guidance in dealing with probationers.

Another surviving trait was the fear of frankness, rationalized by the theory that judgments of policy and especially of personnel were too complex for open discussion and too sensitively disturbing. Personnel committees and appointments committees tended to be secretive, and even representative faculty councils resisted attempts to make their meetings open to any members of the faculty that elected them who might wish to be spectators.

The formal procedures that the new complex organization

required were sometimes felt as cumbersome by those habituated to other ways. In an authoritarian organization no discussion of policy or personnel by department members had had other than informal status. It even became popular for a time to ridicule the formalities of democracy. But with formality of procedure came increasingly impersonal discussion and the possibility of frankness without rancor.

On the other hand, morale among both teaching and non-teaching staff was tremendously improved. Cooperative discussion began to replace dependence on favor. The basis of initiative was tremendously broadened, and inroads were gradually made on the feeling so prevalent in an authoritarian organization that whenever one has an idea someone else ought to act on it. For "the college ought to do this" was substituted specific steps to bring the idea before the appropriate body. Initiative was required in each department to face all the problems of government—the reconciliation of rule and discretion, the Scylla of rubber-stamping, and the Charybdis of the department fumbling with innumerable details. It was not a question of testing democracy but of perfecting specific techniques. Immediately, there began a growing revision of curriculum, particularly of basic courses, with an eye to student needs.

In April 1939 Tead wrote of the reorganization: "It has brought with it a common disposition to think about problems of college government and policy and of control of departmental affairs that was not there before. There is even in these few months an awareness, a concern, a sense of responsibility about the educational process among scores of faculty members who before were quite content to let their classroom work stand as the sum total of their contribution to college education."[2]

This spirit was manifest from the very outset. The first task—recommendations on reappointment and promotion—led many departments to attempt to formulate standards.

Questions of objectives were explicitly raised, often for the first time. In one case members formally refused to be considered for promotion because they felt that insufficient attention was being given to standards. Of the result of this first budget, Tead wrote in the article quoted above: "A certain number of grievous old-time inequities have been sought to be removed by the new recommendations, which means that the number of promotions proposed may be higher than it will be two or three years hence. With this exception noted, the requests are certainly not exorbitant as they have reached the Board." In short, democracy had not meant releasing the passions of the multitude for personal gain, which the anti-democratic tradition in political philosophy has always taken to be characteristic.

To counter the tendencies to secrecy and the fear of openness required a positive campaign at both the college and board level:

> A vigorous Union campaign to make public the decisions of the newly elected Faculty Committee on Personnel and Budget at the City College was climaxed last Thursday by an open meeting of the City College chapter at which Acting-President Mead personally announced that the results of the Committee's deliberations would be disclosed to all members of the staffs whose cases were considered. Dean Morton Gottschall also addressed the meeting, at which many heads of departments were present.
>
> The Union's campaign began when it became known that the Faculty Committee on Personnel and Budget had decided to make its proceedings secret. Union delegations visited Acting-President Mead and Dean Gottschall to inquire the reasons for the decision and to protest the ruling as a violation of the spirit of the new democratic reorganization.[3]

Hunter College from the outset had provided for periodic reports from the Committee on Personnel and Budget to the faculty council. But the situation generally appeared to have been serious enough to call for board action. On January 16, 1939, it resolved that "as a matter of policy with regard to future budget procedure, the definitive decisions of the respective Committees on Personnel and Budget and the President's revisions thereof when completed, shall be made available to the respective Faculty Committees on Personnel and Budget and to the members of the departments through their department chairmen." The board also promised open hearings on the budget, and subsequently the hearing was included as a regular procedure. It also set up college committees on faculty–board relations, specifying three members of the permanent instructional staff, elected by faculty councils for a three-year period. The committees included the president and academic dean, and were to meet once a semester with the board's administrative committee of each college.

The democratizing process gained momentum as it functioned during the academic year 1938–39. Its various mechanisms were observed in action, and their merits and defects open to view. For example, appointments committees within departments sometimes cut themselves off from any form of responsibility to the department, seeing their democratic election as the sufficient basis for their independent judgment. Some committees refused to report their proceedings to the department for criticism and suggestion before sending recommendations beyond it. Some departments controlled their committee's procedure on the ground that procedure involved educational policy, though they could not control committee judgments. The faculty Committee on Personnel and Budget proved to be inadequately structured. Consisting of departmental chairmen, it had all the difficulties of departmental interests and mutual deference. The variety of its functions— budget, consideration of personnel, and hearing of appeals—

created further difficulties. It was not always clear, for example, whether in passing on departmental recommendations for promotion the committee was denying some on the basis of merit or budgetary necessities. Again, appeals against its decision were considered by it itself; and where the appeal involved overruling a department chairman, there was reticence to overrule one of their number.

In the long run, a functioning democratic system can experiment with different mechanisms and see which work out best. This, however, involves a certain community of underlying objectives and policy. It would not be profitable here to explore the specific problems in the variety of mechanisms. Many of them can, in the half century that has passed, doubtless be studied from the repertoire of mechanisms in colleges and universities throughout the country as well as at the city colleges. Perhaps the new democracy of the city colleges would have solved these problems of mechanism more immediately if it had continued with its initial vigor. But basic conflicts of various sorts soon emerged.

At first sight, the problems that arose in 1938–39 had the appearance of unfinished matters to which the new democracy could be applied. For one thing, there were many grievance cases. Central among these were probationers, and the question at issue, where it was not some special discrimination, was whether probationers had any presumptive rights of continuance in virtue of the quality of their service. The prevalent administrative view was that they did not: To discontinue service involved no reflection on the teacher's ability or scholarship. No reasons were required; a department might continue to shop over a long period, giving tenure only when it found an exceptional person. The opposing view was that standards might be set high in the first place, but that if the probationer satisfied them, he or she had the right to tenure. To decide in the absence of explicit reasons was dangerous, for it opened the way to possible bias on irrelevant grounds.

A second serious conflict concerned the nonteaching staffs. At the time they were covered by state law with respect to salary schedules, and not set off in a separate system. In many relations—as between science teachers and laboratory assistants—teachers and nonteachers had achieved a sense of unified effort rather than that of a superior and a service system. In October 1938 the board introduced and eventually (July 6, 1939) carried through a transfer of the nonteaching staffs to the Municipal Civil Service system. This clearly had strong financial motives, for the new salary scales were lower, and retrenchment was in the air. The Legislative Conference of the City Colleges introduced a bill in Albany to provide the tenure that had been agreed upon. When it included the nonteaching staffs, the board opposed the bill, which consequently failed to pass.

During the spring and early summer of 1939, it became clear that serious financial retrenchment for education in New York City was under way. In late June and early July, the board placed stoppages in the salary scale of instructors and assistant professors at given increments within their automatic range. To leap this hurdle it would be necessary to be recommended as "a teacher of exceptional teaching ability who is also a distinguished scholar or creative worker." This extravagant language strengthened the wide impression that scholastic excuses were being used to keep salaries down. Interestingly, several years later, a court decision found that the stoppages violated state laws.

A group of changes in the board's bylaws proposed at the end of the 1938–39 academic year were kept private until passed. They turned out to take considerable steps toward restoring presidential power in the colleges. The Legislative Conference of the City Colleges, later analyzing the changes (November 6, 1939), said:

> The most significant group of changes has the result of markedly increasing the powers of the President, while relegating the Committee on Faculty Personnel and Budget and the Department Committees to the position of advisers to the President. It should be noted that, while the organization by-laws were originally formulated only after extensive deliberation and consultation with the college staffs, these changes, which involve the abandonment of many steps in the democratic procedure, were adopted without an opportunity on the part of the staffs to offer suggestions on a matter which so vitally concerned them.

The changes involved systematic combing of the bylaws to enhance the presidential role. For example, in the section on the Committee on Faculty Personnel and Budget, the sentence "Its recommendations, together with the recommendations and comments of the Presidents, shall be submitted promptly by him to the Board" was replaced by "The President shall consider such recommendations in making his recommendations on such matters to the Board." To the sentence reading "The Committee shall receive and consider petitions and appeals from members of the instructional staff with respect to matters of status and compensation" was added "and shall present its recommendations to the President. Appeals from the decision of the President by a member of the staff or any faculty committee shall be made in writing only to the respective Administrative Committees of the Board and shall be transmitted through the President." Departments were now instructed to consult with the president before taking final action in making recommendations to the Committee on Personnel and Budget.

Given these changes, the extent of actual democratic functioning would depend to a large extent on the character of the presidents of the colleges. If they encouraged participation, it could grow. If they wished to use the instruments the bylaws now placed in their hands, they would have free channels for autocratic power. There remained, however, substantial democratic gains in both structure and spirit. Departments retained the internal structure they had won, and the election of chairmen stayed with the department, although the president now had the right, in the interests of enhancing the educational character of the college, to bring in a person of professorial rank after consultation with the department, and recommend him to the board as department chairman. The democratic control of curriculum by faculties and departments was unchanged, as was election of committees and their responsibility.

We may well wonder what led the Board of Higher Education to abandon so hastily and surreptitiously a sizeable part of the structure it had only a year before established. Various conjectures were offered. Some of the members appeared to have been alarmed by the extent to which grievances arising in the first year came into their hands for solution. Failing to attribute this to deficiencies in specific mechanisms, they may have turned to the typical solution of the business world—leaving matters in the hands of efficient and trustworthy general managers. Perhaps the democratization had served its "cleansing" purpose in the colleges: The old administrations were gone and more trusted ones installed; the dominant interest was in good administration rather than in the development of democracy. Some pressure for recovery of powers may have existed among the presidents; while this did not hold for Klapper of Queens, who throughout went even beyond the bylaws in setting up procedures in the new college, it was rumored that the changes were demanded by Harry D. Gideonse, the incoming Brooklyn College president. Among the more pervasive causes was surely the critical budgetary situation. The board's action in putting the noninstructional staff on Municipal Civil Service, its abolition of Townsend Harris High School, its establishment of stopping points in the salary schedule of the college teachers, reinforced the general lesson that reform administrations may be both high on ideals and vigorous in reducing costs. The rising faculty democracy was headed for expansion in its attempt to correct long-standing injustices and its recommendations of better conditions of work. Frictions and unceasing tensions would probably have been unavoidable. (The budgetary situation was evident in the city as a whole, not merely in education.) Ultimately, the board would have had to decide whether its role would be to interpret the needs of higher education to the city and state authorities or to interpret the demands of the latter to the college staffs. The lessons that may be learned about the bearing of these broader questions will be considered in a subsequent chapter.

During 1939, after the changes in the organization bylaws, and during the whole of 1940, experience continued to grow about the operations of democracy. At many points the opposing directions—the broadening of democracy or the increase of authority—had to be faced in disputes about interpretation. To take a particular example of detail, the Committee on Personnel and Budget at Brooklyn College decided that where there was a tie in a department committee the department chairman should have a second vote. The Brooklyn faculty overruled this, affirming instead that in case of a tie the question should go to the department. But the faculty parliamentarian and the dean, presiding in the absence of the president, ruled that the faculty was only a body to review decisions of the faculty Council and could not properly consider a decision of the Committee on Personnel and Budget!

On January 8, 1941, a bulletin of the union's Educational Policies Committee issued an alarm. Delegations conferring with some of the presidents had learned that further revision of the bylaws was under consideration, that it had been proposed to substitute appointment for election of the department chairmen. The committee offered the interpretation that difficulties in the operation of the bylaws could be solved by expanding rather than contracting the democracy, and called for broad cooperative discussion of any proposed changes. It soon became clear that what was involved was a general reckoning with the organizational system. A story in the *New York Times* was headed:

CITY COLLEGES ASK FACULTY CRITICISMS

Opinions Sought as 3-Year Trial of 'Democracy' By-Laws Nears End

Teachers Now Govern

Lodging of power with them was hailed as their 'Magna Carta'—2000 affected[4]

The story told how Ordway Tead had called on the presidents to review the bylaws now that three years of their use had passed. The presidents invited faculty members to suggest changes in the light of their experience.

Staff response was widespread and strong. At City College about 275 teachers answered a questionnaire prepared by the Faculty–Board Relations Committee. At Brooklyn College about half the instructional staff answered a questionnaire circulated by a special committee. At Hunter the Faculty–Board Relations Committee received many suggestions without special solicitation. It appeared that the majority of those who expressed themselves were fundamentally in favor of the democratic changes of three years earlier and wanted to maintain them. A *New York Times* item reported that Klapper favored revision to ensure greater flexibility, but was in complete agreement with the democratic spirit of the bylaws. "As evidence of this, he points out that Queens College has, since its inception, been organized on a more democratic basis than is required even under the by-laws."[5]

The union's Educational Policies Committee issued a series of bulletins dealing with specific items of the bylaws. It found the faculty council to be one of the most successful parts of the democratic organization; to its departmental representation there should be added representation of other segments of the staffs, such as the evening session, the administrative staffs, and, where present, the elementary and high schools. On departments, the union committee supported extension of participation by nonvoting members and general departmental control of the bylaws of its committees where not at variance with the board's bylaws. It found the personnel and budget committees the most unsatisfactory and suggested the substitution of a variety of mechanisms for their different functions. On personnel, it proposed that departmental recommendations should go directly to the president, giving that post responsibility commensurate with the power the board had in effect delegated. Appeals should be handled by a committee of nine, elected at large, which would attempt to resolve most problems within the college. (Department chairmen should not be eligible for this committee.) Its recommendations should go to the Administrative Committee of the board together with the president's recommendations. Budget should be handled by a standing faculty or faulty council committee, and where there are several schools, a college-wide conference, representing also all different kinds of staffs.

The weight of staff opinion proved decisive when the board held a hearing and finally acted. Most significant was the fact that the department chair continued to be elective. From this point on, the basic democratic structure of college organization was maintained. Indeed it became commonplace that educational matters should be in the hands of educators.

The question of structure was now settled, but questions of power and of freedom—academic freedom—remained. The long-postponed tenure law was passed by the state, giving greater legal protection than the bylaws of a board could afford. It contained the provision the bylaws had included, that conduct unbecoming a teacher should not be construed in such a way as to violate academic freedom. It was just in time, for a storm was about to break.

The incident that provoked (or perhaps just signaled) the storm was the appointment of Bertrand Russell to the philosophy department at City College. World War II had begun in September of 1939. The Russian–German pact, which allowed Hitler to attack the western countries more freely, and the Russian–Finnish war made anti-communism a central political issue in the United States. It soon became an attack in the community at large upon progressive action and liberal thought: within labor, upon the labor left; within liberalism itself, on all popular front and left–radical thought. In New York it added strength to the extremist groups that had attacked the democratic reorganization as a communist plot. Within the labor organizations it led to expulsions of the more militant unions. The city's teachers union and the colleges' teachers union had supported unity with the CIO while they were still within the AFL. They were expelled and joined the CIO. As political hysteria deepened, the CIO in turn expelled its own left-wing unions, including the New York teacher unions. The latter became allied at that point with the State, County, and Municipal Workers Union.

The Russell case showed the growing power of the hysteria. Russell had been a pacifist in World War I, though not in World

War II. He had written against religious dogmatism and for sexual freedom. When his appointment became public, Anglican Bishop Manning denounced him as an immoral atheist; a right-wing Catholic group attacked the colleges for the appointment; and a Jewish woman filed a suit alleging the dangers of corruption to her daughter if she went to the college. It was thus a "united front" and soon became a "popular front." And most surprisingly, when it was adjudged in court, the suit won out. The McGeehan decision argued that Russell's brilliance as a teacher would lead students to read his books; it quoted selected passages concerning his pacifism, sexual beliefs, criticisms of religion. Particularly on sex, it inferred that a girl under eighteen might be tempted to sexual experimentation, which, under the laws of the state, would be construed as "constructive rape." Accordingly the appointment of Russell to a public institution was a violation of state law and invalid. It was branded "a chair of indecency."[6] Although a small part of the Board of Higher Education supported this attack, the majority were outraged and wanted to appeal the verdict. The city's legal officer refused to do this; it was argued that in the current hysteria the intermediate court might support the verdict and it would thus become a powerful precedent, whereas it could be bypassed if it remained only a lower-court decision. Nevertheless, the board voted to proceed with the appeal, and its members offered to pay the costs. But at that point the mayor gave up; he deleted the budget line for the post, and without this financing the issue became moot.

Under the impact of the larger situation, the state legislature set up the Rapp–Coudert Committee to investigate the financial situation in higher education and subversive influences within it. The reign of terror that this investigation unleashed in the city colleges is part of the history of the early 1940s in New York. It has well been described as a dress rehearsal for the

McCarthyism of the 1950s on the national scene. Dozens of teachers on tenure were dismissed as a consequence; many not on tenure were quietly dropped or driven away; an atmosphere of fear pervaded the colleges and affected both teaching and freedom of thought and expression. That it was a gross violation of academic freedom has been generally acknowledged. The kinds of laws on which it rested (such as the Feinberg law) were eventually declared unconstitutional. Several decades later the Board of Higher Education gave official apologies. Some of those dismissed were reinstated, and some given pensions they would by then have earned. New York had had the same kind of experience after World War I, persecuting teachers in the public schools, with the same kind of later apologies. Yet lessons from the past had too readily been forgotten. In this case, within a few years, the national hysteria of the McCarthy period prolonged the situation that Rapp–Coudert had fastened on the New York colleges.

Under these unsettling conditions, presidential power was largely restored as a matter of practice. It was evident at City College and Brooklyn College, where the presidents supported the political investigation. Nevertheless, the organizational role of the faculty remained theoretically ensconced, and in this sense the basically democratic structure was preserved for later development.

This is the end of the original narrative, insofar as the New York city colleges are concerned. The next chapter examines how at the time we saw the governance scene throughout the country. After that we ask what can be learned from the account, and how we may secure that learning.

CHAPTER 6

New York and the National Scene

OUR NARRATIVE HAS REACHED its temporal limits, but there remains within its period one topic that has not been touched: How did these events relate to what was going on in higher education throughout the country? A few items on that aspect are worth reviewing, once again from the perspective of our awareness at that time. This account falls into two parts: the first, during the campaign for reorganization (1936 to 1938); the second, after the reorganization (1938 to 1941).

Of course in preparing the proposals for reorganization, the Educational Policies Committee of the college union examined what was going on within the broader New York area. We were aware of the greater role that faculties played in the operation of the institution at some of the local, especially experimental, colleges—at Sarah Lawrence, for example—or the sense that many departments at a university like Columbia had that they were in a practice managing their own affairs by common consultation. It was not always clear how firm informal practice would prove in particular situations. Moreover, given the situation at the city colleges, our emphasis fell on overt constitutional provision rather than sociological practice.

Again, in preparing proposals, our primary interest was in getting ideas rather than in mapping the distribution of practices. A good current practice might be helpful in advocacy of reform, but the first thing was to come to know the good. This obviously led us to the then current literature in the field of governance. Such studies for higher education—descriptive and statistical, historical, and theoretical—were accumulating by the 1920s and 1930s. For example, numerous works by Everett C. Elliott and others gathered the charters and foundation regulations of many universities and branched off into special studies. Thus Elliott, together with M. M. Chambers and William A. Ashbrook, prepared, under grant from the Carnegie Foundation for the Advancement of Teaching, a work entitled *The Governance of Higher Education, Designed for the Use of University and College Trustees* (1935), in which one could find sets of questions and answers on various matters. For example:

> Q. Is the faculty sometimes entirely unrepresented in the determination of educational policies? A. Twenty-two presidents of ninety-three who answered a questionnaire in 1919 indicated that the faculty had no voice in the determination of educational policy. (No. 355)

> Q. Is there a trend toward allowing faculties to participate more in the determination of educational policy? A. A study of the same institutions as mentioned above made ten years later (1929) indicated, if any trend, a slight decrease in faculty participation. (No. 356)

Similarly we could learn (No. 358) about whether faculties in general were permitted to select new members of the teaching staff: Presidents of 136 institutions in 1929 indicated that at 36 the faculty actually selected new members, at 83 the faculty or members of it were consulted, and at 15 the faculty had no voice. With respect to faculty role in selecting their own administrative officers other than the president: Of 139 in 1929, faculties had no voice at 78 institutions, were consulted at 30, and actually selected their own officers at 25 (No. 363). The trend was toward more faculty consultation but less actual selection by faculty.

Interestingly, the book went on to report on proposals for change. It told of suggestions (as early as 1913 by J. McKeen Cattell) that instead of a lay board there be a corporation of professors, interested alumni, and members of the community (No. 373). One college dean (Max McConn) suggested a board containing six members of the faculty, elected by the faculty; three students, elected by the senior class; and three alumni, elected by the alumni association. As for organization of the faculty (No. 374), that should be left to the faculty itself. Particularly, inauguration of courses of study and curricular change should be left to the president and the faculty.

The relation of outside lay boards and insiders (teachers and administrative officers) was the special focus of J. E. Kirkpatrick's *American College and Its Rulers* (1926). This was a vigorous critical and historical study in terms of a concept of academic democracy. It showed how the early American colleges had followed a British pattern of a corporation of insiders, with a lay group acting at most in a supervisory capacity, but not endowed with actual control. This had characterized Harvard and William and Mary at the outset, and the pattern of such trustee control almost everywhere had been a matter of conquest rather than an indigenous product. (Outsiders had been used in those two colleges to found them, not to control them.) Yale and Princeton, on the other hand, had outside control from the beginning. Virginia is of special interest: Jefferson gave it self-control, and for its first eighty years it was even without a president as representative of an absent governing body. But in the vicissitudes of the break with the British tradition, it eventually succumbed to the emerging American pattern. Kirkpatrick traces occasional survivals or redevelopment of faculty control—in Union Theological Seminary in New York, in proposals at Vassar, in partial faculty control of university policies at Western Reserve. Surveying the scene as a whole in the 1920s, Kirkpatrick looks forward to a plural or collegiate executive, a kind of cabinet system with individual and joint responsibility, as the next step. He thinks that the introduction of the provost as academic leader, with the president as business head, could be a step in that direction if the provost were given equal status and authority. But beyond that he wants a fuller democratic academic home rule, without which he maintains our educational institutions cannot effectively educate.

The most trenchant analysis in sociological terms of governance in higher education was, of course, Thorstein Veblen's *Higher Learning in America, A Memorandum on the Conduct of Universities by Business Men* (1918). Veblen saw the prevailing mode of governance as reflecting the habits of businessmen in America, and not consonant with the advancement of higher learning as the disinterested pursuit of knowledge. There is a sardonic tone to his report that "the spirit of American business is a spirit of quietism, caution, compromise, collusion, and chicane" (p. 51). American inventors are bold and innovative, but they are not the ones who end up on college and university boards. The system and order of knowledge are logical and organic, those of business mechanical and bureaucratic. The university finds it difficult to reconcile being "a corporation of learning" and a business dealing in "standardized erudition." "The faculty is conceived as a body of employees, hired to render certain services and turn out certain scheduled vendible results" (p. 67). The consequence in administration is bureaucratic departments, hierarchical gradation, standardization of instruction, all indispensable to control from above. Veblen is thus sensitive not only to administrative consequences but to the character of the teaching and learning. The intrusion of business principles in governance defeats the ends of a university. He concludes that the college president (whom he has labeled a "captain of erudition") should be discontinued, and the current type of governing board eliminated.

For the critique of detailed mechanisms, there were the rich reports of the AAUP extending over the decade, particularly those of Committee T, which deals with faculty structure. Already in 1921 (vol. 7, no. 3) we find an address by Joseph A. Leighton describing current practices at the better institutions and what faculties are called upon to recommend on matters of educational policy. He wants those practices more explicitly specified in the constitution and bylaws of universities. "The greatest problem in education as in industry, is to harmonize administrative efficiency in large concerns with humane values of self-determination and self-respect in the life of the worker, without which his work will surely deteriorate in quality." And he is wary of boards succumbing to influence and acting solely on the advice of presidents, who may not be great scholars or educators nor sound judges of scholarship.

Unanimity is by no means to be found in these controversies. There is a counterargument that faculties are less suitable for control because they have vested interests. For example, in the struggle to have science more widely introduced, obstacles came from the vested interests of older curricula adhered to by the profession rather than from presidents and trustees. Indeed, it was argued, the presidential system is needed for the great task of weeding out incompetency. (We shall have to consider these serious criticisms in a subsequent chapter when we come to the evaluation of claimants to governance.)

Again, agreement that the faculty should have a role in matters of educational policy would have to be spelled out in terms of specific powers: how far this would go into matters of budget, not merely of curriculum, how far a sharp line would be drawn between educational policy and administration.

These studies left us with the belief that while there was widespread aspiration toward a less authoritarian and a more democratic structure of governance, there were no visible models for the kind of situation we were facing. We had to plunge ahead and work out our own constitutional proposals, and learn by our own experience.

After the reorganization, during the 1938–39 academic year, we were fully occupied with the current problems of making the new structure work. By August 1939, however, when the national convention of the American Federation of Teachers met at Buffalo, attention was turned directly to the governance situation throughout the country. There were at the time around fifty college locals in the federation, and the interest in what had happened in New York was great. A national Committee on Democracy in Higher Education was set up and charged with drawing the lessons of the New York experience. As chairman of that committee, the present writer then had the general task of corresponding with interested members of the locals and, in part, getting a picture of the current scene.

Dramatically, within the last days of the convention, the Nazi–Soviet pact was announced, and in a few days the European war was on. The United States did not enter the war until the Japanese attack on Pearl Harbor, on December 7, 1941. During these two years, individuals and groups in the country had to ask themselves how far their existing projects should be continued or put aside in the light of the clearly approaching shaking of all social foundations. In the new committee, we continued the work partly as a task assigned and undertaken, and partly in the sense that under the conditions of the time anything that had to do with the advance of democratic ideas, when democracy was under attack, was worth persisting in. By the end of 1941, however, the New York locals were no longer in the American Federation of Teachers, having been dropped in inner conflicts within the federation; and in any case, entry into the war would have enlisted all available energies.

Nevertheless, there had been time enough to get a partial view of the state of governance in the country. Few formally enunciated democratic college organizations came our way, except in smaller private institutions, as with the elegant 1935 Vassar Statutes of Instruction, or in the construction of an experimental college such as at Antioch. We did find varied partial mechanisms, such as a faculty–trustee committee, an advisory faculty committee, a practice of asking for faculty advice, and so on. Sometimes these were traditional or a matter of habit, sometimes the instigating effort of a genial administrator. Often they were part of a fresh program, in some cases stimulated by the New York experience. At Ohio State University, where active leading spirits in the AAUP were obviously at work, an annual report in January 1939 listed as faculty organizations looking toward increased participation the following: Temple, Western Reserve, Texas A&M, Alabama, Cincinnati, Toledo. Emphasis fell on getting a faculty committee to confer with the administration and the board of trustees on matters of general university concern. In Cincinnati there was an effort to establish a whole-university faculty, with representation from the various college or school faculties, so as to have a faculty group that could address fundamental whole-university problems. At the University of Chicago, the Chicago College Teachers Union was concentrating on tenure, and seeking revision of rules of appointment to have recommendation by department rather than by department head. In the California university system, there had been a slight liberalization in governance in the shift of presidents, only to have it withdrawn by the next president. At Pittsburgh, the situation was unusual: With neither the union nor the AAUP chapter venturing to make a move in what they regarded as an autocratic atmosphere, the trustees were feuding with the chancellor because the reputation of the university had dropped; the trustees now suggested greater faculty participation to encourage initiative.

What happened at Harvard in 1939 and 1940, just after the New York experience, went to the heart of the governance situation in American universities. The story is told in the *Bulletin of the Cambridge Union of University Teachers*. The March 1939 issue (vol. 1, no. 4) gives the report of the union's Committee on Appointment and Tenure and Committee on Departmental Procedure in Appointment and Promotion. It proposes greater security and democratic participation, with special regard to the particular problems at Harvard. The May 1939 issue (vol. 1, no. 6) tells of the publication of the report of the president's Special Committee on "Some Problems of Personnel in the Faculty of Arts and Sciences." The union bulletin compares the recommendations of that report with the union's proposals. It finds some community but also some differences: For example, the president's committee reaffirms that department chairmen be appointed, and is not concerned with the issue of departmental democracy. Its effect, the union argues, would be "to crystallize the increasingly sharp distinction between impermanence and permanence, between a quick turnover in the lower ranks and a highly publicized system of importation in the higher reaches of the faculty." The union does not believe this is the best way to achieve the "laudable aim of avoiding intellectual stagnation at Harvard." Basically, the union points out that the proposals are not set in a consideration of the larger social and economic trends that have brought the problems into present concern.

A month later (June 1939, vol. 1, no. 7) the issue of the *Bulletin* is an open letter to the president's Special Committee. It complains about the haste with which those recommendations have been implemented and the somewhat devious way in which it was assumed that they had faculty support. "It is safe to say that no other period in the history of the University has seen so many final decisions, respecting the future of such promising scholars reached in so short a time." The tenure provisions of the report have been applied immediately "with remorseless retroactivity."

The October 1939 issue (vol. 2, no. 1) is clearly a rearguard action after the battle has been lost. It argues for increasing the associate professorships, doubtless in the hope that it will lessen the number of dismissals. But there is a serious question of policy involved. The administration has ruled that no one will be promoted to the associate professorship unless there are visible funds for his subsequent promotion to the full professorship! This thrusts aside the option of continuing as associate professor while waiting for budgetary improvement. The union attacks such sacrificing of educational values to supposed financial exigencies. (This whole argument, we may note, is a clear case of the need for faculty concern with budget, as part of educational policy.)

That the policy of rotating people in the lower ranks became a standard operating procedure at Harvard is a matter of history. (It became know as "folding chairs.") It was palliated somewhat by its explicitness, so that not being among the chosen at Harvard was not a ground for derogation of ability, and teachers found it worth serving there for a while, and indeed it proved in many departments a helpful step toward a job elsewhere. In this way Harvard traded on its reputation, so that it could do blithely what elsewhere was condemned as simply a budget-cutting device.

Defeat often brings reflection and fundamental wisdom. The March 1940 issue (vol. 2, no. 4) was chiefly devoted to an analysis of "Non-Resident Government at Harvard": "that Harvard, like most American colleges and universities, is a very model of undemocratic administration, that the Faculty has responsibilities and certain academic privileges, but no real power, except the right to recommend or suggest, and that the autocratic powers of the President are derived from an absentee, self-perpetuating government, the Corporation, of which the faculty members are servants and employees." It went on to contrast European democratic self-government in universities, and how power passed in the United States to outside boards. It refers to Kirkpatrick's book, and to controversy over the meaning of "fellow" in the original charter. (At one point, the "outside" controlling board, faced with the regulation that it have a "fellow" as member, simply appointed one of their number as "fellow" to secure the required representation.) The *Bulletin* traces the victory of presidential power through control by outside boards, and the perennial criticism of its educational consequences. It notes the renewed criticism of business leadership since the depression. And it appeals to the New York college experience to show the capacities of faculties.

Such an experience at so outstanding a university as Harvard, immediately after the New York colleges were democratized, suggests that the New York changes of 1938 were certainly not commonplace. Whatever the convergence of features and causes, the resultant had a distinctive character. In this sense Flynn and Tead were correct in their proud estimate of its significance. What distinguished it, however, was not entirely novelty, nor general theory, nor even a tie-in with democracy. It was rather the fact that it was a *detailed* program with a central thrust of increased faculty power; that it was developed not as a general reflection on the state of higher education but as a militant program to deal with hosts of specific grievances; that it was backed by a labor union that grew up to strengthen the staffs and struggle over the grievances. The contrast with the procedure of the AAUP at that time is instructive. When a local chapter of the AAUP thought that a teacher was dismissed unjustly, the central office would have an ad-hoc committee investigate, and considerably later the institution might be censured by the association. In the New York colleges the union fought grievance cases immediately and on the spot, raising together all the relevant issues, whether of discrimination, injustice, procedural violation, or inadequacy in existent regulations.

Another important element in the New York situation was that the battle for tenure had, as a practical matter, already been won by the time that the governance program was seriously considered. A share in governance assumes that the persons involved are part of a stable community. For teachers this requires tenure. Without the guarantee of tenure, teachers rarely venture into an area of possible controversy in which they may be putting their jobs on the line.

Finally, it was novel to have a large public system, such as the New York city colleges, adopt in a formal way and entrench in its bylaws (and in the case of tenure thereafter in state law) a system of governance characterized as a democratic reorganization. So far as we can see, this was the first large-scale event of this sort in the United States.

CHAPTER 7

A Half Century Later

WITH THE ACCOUNT of the democratic reorganization and its immediate career behind us, the task ahead is its lessons for a philosophy of governance. In part this was begun in concurrent evaluations made within the body of the narrative: the evils it overcame, the opportunities it opened for educational initiative, the cooperation it encouraged, the general awakening it involved; but at the same time the energies it consumed, the difficulties it gave rise to. It would be tempting, though simplistic, to extract the democratic structure as a kind of model and then follow it at New York's city colleges through the remainder of the half century, charting the benefits it bestowed and the costs it involved, hoping perhaps for a bottom-line summing as we neared the end of the century. Such an inquiry would ask what role the achieved structure of 1938 played in the governance of the colleges during subsequent decades, whether the faculties used or abused their new powers, how presidents adjusted to the changes (how far by new forms of leadership, how far by devious assumptions of power), where departmental democracy produced cooperative intellectual advances or where power cliques, whether faculty councils exhibited creative deliberation or inertia, what fresh forms of organization were tried as the colleges grew into a university and as students were given a role in governing, and how all these aspects related to the educational policies under the growing needs of the community and the country for expanded higher education.

To some extent we may hazard guesses to such questions, but the difficulties are enormous. For the governance forms do not function as independent mechanisms, even though some of their consequences can be traced. What happens to higher education at each point depends more fundamentally on kinds of resources and general purposes in the community, on the composition and character of the student body, on the extent of social crisis and whether it is faced or ignored, on the advance or sluggishness of research in general. Consider the following critical events in the last half century's history of the city colleges, some local, some response to national turmoil, each of which affected governance and each of which could well receive as detailed a treatment as has here been given of the 1938 revolution.

First, there are the broad changes that World War II brought to higher education in general, and the expansion that took place. The city colleges multiplied: Lehman in the Bronx, Richmond in Staten Island, York as a second college in Queens, a multiplicity of community colleges, a graduate school and various professional schools and programs—eventually a unified university system. The structure of the board was revised, eliminating the separate borough-based administrative committees and encouraging more unified policy. A chancellor's office was placed above the host of presidencies, operating from the board. A university-wide faculty senate came into existence.

Second, the McCarthy period on the national scene, coming before the effects of the Rapp–Coudert turmoil had subsided, extended the long period in which many aspects of the new governance forms remained subject to practical presidential power. Studies of the effects of McCarthyism in bringing universities and colleges throughout the country to the point of breakdown with respect to academic freedom are clear enough, and the New York colleges bore a double burden.

Again, just as student movements in the 1960s throughout the country's universities and colleges brought a rewriting of governance with student demands for some share, so, for example, City College adopted a fresh charter in 1972, establishing a senate relating the various schools of the institution, and also setting up an undergraduate senate and a graduate student association, with definite representation in governance functions. (It was written on the basis of a referendum in the spring of 1972 and approved by the Board of Higher Education.)

College teacher unionism moved closer to problems of governance. A new, much broader union emerged from an alliance of a now-extended Legislative Conference and the United Federation of College Teachers, which had succeeded the older union of the 1930s within the American Federation of Teachers. Whereas the college union of our chronicle had operated only through education and public pressure, this new union was eventually recognized and engaged in collective bargaining from 1969 on. We shall consider later the relation of such contracts to the governance system.

Direct community action entered into governance through the determination of broad policy when, in the latter part of the Black liberation movement, City College was occupied by Black students with the support of the Harlem community. This demand for greater opportunity in higher education led to the open admissions policy, with a variety of mechanisms to accelerate the entry into the colleges of hitherto submerged strata of the population.

Government resources, state and municipal, were brought into play at a crucial time when the university was threatened with collapse because of the financial difficulties of New York

City. One possibility was to put it under the state university system, which would have altered its governance mode to the highly centralized state controls. Instead, the solution adopted in 1979 was to add state to city financing (the state to support the senior colleges), but maintain city control. A moderate fee was introduced, thereby ending the free college system.

Each of these episodes, as prosaically listed here, was a drama in its own right. Hopefully, some reflective participants will record them, as I have attempted for the 1938 episode.[1] Until we have a much fuller history of the colleges in the half century, the lessons of that half century for a philosophy of governance can be at best partial and fragmentary. There is no reason, however, why we should not draw what we can from the earlier part of the century. The account was given through the consciousness of the time; we have now to look at it with the critical awareness of the present. We need to thread our way through it not as we saw it at the time but by reflecting on what we were doing, what implicit choices we were making among alternatives that at the time did not even come to our minds, and by asking why those alternatives were bypassed, what the ideas we invoked meant to us then and how they have been enlarged or deepened by subsequent experience—particularly the idea of democracy and its constituents. Such looking back is not just to recall and retell. It is to recognize what the half century of subsequent experience has brought to understanding: various possibilities where once there seemed a single straight path, complex relations that affected outcomes, the place of past events within the matrix of now visible larger social change. Ideas then invoked are now seen not merely as goals of action or as banners and weapons, but as experimental programs of practice, from which methods and lessons may be derived for future action. Alternative possibilities, complex situations and relations, social change, ideas in action, become the themes of such reflection, unified by the attempt to see what democracy can mean for higher education in the life of a society. Thus we are brought into the midst, not just to the threshold, of a philosophy of governance.

To go along this path is the aim of the next chapter. Such retrospection on exciting events is doubtless attended by some risks. Memory makes tacit assumptions that have grown over time, and there are traps. Recent physiological theories of memory suggest that it is not just a filing system but a construction in which subsequent experience plays a part. The historian's standard work has comparable difficulties, but when persistently pursued it helps its own correction. Think, for example, of the investigator who explores ancient slavery on the assumption that the slaves understood as well as longed for freedom, and then turns up evidence that the freedom ancient slaves dreamed of included being able to own slaves themselves! Our inquiry in the next chapter has fewer risks, since its aim is less to establish historical fact than to elicit possible lessons of present concern.

It remains here only to note that the issue of governance is heating up today in both higher education and public education generally; and that, moreover, the contrast of concentrated authority versus democratically dispersed power seems to be a central point of contention. Thus the need for a clear philosophy of governance is a pressing one. This present prominence of the issue is evidenced in journals and even the daily press, and indeed in formal foundation commission reports.[2] Take some striking examples.

Coincidentally, one of the most striking I have come across is again from a Harvard source. We ended our brief view of the country-wide scene half a century ago with Harvard's firm exercise of trustee–presidential power, and now, half a century later, we find it actually taking pride in that phenomenon. An

99

essay by Henry Rosovsky, former dean of the faculty of arts and sciences at Harvard, appeared in *On Campus,* an official publication of the American Federation of Teachers, AFL–CIO, with the masthead slogan "Democracy in Education/Education for Democracy" (vol. 7, no. 4, December 1987/January 1988). The title of the essay is "Nobody Does It Better: The Best Higher Education in the World is 'Made in America.'" It seems that two-thirds to three-quarters of the world's best universities are located in the United States. This, Rosovsky points out, is doing much better for higher education than the country does today for steel, sports, or automobiles. Now Rosovsky had a notable record at Harvard, particularly at a time when its curriculum was being revised. It is therefore significant to see how he explains the superiority. He lists a number of factors, stressing competitiveness and great caution with respect to tenure. "At Harvard we ask a traditional question: Who is the most qualified in the world to fill a particular vacancy? Then we try to convince that scholar to join our ranks." But most of all he attributes the result to the American system of governance in which "ultimately one person—a president—is in charge. Typically, educational policy—curriculum, nature of degrees, selection of faculty, admissions, etc.—is initiated by or delegated to academics. But budgets, management of endowments, decisions on new programs, long-range plans and similar matters are in the hands of a hierarchy headed by a president who is responsible to a board of trustees." He stresses the fact that chairmen, deans, provosts, and other administrators are appointed, not elected, and can be dismissed. Second, trustees give protection from political interference even to state universities. Universities that are state run or that are democratically run, he contends, provide weak leadership and sacrifice excellence.

If Rosovsky is correct in seeing presidential power as the

dominant pattern, then the New York city colleges' democratic reorganization still remains a special case. There is a paradox, incidentally, in the American Federation of Teachers publication featuring the article, for at the same time its New York local was engaged in trying to get teacher participation in the appointment of principals in elementary and high schools as well as greater teacher participation in administration.[3]

For contrast, take an item about the New York colleges. A story in the *New York Times* (1987) under the headline "Queens College, 50 Years Old, Seeks to Rebound" refers to an evaluation team expressing "astonishment at the power of the faculty. 'Put summarily, faculty do govern the college to an extent almost unknown in American institutions of higher education,' the report stated. 'Faculty deliberations have come to be de facto determinative, not only in many areas of educational policy, but also in many operational areas,' it said."[4] The same story stated that the president recently "sent shock waves through the faculty by setting forth that it is she, and not the teachers, who run the college."

Take now a more systematic indication that questions of governance in higher education are coming to the front burner. A reader of the *Chronicle of Higher Education*, scanning its pages for reports of trends in the 1980s, would find that a report on academic governance by the Carnegie Foundation for the Advancement of Teaching emphasized strengthening the governing board as "the keystone in the governance of higher education."[5] It recognizes that decision making is spread among trustees, presidents, and faculty, but concludes that the trustees' role should be strengthened even beyond setting policy, electing presidents, and approving budgets and key personnel appointments; "trustees also must participate in shaping educational priorities for the future and actively involve themselves in the review of the quality of the institution." It is proper to delegate a large share of the work to administrators, faculty, and students, and their decision-making structures should be improved. But the corporate authority of trustees should be maintained, and any representation of campus groups on the board should be only advisory. Collective bargaining, where it exists, should relate to issues of compensation and due process. The report recognizes that difficult strains have arisen under economic recession and budgetary limitations. Its basic model remains that of business management, which is called on to stress high quality as well as to utilize the variety of expertise in the enterprise.

We cannot, of course, assume that the problems of governance that arise today are precisely the same as those faced half a century ago. The character of higher education itself has changed immensely since World War II; its social role has shifted from a partial benefit for some to a necessary component in the operation of a highly technological and increasingly information-oriented society. Some of the problems of governance may be perennial, such as the dangers of autocracy, which, however, assume fresh form as ideas of management take on a scientific guise, or the dangers of vested curricular interests, which, however, are altered in a setting of rapidly changing scientific frontiers and increasing interdisciplinary necessity. Other problems of governance may be fresh: for example, the extent to which teacher union contracts, a novel phenomenon stretching back barely two decades, are likely to make inroads on institutional self-governance.

The multiplicity of such issues, the concepts in which they are framed, and the doubt whether a systematic answer can be given, all point again to the need of a philosophy of governance that will not just ask the descriptive question, who in fact governs, and the normative question, who governs best or ought to govern, but the deeper prior question, what is the nature of governance itself and what human purposes shape it.

CHAPTER 8

Looking Back for Lessons

How did the question of governance arise in the first place when what we set out to consider were criteria for teacher competence in the case of a probationer up for tenure? The inquiry might have stayed with standards or as readily turned to justice or professional rights or power.

Finding a lack of general criteria, the Educational Policies Committee might have gone on to devise them, carefully parceling such areas as knowledge of the subject, degree of specialization, kinds of courses in demand, progress toward the doctorate, publication and research, appropriate type of supervision or guidance to be exercised, and so on. We did begin in this direction, and even went into criteria for different fields of subject matter.

Of course department heads were capable of articulating grounds for their judgment when they wanted to. One head of a science department, faced with a battle over the dismissal of a probationer, wrote a forty-seven-page report explaining his action, which was sufficiently convincing to lead the union to drop the case. Looking back, the issue was not what standards to use, but whether department heads were to be required to give reasons based on standards. The union argued that lack of reasons often covered arbitrary decisions or actual discrimination. The administration replied that a policy of not giving reasons would not prejudice the probationer's career, since departments might simply be acting in response to a variety of specific needs, not charging incompetence.

Again, the inquiry might have moved directly to *justice*, for a probationer has a right to a *fair* judgment. How strict or how compassionate should a fair judgment be? Should there be warnings and a second chance even without formal reasons? If not, perhaps some severance pay, even after only three years. Perhaps a person's career would be less affected if the city colleges followed the Harvard procedure of folding chairs, noted earlier; but then they should not be construed as "probationary," just, say, three-year appointments. Whatever the results along the avenue of justice, they would not have touched the problem of democratic administrative organization.

Faced with the refusal to give reasons as the central issue, we might have moved into the claim of professional rights. Admittedly, employees have some rights, and professional employees operating with the freedom of expertise might reasonably be expected to be told why they were not being continued. Surely an associate or full professor who had come from elsewhere, trusting the assurances of a department, should not be dropped later by presidential judgment without explanation. And if a higher-ranking professor, then why not an instructor with a Ph.D. as the mark of a professional? Then why not a tutor doing comparable work?

Perhaps more readily, the refusal to give reasons in dropping a probationer might have been seen as a simple exercise of authority. From the point of view of department heads, to be compelled to give reasons would be a limitation of their *power*. The union's experience suggested this, for in the accumulation of varied grievances there was marked arbitrariness, often with disregard of educational considerations. In the mid-1930s the City College tutors sent a delegation to the president to complain about their low salaries. He told them that he treated hiring and dropping the lower instructional staff as purely a market matter (and this in the midst of depression unemployment), exactly, he said, "like buying bags of coal."

The social atmosphere of the time made power conflicts central. Internationally, dreams of peace through the League of Nations or through treaties had broken down; Hitler was rearming and Japan already making inroads on China. The confrontation of *isms* on the European scene seemed one of armed strength rather than rational social policy. Even moral philosophy was on the verge of converting morality into a power struggle, a conflict of ultimate opposing attitudes that admitted only of emotional proselytizing, not rational argument. Most of all, political theory was being swept into viewing all social life in terms of power struggles. This is evident in Harold Lasswell's *Politics: Who Gets What, When, How?* (1936). Everything else—ideals, programs, statements of needs and decencies—was just a counter in the struggle for power.

It was then a short step from thinking about standards, justice, professional rights, to recognizing the basic fact that the staffs of the colleges were faced with an arbitrary power system. Even here the usual reaction within society at large was not to change the system but to build up countervailing or balancing power. Thus in the labor movement, since the days of Samuel Gompers, the American Federation of Labor had carefully drawn the line at claiming a share in management. If miners in the first decade of the century wanted relief from conditions in which they were paid in paper redeemable only at the company store, lived in company-owned housing, and could be fired and turned out by company-controlled force in mining villages, they joined a union and went on strike for remedies by contract; to ask for a share in management at a time when strikes were being checkmated by court injunctions or broken by force would have been a utopian dream. If labor unions were compelled to be adversarial, it was simply to gain sufficient strength to bargain collectively with a fair chance of equality. This was the outlook eventually embodied in the National Labor Relations Act recognizing and supporting the growth of union organization. It was to make possible a fairer balance for fair bargaining.

Indeed, when the Educational Policies Committee of the college section of the union sought advice from the most experienced of the primary and secondary school teachers of Local 5, we found great skepticism about seeking to democratize the college system; it was better, they urged, to have a strong union that could resist injustice and negotiate from strength for better working conditions; better not to take responsibility in governance in which the governing group might be used to hold back the teachers at-large under pressure from city and state administration, in endless compromise.

It is worth contrasting what happened in the colleges with the path taken by the elementary and high-school union in New York (both Local 5 in the 1930s and the United Federation of Teachers, which became established and recognized in a later period). The issue of teacher participation in determining educational policies in the lower schools seems only now to be coming to the fore, half a century after the revolution in the colleges. A reader looking at a 1987 column by Albert Shanker, president of the American Federation of Teachers, might have been amazed at the exultant tone in which Shanker reported that the new contract of the New York local gave teachers "the opportunity to challenge the educational decisions of their supervisors in areas such as grading policy, textbook selection, and curriculum mandates."[1] A process of conciliation would try to bring the sides together. Shanker comments that it will encourage professional dialogue on what is best for the students. This looks as if the public schools are just starting piecemeal on the road to democratization that the colleges had traveled over in a single sweep. Actually, such an interpretation would oversimplify. In the same column Shanker told of other gains: a plan allowing teachers to modify union contract regulations and board regulations to meet local school conditions, by agreement of the principal and 75 percent of the teachers; and an opportunity to work with teachers thought to be unsatisfactory by principals, as part of due process. Other press reports soon made clear that the union was calling for a voice for teachers in the selection of principals. Finally, when it actually played some role in the selection of a new chancellor for the New York public school system, Fred M. Hechinger, a veteran *New York Times* specialist on education, gave a historical exposition of what was going on (January 10, 1988).[2] The union has become a power, both in numbers and in influence. It obtained the right to bargain collectively for the teachers in 1960. In 1969 it began putting educational policy and school reform into its contract by asking for more effective schools, with smaller classes. It exercised some influence in the community boards that were given local powers in schools throughout the city. It is now moving on a wider front toward a share in making educational policy, both in selection of administrative officers and through actual teacher participation in policy decisions. On the very same day as Hechinger's story, page one of the *Times* told from Miami how Dade Country public schools had turned over the running of thirty-two schools to teams that include teachers and parents, and described detailed administrative changes that took place. This was a last desperate step in a school situation that was proving intolerable, in short, not working. The publications of the union since then have had numerous accounts of experiment and advocacy of "shared decision" in school administration.

The elementary and high-school teachers union clearly

stayed with the analysis of the situation as one of building up countervailing power. It apparently postponed demands for participation in policy determination until its power became sufficiently formidable, meanwhile making criticisms and formulating demands on the content of specific measures. In now seeking participation, it does this not through a statutory part in the governance pattern but through the collective bargaining contract. Its bid for participation is aided by the desperate condition of many of the schools in urban centers: the large percentage of dropouts; the spread of illiteracy, whether the inability to read or so-called functional illiteracy; in many areas the problems of new incoming groups and multiplicity of languages; in the large cities even questions of drugs and violence in the schools.

The decision of the New York city college staffs half a century ago to go ahead with a program of democratization thus stands out as a bold initiative; retrospectively, it was a watershed. It is not easy, thinking back, to locate the determining influences, probably because they were many, not one. The role of the idea of democracy itself was not negligible, for to demand democracy was in part a reaction against the attacks on democracy that were being made in the advance of fascism at the time. Even more, to many the new use of governmental power in the Roosevelt New Deal on behalf of the general welfare seemed an object lesson of how a change in the power system of the state could bring benefits to people at large. Particularly to those working in the union, the surge of labor organization in the mid-1930s seemed to augur beneficial changes in the economic relations of the country. To all this may be added the professional pride of the college teachers and their feeling that they, rather than the nonteaching administrators, *were* the college and ought to have some share in determining its policies. Here and there too were individual teachers who had had

experience of other ways—for example, of the older universities in Britain such as Oxford or Cambridge, where teachers
("fellows") constituted the college and administered it. For
them, the status of employees under authoritarian management was irksome, even at best. In any case, once the idea of
democratizing governance was put forward, the enthusiasm of
the response was sufficient to give it momentum, whatever the
mixture of influences in its initiation. It had the character of an
idea "whose time had come."

Once the campaign for democratization was under way, the
objection was sometimes offered that it would politicize the colleges. As one professor of English put it later, "At lunch we used
to discuss Shakespeare; now we discuss how to vote at the next
departmental meeting." It took time to realize that the issue
was not to replace a nonpolitical order by a political system, but
one political system by another, and that the luncheon discussion might as readily have been directed to removing long-range
frustrations in the teaching process itself. This required two
lessons in practice: to cope with the influence of sheer habit or
tradition that had made the existing way seem just a natural way
of doing things; and to understand the existing conditions as
themselves already constituting a definite system.

The tremendous hold of tradition, custom, and social habit
as authoritative is sometimes underestimated in a world of
growing technological change and rapid scientific advance. It
may show itself particularly in times of social crisis by desper-
ately holding on to the past. A farcical example pointedly conveys its character. In the late 1940s, when investigations of subversion were spreading, with the same destructive character
they had had in the Rapp–Coudert hearings, the *New York
Times* reported the appearance of Edward C. Condon, of the
Bureau of Standards, before the Committee on Un-American
Activities. He said of his hearing:

For example, if I did not have a transcript to prove it, I doubt if any of you would believe me when I tell you that in my own loyalty hearing I was asked about an accusation that "You have been highly critical of the older ideas in physics."

When I heard this I could hardly believe my ears. However, there is one thing that one must not do with inquisitors, and that is to appear not to take them seriously. So I went into an impassioned affirmation of faith in Archimedes' Principle and the general correctness of Newton's law of Gravitation.[3]

Perhaps he should have answered that "being critical of the older physics" was what he was paid for, that it was his job.

To recognize that an area of social activity exhibits a system or constitutes an institution is a subtle matter—as startling as Monsieur Jourdain discovering that he had been talking *prose* or ordinary users of language learning that they are employing grammatical rules or that their utterances have a "deep structure." Michael Oakeshott remarked that a conservatism that begins to formulate itself as a philosophy is already slipping; that is, it becomes self-conscious when it is no longer being taken for granted. The same effect is produced when an entrenched way of doing things is challenged by a program that is itself presented in an organized way. It brings to the surface the systematic character of what it is attacking. Thus to think of democratizing college governance, however inarticulate the concept of democracy might be at the outset, etched the existing system as monarchical, autocratic, or authoritarian. Of course the terms in which it is described may carry a criticism in greater or less degree. To label an institution autocratic, or a culture repressive, is tantamount to calling for its reform. On the other hand, to describe an institution as having a well-demarcated pattern of authority, or a culture as having a strong pattern of controls, invites an evaluation in terms of its effects in operation.

The way ideals work out in practice may also show the character of an institution or a culture. The ideals of liberty and equality used in legal contexts since the 1930s gave body to American individualism. Freedom of movement across state lines was reaffirmed (in a notable case during the depression when California attempted to bar impoverished farmers from other states from moving in); constitutional protection was given to freedom of speech against restrictive city ordinances; lower-court injunctions against peaceful picketing were overruled (one injunction had come up with the quaint dictum that "peaceful picketing" was a contradiction in terms, like "chaste vulgarity"). The role of equality in the concrete struggles against discrimination in the major liberation movements since the mid-century scarcely needs recounting. Ideals worked out in practice thus call for institutional change.

The program of democratization in the city colleges was just that kind of proposed change. Moreover, in assuming that a meaning could be found for democracy within institutions, not merely in the more obvious political unification of the whole society, it appears to have been strikingly novel for the time. The general recognition that most social institutions were internally autocratic came with growing cultural sophistication. The military structure was the most uniformly authoritarian; disobedience to the command of a superior had definite and disastrous penalties. It was justified by the need for a training in which not merely victory in war but survival itself depended on split-second obedience to commands without questioning. The structure of business, justified in different ways in a system of free enterprise and private ownership, was also authoritarian, operating with well-defined threats of dismissal for disobedience or inefficiency in carrying out instructions. The family institution, although it served as a residual center of sympathy and affection, was generally governed with authority by the father, many of whose rights were enshrined in law.

Governance in education too was largely authoritarian. In public elementary and high schools most clearly, authority flowed from superintendents to principals to department heads; indeed, training centers such as teachers colleges, in dealing with the theory of administration, explicitly set the aim of turning out efficient educational executives.[4] As we have noted, such a structure did not always characterize colleges and universities. For example, in the older British universities the governing body of each college was its fellows; even their appointee as bursar, who handled the rents from college lands as well as student fees, might himself be a tutor of a regular subject. In Germany, each department was governed authoritatively by its professor (who might act as a dictator for his field), but the rector of the university was elected by the professors, and the university might have considerable autonomy under the state. In the United States, the authoritarian attitude was not limited to administration; it characterized a great part of teaching and learning as well. Challenged to a limited extent by progressive education, teaching for the most part went on as if the teacher had the information and imparted it to students and the students had to learn and be examined on it. The true/false examinations were the epitome of this mode.

When an authoritarian structure is dealt with in contexts of institutional practice and objectives, its acceptance or rejection is not a universal matter but requires local experimentation. There are areas in which it may prove necessary, and others in which it may prove harmful, and in any one of these too, the answer may depend in part on existent conditions. In the extreme case of the military, autocracy may be necessary under large-scale warfare where the overall plan is not known to the various corners of the far-flung enterprise of battle. The situation may be quite different where individual initiative may be more important to the pursuit of fighting, where particular plans have to be made and recast under sudden changes of conditions. (There is occasional comment on the more relaxed relations of officers and soldiers in the Israeli army.) At the present time, when nuclear threats hold back large-scale warfare, and where guerilla tactics have become more prevalent— indeed contemporary terrorism is sometimes described as deregulated or privatized war—the desirability of tight authority may become questionable. In business, the authoritarian system of governance has seldom been questioned in the United States; collective bargaining contracts limit only certain types of action and enjoin others. Inroads on the governance system to give a place to workers have been found to some degree in the Scandinavian countries, and in Socialist countries in experiments with self-management of workers of an establishment in Yugoslavia.

In the revolution in the city colleges, the choice between governance systems led directly to the question which would best carry out the aims and tasks of higher education. Of course a system of governance does not itself answer these ulterior questions. It is rather to be judged by the extent to which it stimulates teachers to concern themselves actively with these inquiries. Certainly the struggle for democracy had this initial effect. Divisional inquiries into aims as part of the effort to determine standards provoked wide interest. At the Educational Conference of the union shortly before the reorganization bylaws were finally adopted, the panel that attracted the greatest audience was a debate between Ernest Nagel, an illustrious philosopher of science who maintained the independence of theoretical research in science, and Alex Novikoff, a teacher of biology, soon to be an illustrious researcher into cancer, who argued for a close relation of scientific inquiry and social needs. In the case of the physical sciences, later decades could look back on experiences with this complex question and reject an overall answer. They had seen the dangers of political control of research (as in the Lysenko episode in Russia); the major investment of resources along one path, which then discouraged other possible avenues of basic research (as in the predominance of the nuclear option in energy research); and eventually how basic research became recognized as vital on its own precisely after it showed how rapidly it could be translated into unexpected practical gains. A democratically organized department would, at the very least, open the door to the educational initiative of many researchers and many directions. (In the physics department at City College in the 1930s there were several teachers who later played an important part in nuclear research, but at the time had no recognized voice in policy.)

In the social sciences and the humanities the character of research and teaching was subject to much more debate. Of course the teacher's business was to teach the analysis of the economy, Shakespeare, intelligence testing, or the American legal system. Did analyzing the economy mean mathematical economics or the social effects of the economy's operation? Should a course on Shakespeare concern itself solely with literary quality and human quality (it was still early for the full force of the New Criticism to limit attention solely to the text), or should it deal with Shakespeare as part of the Elizabethan renaissance in a particular stage of England's development? Should a course in psychology simply teach the methods and results of intelligence testing or consider the extent to which cultural elements entered into the construction of tests and the effects that had on current judgments of "racial intelligence"? Nazi racialism had of course brought awareness of race prejudice, but should the inquiry be pressed into the inner sanctum of the teaching of theory? Should a course in American government and law study main lines of Supreme Court decisions or conflicting theories of legal interpretation and their legal effects? Robert M. Hutchins, as dean of Yale Law School, had turned against the teaching of detailed law because the law was undergoing rapid change in the early 1930s and what the students learned would be out of date by the time they graduated. But what he then turned to as president of the University of Chicago was the advocacy of a fixed Thomistic metaphysics.

What a democratic organization did was to open the door to debate and stimulate varied experiment. An art department asked itself how far it should be geared to developing the fine arts and how far also the kinds of skills that might find an outlet in advertising artwork. A philosophy department could think through what contribution the study of philosophy might make to different professional careers, and how far to go with the growing area of "Philosophy of . . ." courses. A psychology department redid its laboratory work, which had consisted in having the students go through traditional important experiments. Realizing that this could be done in lecture demonstrations, it added social psychology to its "laboratory" so that students could carry out fresh inquiries, for example, by surveys in the community. Papers even began to appear in psychological journals in which students were coauthors. A speech department was aware that part of its aim had been to alter the accent of students, native though it was to parts of the city. It felt justified in doing this because the Board of Examiners for prospective teachers might fail students with foreign accents although they had done well in the written examinations. Now at least some members of the department began to consider whether the department might not better throw its weight to changing the attitude of the examiners as well as to assessing the values of cultural uniformity in mode of speech. Some members of the hygiene department made a comparative study of methods of exercise under different social systems, considering the possibility that modes of group exercise had a disciplinary social effect. In department after department, at least in the early period of the democratic reorganization, traditional intellectual differences about the nature and methods of the disciplines came to life and entered into the planning of courses and teaching.

In one area the democratizing process proved less happily educative to the staffs. This was the complex relation of college needs to economic sources. The installation of a democratic decision process carried a promise of reform and improvement, and improvement is usually costly. To secure fair salary scales, to remedy long-standing grievances, to keep class size reasonable, to make room for educational experiment, to provide adequate nonteaching services, all would push up the budget. It came as somewhat of a shock to the staffs that the same board that had opened the gates to reform should then proceed to a whole set of budget-cutting measures. As noted, it transferred the nonteaching staff to the municipal civil service, with a lower salary scale; it tried to rotate tutors to save money; it abolished Townsend Harris High School; it set stopping points within the increment ladder and specified extravagantly high conditions for anyone to go beyond them.

Now no city employees were so naive as not to be aware of the budgetary difficulties of the city administration, of the sources of its revenue in real-estate taxation, of the powerful pressures of real-estate interests to keep down the tax rate. Under the old system they assumed that presidents and boards presented the needs of the colleges, engaged in political maneuvering, did the best they could for the colleges, and then had to live within the bounds of achievement or failure. What they had not realized and now learned was the amount of *preprocessing* that had gone on—how what was asked was itself a function of what higher-ups were ready to grant. In short, even what was asked for was what the system allowed to be asked, not what the colleges needed for essential work.

The democratic revolution brought this situation into the open. Under open deliberation, the administration would have to interpret the needs of the colleges to the board and the board to the city. If there was to be agitation over the budget, it should be public, with the board arguing the case for the colleges. The community would then have to decide through its political channels whether, if necessary, taxes should be increased. Of course at that particular moment the situation was tense—still the depression, and recovery slow.

In the long run, as we know today, the whole struggle was bypassed by the growth of teacher unionism, for unions (in all city departments) succeeded in bringing the whole budgetary process into the open. Overall budgets are proposed not only by the presidents and the board, but they involve collective bargaining and contracts, and the union frames its own budgetary recommendations as well. (The budget in any case is now more complex, for there are student fees and state support as well as the municipal contribution.) The net effect of democratization and union growth was thus to give freer rein to presentation of the interests and needs of higher education. Learning did not stop at this point, for there remained the wider arena of pressure and conflict from other needs and interests in the life of the city. Democracy in higher education had to learn to cooperate with these, and help shape public needs for the city at large toward a fuller understanding of desirable public policy.

In general, then, the democratic revolution had a vital role in giving the staffs a sense of active agency in which they shaped the development of the colleges, in strengthening their sense of responsibility for educational and social policy, in initiating them into the complex social relations of higher education, and in integrating the objectives into larger social needs. How long this renaissance would have gone on is hard to tell. The events of the counter-revolution and the pressures of the war period brought many trends to a halt. After the war, stimulus to face the problems of higher education came directly from the social changes and the rapid expansion of higher education itself. By then being ready in place, the democratic system opened the door to broader staff initiative and contribution.

The rapidity of change has been the great lesson of the twentieth century. Change was less noticeable when it came over many generations, but in the late twentieth century it comes repeatedly within a single generation. A generation that has witnessed the popular spread of air travel, the communications revolution, and now the computer revolution, almost takes this for granted. Margaret Mead epitomized the situation in a striking metaphor (in her *Culture and Commitment*, 1970): We are all now immigrants in time, as people who came to America and saw their children grow into a different culture were immigrants in space. The changes are not merely technological; they are social and institutional as well. Hence one generation cannot simply impose a mold of life on the next, as it did in the past. Education must prepare the next generation to make creative and innovative decisions. In our system of education, this task falls largely on higher education.

We noted that in the 1930s many of the faculty and even members of the board felt basically insecure about the existence of the city colleges. It was taken to be precarious; there was assumed to be constant danger of abolition if too great a public storm arose on one or another matter. At the time of the Russell case some suggested that the colleges be abolished and the money used for scholarships so that students could go to the private colleges. In short, the widespread perception of the colleges was that of a luxury. In a budget hearing in Albany in the early 1940s, representing the college union, I was allotted three minutes to present (for the first time) the views of the college staff. In an atmosphere of genial smiles I suggested doubling the budget because higher education was coming to have a vital role in the continuity of modern social life and in equipping it for oncoming change. This was then dismissed with a remark about impractical dreams; yet within a few years the budget was more than doubled.

The social role of the colleges was also changing. In the 1930s the city colleges enabled the children of the lower economic classes to work their way up into the middle class. The colleges prepared them to move into the professions—medical, legal, educational, scientific. Statistical studies of graduate work in relation to undergraduate college showed that they did this well. This social role continued and was intensified over the years, particularly as different ethnic groups in New York entered college in greater numbers. What changed was the whole role of the colleges, within the short period of the war.

At first it might seem to be change under emergency conditions. College scientists worked on the Manhattan Project; there was teaching for army officer training. The armed forces required a variety of skills (e.g., mathematical, psychological), and teaching ability itself proved important. By the time the war was over, college education was on the way to becoming a social necessity rather than a luxury or social privilege or just a social ladder. Further too, the promise of a good education open to all had been made in the manifestos of the war period, as a matter of right. More important, the United States had moved into a full-fledged industrial age; skills of all sorts were now widely required on a more advanced level than high schools, academic or vocational, could offer. An incident on the New

York scene is indicative. The Board of Regents had worked out a plan for vocational post–high school institutes, and found that organized labor feared it might be a training school to flood the labor market, and weaken the strength of labor—in short, a "school for scabs." A conference organized by the teachers union brought top labor leaders and state educational leaders together to discuss the situation. Most effective was the state commissioner of education, who explained in detail how even the care of a diesel engine now required advanced training. Labor was convinced that the institutes represented a new era, not an anti-labor device, and gave its support. Nuclear research tied to issues of national security added a strong impetus to scientific schooling. Finally a political motif capped the general social necessity: Within little more than a decade the Russian launching of Sputnik spurred higher education as a competitive need. State university systems expanded, community colleges proliferated, and an opportunity for higher education became recognized as a basic social need in the United States.

Social change, even when rapid, usually takes place with a background of continuing, more or less stable, attitudes and values. Whether these make room for adaptation or resist every change as a hostile undermining of society itself reflects the character of the culture. For example, it has been noted often that although countries achieving national independence have sometimes copied the American Constitution as basic law, this has not saved them from internal discord and revolutions ending in dictatorships. In the United States, in spite of civil war and social crises, there has been a strong continuity in the growth of political democracy.

The role of entrenched values in relation to formal mechanisms is well illustrated in some of the detail of our narrative. Tenure for the city college staffs was first granted in the form of bylaws of the board, and then written into state law. This gave it a greater security, and though it did not save jobs in the

Rapp–Coudert dismissals, the board had to find other grounds and follow the law in providing trials in order to carry through its purge. The democratic reorganization was not written into state law. It remained in the bylaws of the board, and so was subject to revision simply by the board's action. Here it was the strength of the colleges' reaction, particularly on the question of electing department chairmen, that stopped an even more extensive revision. Even today, after half a century, the board could, on its own, extend presidential powers in many directions that would nullify the reorganization. The board's own powers rest on state law, just as those of trustees of private colleges may rest on charters of incorporation.

In the long run, the bases of stability are not themselves unvarying. Habits may die out, values may change, laws and charters may be reinterpreted even within the legal process. The stable and the continuous at any time are those parts of the structure in which change is slowest.

So far we have spoken in general of the idea of democracy. Democratic participation in higher education meant at first giving members of the college community a definite part in decisions of policy and to some degree in controlling subsequent administrative decisions. It was the same general meaning of democracy that had guided historical battles for the extension of voting rights to Everyman and Everywoman, that had opened political office to candidates from all social classes, that had prompted experiments with political techniques as varied as modes of representation (direct, proportional, etc.) and referendum and direct initiative for legislative measures. What democracy would mean in practice in the governance of higher education required working out in a detailed program and, even more, assessing how it then operated in practice. That is what our chronicle showed, even in the few years that it covered.

The basic elements of the general idea of democracy can be

readily listed. At the foundation is the *moral recognition that everyone counts,* what is widely called "respect for persons." This installs a basic individualism, but within a community of persons and with a mutuality of responsibilities. The *traditional ideals of democracy*—liberty and equality (the third member of the trio, fraternity, being now broadened and merged into community)—provide a matrix of opportunities in which each person can find room for maturing distinctive abilities and interests. The *principles of democracy* constitute a structure of organization (within the political realm of government) that gives shape to these ideals: For example, everyone counts as one and so has one vote; in legal matters an accused is given a fair trial whether rich or poor. Bills of rights are attempts to formulate these principles, often with an eye on typical trouble-spots of that time, and their interpretation has the task of reconciling possible inner conflicts. *Democratic attitudes* are states of character and dispositions that give body to the ideals and substance to the principles in the actual relations of people. They concretize a basic decency in different contexts and with different names: care and sympathy and helpfulness, where troubles or difficulties are present; civility in discussion and controversy over measures of action; politeness in ordinary human relations. Finally, there is the endless devising of *democratic techniques* in one realm or another, to give greater or smoother expression to democratic ideals, principles, and attitudes. These can be proposed in any context, from the regulation of the size of election districts in order to ensure that every person's vote is roughly of the same weight, to the practice in debates of restating an opponent's argument to his or her satisfaction before attacking it.

It is difficult nowadays—fifty years after the 1930s—to realize how limited was the idea of democracy before World War II. It was not a question merely of having the idea and not following it in practice: for example, preaching the equality of humankind and discriminating in a multitude of ways against Blacks, women, and the foreign-born. (As a matter of fact, when some teachers attempted to comb the school textbooks to remove such prejudice, it was taken as evidence of radical subversion.) It was rather that the practical interpretation of democratic ideas was narrow. Liberty tended to mean the absence of legal restriction, rather than ensuring generally necessary conditions for action; equality, the absence of formal (legal) hindrance, quite compatible with the most extensive differences in actual opportunities. It took the experience of Nazism with its holocaust, and even after that the liberation movements of the 1950s and 1960s and beyond, to give a practical meaning to liberty, just as it had taken the Great Depression to bring the lesson that economic security was no longer a function of being willing to work but required a social concern for the state of the economy and (in even the most conservative formulation) a social net below which no one should be allowed to fall—and this as a minimum provision of equality. It took the whole human rights movement, from the United Nations Universal Declaration on, to give systematic expression to these practical changes. In many respects, higher education provided a clear instance of the enlarged ideal. In the 1920s and 1930s, while formally open to all, a college education extended to very few. After World War II, beginning with veterans' educational benefits and the expansion of community colleges, the program for universal higher education—at least for all who were ready to take it—was pioneered in the United States to the point of casual acceptance. It is still not a program in corporate Japan or socialist Russia. In the 1930s free higher education in the New York city colleges was an exceptional instance. It is not surprising that it was the scene for concrete lessons in the meaning of democracy.

Practical questions of equality and liberty came thick and fast in the concrete experience of transforming college participation. Who should have a vote within a department: instructors as well as professors? Permanent tutors as well as instructors? What is the place of expertise: Should the votes of the experts have greater weight, or should they have to carry their weight by convincing and persuading? On curriculum: Should a basic required course be worked out by the professor who gave the mass lectures or together with all instructors who carried on the discussion sections? Perhaps in some fields mass lectures should be abolished and individual teachers be allowed to experiment in different ways—putting aside a dean's insistence that a single textbook for all was managerially the most convenient! (Compare the proposed liberty to experiment and the program, still prevalent in some state public school systems, that the same lesson be taught at the same hour in every high school in the state, according to state plan worked out by state curricular experts.) We could see the general idea of respect for persons working its way through in the feeling that all persons at the college should be seen as part of a community, not just as hired hands for a limited job. This feeling was soon put to the test in the relation of teachers to nonteaching staffs (administrative, laboratory assistant, etc.). In the course of the struggle, all groups worked effectively together, and the sense of community prompted the teachers to support the administrative staff strongly (though to no avail) against the board's measures to incorporate the administrative staff into the separate municipal civil service.

The ideal of liberty was strong in student demands, which teachers supported. Students played an active part in the democratic revolution, as we have seen, and they continued ready to strike or at least to demonstrate when they discovered or suspected discrimination of one kind or another, particularly racial or political. The democratic revolution recognized the liberty of students to organize on any field of their interest; any required faculty relation was to be purely advisory. It did not move on into the question of student participation in governance.

Emphasis on the practical meaning of democracy as a program for the structure of social life or of a specific institution is made necessary not only by the demands of social action, but by the controversies of social theory. The latter concern both the specific idea of democracy and the general theory of ideas.

The idea of democracy is often narrowed in terms of a specific sociological or specific psychological analysis. Thus, Aristotle in his *Politics*, seeing the pervasiveness of the struggle between the rich and the poor, understands oligarchy as rule by the rich, democracy as rule by the poor. In the early twentieth century, an influential analysis of social behavior enunciated an "iron law of oligarchy," that what began as an attempt to have widespread democratic or popular rule invariably ended up as power in the hands of a few. Robert Michels, in his *Political Parties* (English translation, 1915; first German edition, 1911), studied this process in organization, paradoxically, for labor and socialist parties, where the ideal of democracy was prominent in the movement. Accordingly he redefined democracy as a political system that was open from below, as contrasted with one open to a limited upper class. The ideal of rule by the people he found meaningless.

More generally, controversy centered over what ideas and ideals were supposed to be doing in social movements. Many theorists tended to debunk ideals, regarding them as almost the surface froth of the deeper currents of particular group interests. Others saw them chiefly as weapons, linguistic devices to take hold on the emotions and loyalties of people and to make claims. Such interpretations recede into the background

when ideas and ideals become translated into practical programs for the structure of institutions or for the direction of
legal interpretation. This has been evident in the second half of
our century in the career of *equality* in constitutional interpretation, as well as that of *democracy* in political struggles—well documented, for example, in the 1987 congressional
hearings on the Iran–Contra affair.

In the long run, the most important contribution that a democratic structure may make in higher education is that it provides a readier path for innovation and experiment. It is commonplace that the growth of knowledge calls for change in
content and ways of teaching, and that changes in the life of a
society require adaptation in how higher education is carried
on. A democratic mode of governance has the greater poten-
tiality for such processes, for their encouragement, and for
change by consent rather than by conflict. The important
point, however, may too often be overlooked. It is not merely
that change within higher education is of significance, but that
higher education itself is now the seedbed of change for the
society as a whole. It is where research is carried on, productive
ideas are expected, and new paths worked out. This role is
clearest in science and technology, in medicine, in agriculture.
Obviously in the social sciences and the humanities we do not
expect the broader agreement that is found in the other fields,
but we do expect the interplay of different concepts, theories,
and perspectives. Such importance of higher education in the
life of the contemporary world is what ultimately bestows significance on evaluating modes of educational governance. It
makes outside dictation to higher education, the denial to its
members of participation in basic decisions, a contradiction in
terms.

The role of the innovator has not been an easy one. If the
history of the 1938 revolution shows how it prepared the col-

leges for the more systematic contributions they were about to make, the episode of the Russell case and the Rapp–Coudert investigation show how precarious is the position of innovators when they run up against entrenched and powerful interests. Particularly where it requires adjustments in traditional habits of thought and feelings, threatened attitudes will lead people to strike out, or they will be incited to strike out. In twentieth-century America, with the intensity of accelerated technological and social changes, the ideological form of such resistance has been the Red Scare, the cry of communism, from the reactions immediately after World War I through the hardened slogans of the cold war to the present. On such occasions education suffers particularly, and political repression chills the academic atmosphere, stifles innovative ideas, and drives out the boldest spirits. Fortunately so far there has been recovery, though belated, on each occasion. The most serious, of course, was the McCarthy period in the mid-century. This has been much analyzed in great detail.[5] Sociological study has shown how the colleges and universities were on the verge of intellectual breakdown under the impact of the persecution.

We have no need here to restudy these episodes. Perhaps the most striking moral comment can come not from the reflections of those who were persecuted, but from one who held the power of government and then saw it used for repression. Francis Biddle had been attorney general under Roosevelt, and then witnessed a successor under Truman promulgate the attorney general's list of subversive organizations for examining the loyalty of government employees. Biddle's *Fear of Freedom* (1951) traces the history of the persecution of dissenters in Britain and America in considerable detail, exhibiting its devastating injustices. He is led to distinguish sharply between loyalty to the government of the United States and loyalty to the United States. Government is the servant of the people, and so loyalty to the government asks the master to be loyal to the servant. Loyalty to one's country involves, on the contrary, full freedom of belief and thought. There can be no defined system of patriotism, only the freedom for an individual's ideas and choice of causes.

To this principled defense of freedom can be added the instrumental values of freedom we have considered—keeping a society open to change, both response to unavoidable changes and controlled changes and initiative in thought, deliberation, and action. A closed society clings to a fixed pattern and changes unconsciously or surreptitiously. An open society accepts but evaluates change.

The recognition that new ideas and initiatives are constantly required in society is also found today in the popular emphasis on creativity in educational discourse and, at least in theory, the demand that students learn how to think, to deal with problems, and not simply to store information. Japanese educators sometimes attribute such encouragement of initiative to American education, even while American educators envy the learning scores of Japanese students. It is, of course, one of the most difficult areas of educational theory and practice, not only because of authoritarian habits of the past, but because opening the way for initiative in thought so readily challenges cherished beliefs.

In a normal and peaceful development, democratic governance at the city colleges might have been evaluated as an experiment, assessed and modified in terms of strengths and weaknesses exhibited or envisaged. A process of self-criticism, of refining and improving mechanisms, would have been part of the structure itself. There was a suggestion of this in Tead's call for a review at the end of the first three years. But, as we have seen, it was already in the midst of a somewhat secret attempt to undo major democratic features, which only the reaction of the colleges in good part thwarted. The turmoil of the years that followed scarcely provided an atmosphere for experimental judgment.

There are many aspects of any change in social forms that a patient, inquiring attitude could deal with if action were not compelled by a situation of conflict. An obvious one is that of *side effects.* Too often an obvious evil is dealt with by an obvious cure, only to find that some other balance has been upset in the process or some other evil installed. (The story of DDT or of the unanticipated social consequences of the automobile are familiar enough.) This need not mean that the change should not be made, but perhaps it should be done in a different form or with some cautionary accompaniment, and above all in a critical experimental way. Democratizing departments was certainly an effective way of getting rid of the arbitrary power of appointed department heads. Was there a danger that a department majority might then perpetuate a one-sided school in a given discipline in which there happened to be sharp theoretical conflicts? Actually, the same danger was exhibited in the European system of the dominant professor in each given field. Hence it is not a function of democratic structure as such, but rather a point where caution or some remedial mechanism should in any case be incorporated in a democratic structure—for example, periodic external evaluation of one kind or another.

Caution is also required against reliance on a single specific model without trying out alternatives. For example, to regard the human body as a machine with isolable replaceable parts may be helpful for some problems, but for others we would do better with an organic metaphor in which each part depends on the totality of its relation to the whole. (Compare, perhaps, the provision of an artificial limb with a case of organ transplant.) What is more, the very idea of a machine changes when it moves from the mechanical to the electrical. Now the authoritarian structure of governance has often been treated as an obvious mode of *management,* just as a business is managed. Or else the idea of democratic governance suggests that we are using a *political* model. These sound very different, and doubtless are. But from some angles they may yield the same results. Suppose we look at both these models from the standpoint of the consumer as locus of decision. In business management, the managers need not be cast as ultimate deciders but as trying to predict what the consumer will want. (When women bobbed their hair in the early part of the century, hairpin manufacturers went out of business with dramatic suddenness.) And in a political model, the ultimate decision is by the voters. Does it follow that on both models, when applied to higher education, ultimate decision lies with the students? Of course business managers interpose advertising as a way of controlling consumer decision, and teachers interpose a tradition of learning and culture. Impartial spectators might be led to ask what was *good* for the students, thus raising broader ethical ideas as relevant to determination, and posing the question whether the managers or the teachers were more likely to have a better basis for judgment. In short, models may be allowed to help along the path of inquiry, but never to straitjacket inquiry or close the doors to other paths of relevance.

A caution running through all consideration of change is to guard against the possibilities of vested interests. Yet even vested interests may contain legitimate elements. For example, in India the metal plow was resisted not just because the wooden plow was habitual, but because there were social and ritual relations with the makers of the less efficient wooden one. How rapidly change should be attempted is not always easy to decide. Clearly a medical school would not teach old procedures when better ones have been instituted in practice. But the educational effects of the computer revolution do not have comparable clarity as yet. In teaching the humanities, the fact that the world has broadened to make the European–Western tradition only one in a variety of world cultures is still to have far-reaching effects. This is most evident in controversies about content—whether to teach the classics means now to teach Greek classics or also Chinese and Indian. Or the controversy takes shape as a struggle over values—claims for elite culture as against mass culture. Often this is largely the battle to hold on to the interests and values of the past without careful assessment of the values brought on the new horizon. The guiding purpose is to secure a cultural community without ethnocentric bias.

Such debate suggests a general caution concerning the development of a practical program: that there is a cost not only to doing something new but to not doing something new. This has been learned more readily in the economic domain, but it has wider scope. Nowadays no serious social proposal comes without an account of what it will cost if we undertake it and where the money will come from and what effects that will have on our economy. We also need to acquire the greater wisdom of asking what will be the cost of *not* adopting the proposal. Thus recent proposals for the extension of preschool education and child care point to the greater cost for a subsequent adult population that has not had these services. It will have to support more unemployables, a greater prison population, and so on. Such a line of thought leads us to a greater appreciation of innovation. We begin to realize that much of the present is made up of innovations in the past. The idea of a group legislating or establishing laws by a majority vote, or for that matter using a two-thirds vote for some purposes, had its date and place in historical invention. Teaching itself as more than imparting information, Socratic questioning, public schools, systematic adult education, universities, were new ideas in their origin. Innovation is not a radical upsetting of present arrangements—though it can have that effect at times—but an attempt to solve problems that are coming to a head in the present course of events and that cannot be solved by more traditional means. While it becomes a pivot for reorganizing present conditions, it itself requires integration into the world in which it arose. Democratic governance has been precisely that type of innovation.

A last caution concerns the relation of means and ends. Insofar as a democratic system designates accountability for procedures, not results, it would appear to have the character of a means, with its worth assessed by the kind of results it achieves. Insofar as it gives teachers or students or nonteaching staff a place of dignity in the work process, it has the character of an end. Both of these need qualification by looking at the kind of dignity and the kind of results. A democratic system that saw the dignity of the teacher to lie in becoming a little manager, rather than as reflecting a change in the character of the "labor force" from replaceable individual parts to a cooperative professional dialogue, would miss the mark. The ultimate results hoped for from a democratic system—wider creative initiative in educational matters—obviously become more important as the role of higher education itself becomes more important in the life of the time. The significance of a governance system in higher education today thus comes from the fact that institutions of higher education face radically different situations: the need to address, and the potential to handle, new technologies; the need for lifelong learning rather than, as in the past, a few years assumed sufficient to prepare for life; the organization and transmission of vastly increased knowledge as well as the advancement of knowledge itself; the cultivation of a will and attitude to self-education far beyond dependent instruction; the normalization of criticism and self-criticism, of correction and change. Collective participation in such tasks merges means and ends into a constitutive structure for higher education.

In seeking the lessons of the New York experience, we have traveled from a particular question of educational decision to the meaning of democracy and the social role of higher education today. In this light, the 1938 democratic reorganization stands out as a striking episode in the rise of professional consciousness of teachers, both within higher education and within the labor organization of teachers. Occurring under unique conditions, it distinctively raised the curtain on the whole unfinished drama of educational governance whose discussion still troubles us today. A more systematic analysis of governance is required.

CHAPTER 9

Governance—Whose Business?

IF THE STORY we have reflected on shows the rise of teacher consciousness about governance in higher education, then many of the subsequent events on the American educational scene can be read as "consciousness-raising" for others as well. The 1960s were admittedly a period in which students became conscious of their power and role in colleges and universities. On the other hand, the struggle of Blacks, of women, of the handicapped, was rather (in this context) a movement for greater educational opportunity; but it impinged on governance when it had to face entrenched resistance or traditional inertia. Government itself encountered governance issues in legislation, as vast state systems of higher education were set up or extended throughout the country; often political mechanisms of management and financial control were simply transferred to the colleges and universities as if they were departments of state government. In a far different direction, labor organization extended its scope, from cafeteria and library employees to teachers. It met governance power head-on in contract negotiations.

Since higher education today operates as an established social institution, a philosophy of governance has to work out an integrated view of the different social groups and the extent to which their needs and functions with respect to higher education may give them some regular role—from bare voice or advice to varying influence and up to active participation—in determining the shape of education. To ask "Governance— whose business?" will give us a fresh starting point with perhaps a novel view of the field. A view from this angle is comparable to the shift that took place in political theory when political rule ceased to be understood simply from the nature of ruling as the exercise of power and became understood also in terms of the interaction of groups within society with a variety of needs and demands under specific conditions of life and economy. At any rate, the theory of governance in education today is much in need of new directions.

It is appropriate therefore at this point to survey (in some cases, resurvey) all claimants for a part—from influence to a definite share—in the governance of higher education: trustees, president, teachers, students, unions, parents and families, communities and community groups, evaluation agencies (e.g., accrediting groups), organized governmental entities (cities, states, federal government). In each case we may look for strengths and weaknesses, judged of course by the basic standard of how far they contribute to achieving the aims of higher education.

Three qualifications are needed in approaching this task; they concern the standard itself, the variety of institutions, and evidence of success. As to standard, it is not surprising that different claimants may be pursuing different ends in higher education, with correspondingly different emphases in what they would regard as strengths and weaknesses. By keeping this in mind we may through comparison bring out a richer picture of ends and aspirations for eventual conclusions about a desirable pattern of governance. The situation is even more complicated by the fact, noted in the last chapter, that the aims of higher education may not be presentable with finality in advance and may undergo changes in relation to social changes of the period and to the means available for pursuing them.

The variety of institutions and the levels of education involved lie on the surface. What holds for higher education may not hold for elementary and high schools with respect to some topics. The span of higher education may itself be great enough—say from technological community colleges to research-oriented graduate schools—to suggest that difference in governance may be advisable. Even among comparable institutions, material differences, such as financing by tax funds and financing through private contributions, may have significant consequences and impose limitations.

As to evidence of success, it does not follow that a claimant not widely recognized in the United States (because of the prevalence of one type of governance) should be felt at a theoretical disadvantage or compelled to make a stronger case than it would if it were in present power. Similarly, no claimant in present power can properly use that as an argument for the rightness of its claim, unless it invokes the evidence of its success, as Rosovsky tried to do when he argued in the article cited earlier that the authoritative power of trustees had been responsible for the success of American universities. (He stated that thesis there rather than presented the evidence.) Perhaps we would have a fairer starting point for all our claimants if we resumed briefly what we have at various points noted, that the structure of institutional control in higher as well as in primary and secondary education has varied more widely than the present American pattern indicates. Sometimes there has been direct and strong central control of primary and secondary schools, as in France; often local control with state specification of standards, as in Sweden or the United States. European universities on the whole, showing traces of historical origins, used to follow a kind of collegial principle in which the professors—each, however, in almost absolute control of his own area—together determined policy and elected their rector, though a state official might hover in the background. The result was a kind of oligarchy. In some countries (as in Britain) the collegiality of the colleges included a wider group; in others (as in Italy) students traditionally had a share in policy decisions. In our account of the New York city colleges we saw a teacher collegiality under a board, with a president as leader and link. The more general structure in the United States remains one of authoritative management: Under trustees or boards of education, power descends through superintendents and principals, or through presidents and deans, to departmental heads, and to teachers, with students at the bottom.

Trustees

The apex of governance in American higher education goes by different names—trustees, regents, boards of higher education. "Trustees" suggests less than ownership, indeed management on behalf of others; "regents" has a monarchical sound; "boards" conveys more directly the idea of managers. These ruling groups get their basic authority in different ways. In public institutions it comes from legal enactments of state or city, and appointment by officials or election if so specified. In private institutions, it may come from the charter given to an original founding group; often the ruling group becomes self-perpetuating and self-replacing.

Justifying the role of trustees is the traditional assumption that there has to be a unified and ultimate source for decision, and tacitly that it is better for it to be an independent or outside group that can reckon for the institution as a whole, uninvolved in one or another of its special constituent parts or interests. These properties are deeply embedded in the intellectual and practical traditions of the Western world. That control should be unified expresses the familiar assumption of political theory that sovereignty is one, and located somewhere in a community. That control has to have an ultimate locus expresses the methodological assumption of absolute or fixed points, whether in axioms or sense perceptions, on which a system of knowledge rests. (Nowadays it is customary to speak of this as a "foundational" view. It explains also why so much heat is generated over the question of relativism in the theory of knowledge as well as in ethics.) That control should be independent or from outside expresses the traditional theory of rationality, that reason is a distinct element in the self that lords it over conflicting desires and passions; without rational decision, they remain locked in dispersive conflict that ends only with ruin.

We shall examine later, in looking for a more complex model of governance, how these three bases have crumbled in the long history of Western thought. Briefly, what happened is this. Sovereignty in political theory became recognized increasingly as simply the residue of monarchical government. It passes over into a diluted notion of authority, which is itself dispersed into intellectual powers, accumulated knowledge, leadership abilities, and leads further into a refined study of obedience and rational acceptance as properties of the people, not just properties of rulers. Or else, if sovereignty is kept in its pristine unity, it is assigned to "We, the people" and so opens the door to experiment with methods of governance and the expression of needs and aspirations, to some extent with techniques of balance rather than a fixed and located unity. In the theory of knowledge, assumptions of absolute correctness or fixity have yielded, particularly in the philosophy of science, to conceptions of a growing body of knowledge no part of which is in principle unalterable, with the first principles at any time being in effect officeholders in the light of their accomplishments, but ready to yield to fresh theory that advances the whole. (Such an approach is "nonfoundational.") Finally, rationality is identified with the best lessons of experience rather than with an independent power; it is an established, reasonable order of emotions and desires, not a separate intellectual force. In the understanding of life and community, the three changes yield a more hospitable background for democratic theory and practice. There is thus no inconsistency in the idea of divided powers, among trustees, faculty, students, and whatever other claimants may be found to be justified. There are simply the problems of balance, reconciliation, compromise, recognition of overriding institutional interests, and so forth— all common enough in democratic institutions, and existent, though less public, within boards of trustees themselves. Again, there is little justification for absolute judgment or finality in an era of rapid change in the world and society at large, where constant reinterpretation and reformulation may be necessary. Growing experience frankly recognized is a much more secure base.

If appeal to unity and ultimacy does not compel an outside location of governance, the need for independence has greater weight. All self-enclosed institutions may get out of touch with the rest of the world and its emerging problems. Hence some functions of governance have to be exercised from without. Supervision and evaluation and criticism are such functions. Of course criticism of any institution may well be open to anyone, particularly in a democratic society and with media often overready to scrutinize; in short, anything about universities and colleges is "news." Evaluation is initially of results achieved, but is led on to examine methods and processes, particularly where the results are inadequate, but also to learn from special proficiency. A well-functioning Board of Trustees may readily provide a permanent possibility of evaluation, though in fact some types of supervision are occasionally farmed out to a designated board of supervisors or of overseers, or basic reevaluation left to credentialing agencies.

A major strength of a board of trustees is that it links the institution to the community that is in one sense outside it but in another the matrix within which it operates. In public institutions the board may screen the colleges from political interference; in private institutions it may be the chief route for financial support, as well as a channel through which come opportunities for graduate employment. And a well-functioning board may interpret the needs of the community to the institution and an understanding of the institution and its needs to the community. All this requires, however, a high degree of enlightenment, an understanding of the way in which higher education is a seedbed for going beyond the past, as well as a sifting process for preserving the best in the past. A rough test for enlightenment has been the degree to which boards have appreciated and supported academic freedom under attack from community groups rather than become themselves vehicles for repression. Without enlightenment, trustees, in spite of their independent locus, can be just as one-sided, just as reflective of partial interests, just as wise or just as blind, as university cabinets drawn from inside, faculties operating in some systematic organization, or students. On the other hand, sometimes among the trustees are found forward-looking individuals whose practical experience and sense of social needs and oncoming developments may lead them to an early suggestion of directions of policy, especially if they assume leadership roles rather than simply exercise power.

Weaknesses in the trustee system are likely to stem from factors of composition, part-time attention, and overreliance on presidents or on one or a few of their own number. Boards are heavily weighted with persons who have been successful in business and the professions and who often bring the special attitudes of that social segment to their tasks. Moreover, trustees are usually busy in their normal activities, although goodwill may carry them into contributing many weary hours to their educational responsibilities. Hence they often rely on the president of the institution, for inasmuch as they have taken care in presidential selection, they regard him or her as the equivalent of the chief executive officer in the business model. In effect, a trustee system has often become in practice a presidential system with trustee backing.

Trustee organization takes various forms. Often there is a large board, operating through committees of its members. Sometimes a smaller corporation has the legal authority, and extends its operations through a network of boards of overseers for a multitude of special purposes, thereby drawing in a wider circle of often professionally equipped persons for the particular tasks. The result may be, in the most successful cases, widespread community support and guidance for the institution. Private colleges, especially, are likely to employ such a scheme.

Presidents

Presidents derive their authority as executive agents from the trustees. This is what gives them their independent status within the institution. In practice their often supreme authority rests on the confidence that trustees have in their judgment. The actual situation thus is often presidential rule with trustee backing, bounded, however, by trustee interests, vision, and basic policy.

That presidents have a central role in university governance is not at issue in the conflict of democratic with authoritarian conceptions of how that role should be carried out—whether it is one of rule or leadership. In either case, the authority rests on the assumption that there are functions of basic importance for the university that require a one-person unity of deliberation, planning, and decision. Different functions are cited in familiar discussions of the presidential role. Some think in terms of the growth and reputation of the university within the setting of the community or its historical tradition. At the other extreme, in Socratic irony, a president may affirm his or her task to be to ensure that salaries are paid on time and there is chalk on the blackboard in the classroom. In between, with a social psychologist's eye on the human situation, there will be recognition that decision and responsibility are hard and constant needs, and that there must always be someone as a last resort when such burdens are neglected or shifted from person to person or committee to committee. Indeed it is sometimes said today that the tyranny of a president is less feared than a quality of indecision[1]—even though the mark of a good executive may be to know when not to decide but to let a problem mature. The vital presidential qualities may lie quiet during a period of smooth going, but become essential when there is a crisis to be managed.

Different analogies and models are often invoked to suggest the presidential role. The comparison to a chief executive officer in business has been a favorite one, partly because it assigns broad powers that are everywhere applicable. The director of an orchestra might be an apt comparison, in its invocation of the harmony of different instruments, the splendor of the production, and perhaps the recognition that the director is not usually presenting his or her own compositions. If we used the making of a movie as a model, the president might better be conceived as the character who gives unity to the plot than as the director who, from outside, tells everyone in detail what is to be done. Analogies and models are never, however, more than imaginative aids, for they simply transfer problems from one domain to another. How justified is the institution of chief executive officer in business (with what powers?), or orchestra director in performance, or movie director in film production? How close is the comparison of tasks and problems in university and business?

The formal statement of presidential role as executive agent of the trustees in carrying out their policies for the institution needs supplementation from the standpoint of the university's needs. Why does it need a unified central single officer? What in its operation requires a sufficiently high degree of unity to vest tasks and powers in a single person? Thus formulated, the role of a president is not antecedently specified; it reflects the character of the institution and its desirable operations, in particular those elements that require a sufficient degree of unified regulation, that constitute what we may think of as a "structural convergence."

The kinds of tasks that feed into such a structural convergence are manifold and diverse. Take the financing of the university. In private universities, raising money is a major presidential occupation. It has to be unified, for it reaches out in many different directions. It involves keeping the alumni happy about the university, keeping its reputation high and in public view, maintaining smooth governmental relations, gathering both outstanding scientists for the faculty and stars for the athletic teams, making sure there is a next generation of well-qualified entering students. This last task may well involve raising scholarship funds or loans, particularly from government programs, especially as student fees may have to be raised in an inflationary period. All this too may have to be done in a competitive spirit, as the pool of potential students may be limited, and other colleges and universities are engaging in similar competitive efforts.

In a state or municipal university, however, the unity of all these projects may fall apart. Since the source for funding is chiefly the state legislature, and the supporting body for the existence of the institution is the community who look to the college as the avenue of advance for their children, the institutional operations with respect to the legislative budget are quite differently structured. There still remains the general duty to see that no scandal rouse public or legislative passions, and there is a (usually milder) interest in maintaining alumni relations. The president may also be a cheerleader for a winning athletic team. But there is little need for an organized campaign in which deans or other officials travel to various parts of the country to stir alumni in interesting future students. If there were no president, some college or university official could well specialize in the political aspects of legislative relations.

Consider where structural convergence may arise from an educational problem and require unified governance resolution. Rarely today does one find a president seeking to remake the educational program of the institution, as, for example, Robert M. Hutchins, adhering to a special metaphysics of ultimate principles, redid a central part of liberal-arts education at the University of Chicago in that image. Today even a college with a special religious background will generally separate its philosophy teaching from its teaching of religion, lest it endanger its receipt of federal funds. Often too, presidents are too busy to deal with educational problems in the institution, and leave them to academic vice-presidents or provosts. But suppose the question arises whether economics or humanities should be taught in a school of business or left as a requirement to be satisfied by taking courses in the school of liberal arts, or again, whether biology should be taught in the school of medicine for its students or physics in the school of engineering rather than in liberal arts. Insofar as the issue is the kind of teaching involved, what will be stressed and what left in the background, the president is not in a position to adjudicate. Indeed, in recent years, as contrasted with earlier conditions, accrediting committees have begun to include a careful survey of governance and look at whether educational questions are settled by the educators themselves. On the other hand, who should decide such an issue in the given institution is a question of governance, and here the president might well mediate or arbitrate or adjudicate—for example, that each school has jurisdiction over its own required courses, leaving the views of other schools as advisory.

The governance role of the president is not, then, a function of some preassigned power, and only in part a consequence of tasks assigned by the trustees, but rather a requirement of the conditions and problems and state of the institution insofar as its character and objectives produce a structural convergence.

To the specific tasks that fall on the president as agent of the trustees and the requirements of structural convergence we may add a president's general role of leadership, whether in an authoritarian or democratic mold. This involves generating fresh ideas for the university, encouraging others to deal with problems, making sure that decisions are made where they are required, facing crises and taking responsibility in difficult situations (where the familiar "buck" stops), acting as guardian of (but not as slave to) the traditions of the institution, maintaining the moral tone of the university. The strength of the presidency lies in the need for effective leadership. In this, a creative attitude, when present, is unmistakable, just as a heavy hand is deadening. In many respects the role of a president in governance offers great opportunities, but it is also a precarious one.

The chief challenge to the concept of the unified and powerful presidency comes, both in authoritarian and democratic structures, from questioning the necessity for the unity involved and offering alternatives in the patterning of decision. In the authoritarian, a familiar (political) alternative has been feudal baronies, with the monarch maintaining peace among them. (The relation of professional schools in a large university sometimes has this character.) In a democratic structure, the comparison might be of the general medical practitioner keeping an eye on the patient as a whole while the specialists shape the serious deciding, or of the chair of a group of law partners who keeps an ordering eye on the distribution of work to see nothing is left out. The theory of authority in a democratic structure will be considered in the next chapter.

Teachers

The case for a primary position of teachers in governance has already been sufficiently canvassed in the development of the democratic idea within the New York experience. It is clear enough in recent times, with the expansion of higher education, that college education is not a luxury but has become an essential support of a highly developed society, and that the teaching staffs alone have the requisite expertise. The more authoritarian patterns did not omit teachers but coordinated them by selection through a network of deans and department heads under the president. Relaxation of authoritarianism has come through delegation of powers to appointed faculty groups, through greater departmental independence and some consulting share for senior department members about the selection of department head, through the use of special committees, and similar devices. Among these has been particularly the use of organized faculties, senates, and councils, to whom were delegated powers on educational policies but not on the budgetary aspects that make policies efficacious. The resulting lack of faculty interest is widespread, and no critical complaint of so-called democratic lassitude is more widespread than that faculties have difficulty getting a quorum at their meetings. This is only one of a fairly familiar litany of complaints against faculties: that they discuss too much, that they put off or have difficulty reaching decisions, that they overcomplicate issues—in brief, not so much that they do the wrong thing as that they just don't get things done. What is more, the complaints usually come not from outsiders, but from faculty members themselves. Some of these complaints can, of course, be readily handled by specific mechanisms: for example, size by representative bodies, limitations of time by specific self-regulation and more structured committee work. From the point of view of a democratic critique, however, the prevalent faculty complaint may often be a function of the lack of power and the realization that much of faculty processes will not play a vital part in the outcome of university practice generally. The expectation (or hope) is that where faculties are given genuine authority their sense of role will be responsible.

Indeed, a conscious attempt to embody the idea of democracy in empowering faculties and departments can select from a variety of techniques made clear in the development of democratic history. Examples are: collegial forms or a kind of cabinet rule, with an elected cabinet; cabinet proposals for faculty and department approval; faculty and department initiative through committees or directly in bringing proposals up for consideration and in deciding among them; and doubtless many intervening shades. While these may be ranged in order of increasing participatory democracy, they may also be seen as a variety of instruments to be employed under different conditions of the development of a college or university, and not necessarily as retreats from or compromises with the democratic idea. We may compare, in the political domain, the use of appointment rather than election for judges, or for major executive officers, with accompanying modes of ratification; these may be attuned to the state of the electorate, the way different mechanisms have experimentally worked out, and so on.

The most pervasive criticism of the working of faculty and departmental democracy has been that it develops vested interests of its own, of both a material and intellectual sort. This, of course, can happen, but the same thing can happen under presidential rule. What it calls for is the existence of mechanisms for influential evaluation and free criticism, just as departments are often periodically evaluated by visiting teams from accrediting institutions. In intellectual issues, one of the major purposes of academic freedom is to prevent a particular theoretical view or doctrine from establishing itself by controlling appointments and curriculum. For this it is important to maintain an area of freedom for the individual teacher even against the faculty majority, particularly where, as in the social sciences, different sociopolitical outlooks may be involved. On material interests, the most serious issues have arisen when it is a question of abolishing a whole department or division or the entry of a new department in a rising academic field; the usual criticism is that faculties will resist necessary measures that cut down their vested domains. Cases of this sort are often unclear, particularly where the faculty powers are largely nominal. For example, if a cut is being made as part of budgetary contraction, and the faculty has no powers to deal with the budget, it may often be uncertain whether this is the best place to make cuts, whether, for example, it might not be made in the administrative rather than the educational budget. Sometimes, however, where the trustees propose to cut out a school or department, the reasons may be explicit—for example, it is regarded as a training field rather than as an "academic" field, or it is a field in which there has come to be little interest. The faculties are likely in such cases to argue that these are particularly cases in which the educational components are central, and the authority to deal with them falls within their scope.

Let us take a particular example from the New York colleges in 1987. As reported by the *New York Times*, it is headed "CUNY Faculty Fights Teacher-Training Plan."[2] A City University task force recommended abolishing the undergraduate major in education, and faculty leaders "say it infringes on the faculty's right to establish curriculum and degree requirements." The proposal worked through two measures: requiring that students training as teachers major in a liberal-arts or science discipline, not in education; and limiting to thirty the number of education credits they could take. The task force contained seven trustees, five college presidents, two faculty members, and a student. The chairperson of the faculty senate said that while the report included many constructive suggestions, it was "a dangerous precedent for a board task force to attempt to usurp the traditional right and function of the college faculties whose academic backgrounds and experiences qualify them for the making and revision of curriculum and academic programs." The chairman of the trustees responded that new and innovative ideas can come from other places, though ordinarily from the faculties; the faculties would be fully consulted, but it was "ultimately the responsibility of the board to set the fundamental policies of this university." The account goes on to note that university officials said "they could not recall the trustees ever abolishing a major on a university wide basis." But there had been many cases of the board overruling normal faculty prerogatives. An example cited was the board abolishing individual college admissions criteria in the late 1960s and embarking on an open admissions policy.

This comparison is worth pursuing. The open admissions policy was instituted in response to the militant Black civil rights movement. The City College had been occupied and the situation was dangerous. The board advanced by a number of years the plan of broadening admission requirements to provide opportunities for any high-school graduate, with special opportunities for those who had not been adequately prepared. It was thus a whole-city program with city cooperation in financing, to meet the higher-educational aspects of a general, almost revolutionary, situation. The present case of teacher education is quite different. Major dissatisfaction with the elementary and high schools, especially in the inner cities, has focused attention on teacher training, and a widespread proposal has been to insist on more content and less method training, or else have the method conveyed in practice. Many undergraduate majors have been abolished throughout the country, and though important foundations concerned with teaching have offered proposals moving in that direction, there is still more than a touch of teacher scapegoating in the situation. Some universities have disposed of undergraduate education departments and then had to find indirect ways of restoring them. Again, there is a difference between a general policy or direction and the specific investigation of the experience in educational training within a given region. In general, if faculties are prone to hold to the status quo, boards are prone to leap at the latest, most fashionable proposals. The normal procedure of raising a question with the faculties, having them explore it, and in connection with that have a joint exploratory committee of faculty and trustees, would be much more likely to develop a sound and lasting policy.

In this controversy at the City University, further confrontation between the board and the faculty was avoided when, in the words of the chancellor, "the trustees recognized that the faculty's traditional role in developing academic programs had to be acknowledged as part of this process."[3] The faculties of the senior colleges were invited to suggest modifications and innovative alternatives in the report the board was considering, and each senior college to develop a general plan to implement the report's recommendations. Presumably in future planning the faculty would be brought in at the outset.

That faculties in colleges and universities would in a fully democratic structure have basic authority over educational policy does not mean, then, that there would not have to be functions of supervision, evaluation, collaboration, and the like, exercised by other claimants to a share in governance. These have next to be considered. We may add that there remain many questions within faculty structure itself to be answered by collective experience, such as the ones noted in the New York story on the relation of teaching and nonteaching staffs within the university or college.

The elementary and high-school situation with respect to democratic movements also has interesting contemporary developments. In recent years, since teachers had little share in policy determination, the most promising movement was for teacher centers in which they could get together and discuss their own problems. Official attempts to improve teaching tended to be wholly individualistic and competitive, such as merit pay for superior teaching, judged by principals and supervisors, or else increments for taking courses. Even worse, in many cases where teacher centers got going, they were placed under principal or supervisor authority, and so lost their cooperative character. (It was obviously one thing for a teacher to raise a problem of teaching in personal experience to fellow teachers, and quite another where higher-ups could see it as admitting a weakness. Some centers did, however, manage to be acknowledged as teacher-controlled, and even to receive financial support from the schools. We have noted earlier the current campaigns for teacher participation in formulating policy, which now come with strong union backing and can be incorporated into contracts.

Students

In the events of the 1930s, we saw, students supported faculty efforts at democratization, and for themselves they sought and won concrete liberties in their own organizational affairs. Their more basic critique of their educational institutions came in the 1960s. They refused to be the products of the "knowledge industry" and asserted themselves as participant subjects. By the end of the decade the movement had spread over Western educational institutions and had edged its way into secondary education as well. In the United States it was complicated by the special problems of the Vietnam War and the impact of the liberation movements. France had its own Algerian moral dilemma, and Germany the aftermath of World War II. Common to all, including Britain, was the pace of expansion. This was more intensive in Europe as a whole because it had not expanded higher education to the same extent as in the United States. In the old university setting it meant a great increase in lower-echelon teachers, who had no part in governance and who were barely ahead of the students in demanding recognition. Indeed the European response became more sweeping than the American. Some of the German legislatures adopted the principles of a threefold representation in decision-making bodies—from professors, lower-echelon teachers, and students. France gave increased participation to younger teachers and students. (In both France and Germany research was located in separate institutes.) In the United States there has been greater variety, each college or university determining its own policy; but on the whole students have won places in many representative bodies.

Some attention has to be given to detailed techniques. For example: Should there be limits on the kinds of matters students vote on in light of the fact that they represent a rapid turnover in generations? Where is bicameralism (of teachers and students) a better device than unicameralism? How much of administration should be public, how much private? And so on. For example, just as publicity may be judged a good principle of social action but not applicable to certain areas of diplomatic negotiation, so confidentiality might be desirable for letters of recommendation, even if certain risks are involved; to make these wholly public may render them useless. Again, bicameralism may institutionalize confrontation, if there is a likelihood of persistent differences of opinion, and be unnecessarily duplicative if there is not. These are, however, matters for experiment and consequent judgment.[4]

The student body that revolted in the 1960s extended into teaching groups. Graduate students at Berkeley, for example, were very active, and many of them were employed for discussion sections of large classes. In many cases student demand for participation thus embraced also junior faculty demand.

Students in the United States during the 1960s directed a great deal of energy to demands for a place on governing boards, and sometimes won it, only to find that the fruits were scarcely worth the cost. They may have gained an occasional voice on an occasional matter, but on the whole it was not the center of action. Why this was so is not wholly clear. It may have been the cooling down of crisis, distraction by economic recession, the merely token character of much of student representation, perhaps the realization that the effective decisions are often made still farther up the political ladder, or perhaps the discovery of the limits to educational reform without more basic changes in the social structure. Student participation takes its color from the composition of student bodies in different social crises and social structures: Compare the United States during the quiet 1950s and during the Vietnam War, the general picture of Latin America under dictatorship, French students in the early 1960s. Institutions still have to face the question whether to include students on boards and faculties and determine specific representation of varying groups, but there is no formula of a general sort to fit all kinds of institutions. Public institutions probably require the widest representation, whereas special purpose, private, research, experimental, can go in special directions. The significant questions concern the realistic relations of different groups that exercise effective strength in the educational process.

The general contribution that student participation may bring is to stir their initiative and break through the passive student role of traditional schooling. It may also help break hardened traditionalist attitudes in faculties, and spur attentiveness to needed change. One danger is that it may express what is "in" rather than what is scholarly. Another is that parts of the work that require great effort, sometimes almost drudgery, may be shed: For example, student pressure probably accounted for many graduate schools dropping the old requirement of two foreign languages in the Ph.D. program. This often had no immediate relevance, and the growth of translation of foreign works made much available that had not been within reach before. But precisely when the world was growing smaller, and communication with other peoples became more necessary, the United States in general, and individual professors moving more freely into conferences abroad, found themselves at a loss. Often they have been rescued only by the fact that Europeans have proved multilingual. Of course there is no reason why student participation in governance should not be

shaded for different contexts: For example, a student representative in a university may have a part in deciding whether a
course is to be given, but not who is to teach it, or what texts to
use; whether a probationer has a sound educational relationship toward students, but not whether his or her publications are technically competent.

In general, however, student demand for participation in governance has all the force and limitations that consumers have
in any productive process. What force that is depends on the
degree of consciousness and organization. Before the 1960s students were largely in the same position as consumers had been
when it was a matter of *caveat emptor,* let the buyer beware. In
some respects it was even worse, since compulsory curricula
limited their choices. And yet in theory, as suggested earlier, a
full-fledged consumer model could well challenge any other
model of governance. Since the social role of industry in general is to provide goods and services for consumers, the guiding
scheme of what is desirable and at what cost, what choices of
direction should be made and what policies pursued, should
have major participation of consumers. Instead, business management intersperses advertising as a mode of consumer guidance and control, often relying on consumer weaknesses rather
than consumer strengths. Even consumer polling is such as to
yield uncritical consumer preference. There have been occasional suggestions that consumers be elevated to one of three
ruling factors in economic life: owners and managers, workers,
consumers; that representatives of these groups constitute a
kind of legislative council for industry, with government to
break any deadlock. When such suggestions came in the 1930s,
they were too reminiscent of Mussolini's corporate state, and,
moreover, labor was just beginning to get recognition. Further,
the state had been so partisan to business that it was difficult
to think of it as a just mediator or arbitrator; this atmosphere

altered a bit under the social measures of the Roosevelt administration. In any case, consumer organization, when it came eventually, under the impetus of the movement promoted by Ralph Nader, has stressed largely protective steps, making first large leaps into evaluating products and exposing evils. The parallel here in student effort would be winning student course evaluation, as well as the right to suggest course development. We forgo here the task of developing the implications of a full-fledged consumer model and its parallel in higher education. It would have, of course, to fashion a tie-in with expertise in order to save its consumption desires from expressing whim and arbitrary wishes rather than serious long-range and important interests, just as consumer desires in food need the advice of health expertise and as housing needs architectural wisdom. What is lacking in any authoritative as against advisory student control is precisely what students come to institutions of higher education to learn—the accumulated knowledge and wisdom and skill of the past and its concern with contemporary problems. What they are most sensitive to is the impact of the problems. Obviously then, their share in governance has to be finely tuned rather than a blunt partition of power.

It is also possible, as higher education becomes a lifelong process rather than just an isolated period of early life, that fresh institutions, in addition to universities and colleges, will emerge organized precisely to meet student/consumer demand. Extension courses or schools of general studies in traditional colleges or special schools have something of this character. An interesting suggestion has been that cities have centers of learning, giving no degrees and without any organized college or university life, but just offering courses in response to consumer demand. They would operate thus much in the way language schools do for their more limited domain of learning, to speak and read a foreign language.

Within colleges and universities, the heritage of the student movement of the 1960s is that the giant was at last awakened, and it is unlikely that there will be a return to deep sleep. The awakening was a special case in Western history and in American history, expressing the conditions of change in the post–World War II world, the anxieties over nuclear war, the convergence in America of liberation movements, as well as in turn the Vietnam War, which impinged directly on student life. Most important, at its center, was the critique of prevalent aims in higher education itself: It saw students being prepared as items in a military–industrial machine rather than for a worthwhile life of community association. It was this challenge of aims, with sufficient resonance in the lives of many educated contemporaries, that shook traditional assumptions about how higher education should be controlled.

Student generations, however, change rapidly. The activist sixties were followed by the quiet seventies, and then the growingly conservative eighties. Indeed, student activism in the late eighties came sometimes from the ultra right, and even in some places with a growing racist tinge. The question consequently raised by such transitions is whether student participation in governance introduces potential instability rather than a creative novelty.

In the long run, stability in student participation reflects the extent to which students have become a self-conscious *public* with respect to interests that unify them. This is quite apart from diversity on broad and controversial political issues, which can be found in any older community as well. Their permanent interest as students within the university is for acknowledged freedom of inquiry and expression within a framework of civility. This may be broken if the society as a whole approaches a violent split, as happened in the nineteenth century at the time of the Civil War, or again nearly happened at the time of the Vietnam War. On that occasion, students, feeling they were being coerced, controlled, and misled by government, broke the rules of civility and shouted down governmental representatives defending the war.

The positive interests of a student public are seen now rather in the growth of measures within the university that extend their particular participation: in organized forms of course evaluation, in student discipline committees for student infractions, in channels for expression of grievances, in organizing their own activities and controlling their own publications, and in contributing ideas (both critical and constructive) to educational processes and policy. The cultivation of a self-conscious student public thus becomes a university matter, not just a militant student drive. Within a democratic structure of governance, the expectation is that such a positive and continuous process will enable both students and teachers to learn in the long run what can best be done by students in what ways and with what degree of responsibility. In short, the issue has never been one of turning over to students a given fraction of power, but of the university as a whole coming to understand the role of students as a definite public within its framework.

It is sometimes asked of the participants in a university: Who feel themselves *to be* the university? There were occasions in the medieval history of the university when the students simply abandoned one place to go to another—that ended the one and installed the other as a university. The faculty often feel that, as the continuing group, they rather than the students or the president are the university. (For the president to identify himself or herself as such would be the analogue of "L'état, c'est moi.") A story is told (whether true or apocryphal) that when General Eisenhower became president of Columbia University, he made a reference to the professors as "employees of the university" and was immediately corrected with the remark, "They *are* the university." Doubtless, underlying this sense on the part of the faculty are both the duration of teachers' commitment to the institution and the sense that they are the custodians of the tradition of learning, as well as (where research is involved) of the sense of the frontier on the enterprise of knowledge. Yet from a long-range view this sense cannot prove decisive. For one thing, the instrumentalities of learning are growing in the modern world—in some respects the library is a runner-up to the classroom, and television can become a contender—and the possibilities of learning without teaching become proportionately greater. In general, the conceptual shift from education as teaching to education as learning has become marked in recent thought. Moreover, the dependence of the teaching situation itself on the wider technological and social milieu has become greater. A more holistic approach to the university within the society is required to understand the shape taken by its aims and operations. The university, whether public or private, now becomes in effect a social and public institution.

Teacher Unions

Teacher unions, often including other workers in higher education, have grown rapidly in the second half of the twentieth century. Before that, as in the account of the 1930s, they faced the genteel separation of college teachers from labor and its resort to strikes. For the most part, if teachers in higher education had joined any organization to promote teacher interests, they had turned to professional associations, and in particular to the American Association of University Professors. They found by experience that while the AAUP worked out excellent programs it was not very successful in dealing with particular cases. This was especially true in matters of academic freedom during the McCarthy period, when struggle was most needed. In the long run, the AAUP itself learned from the experience of unions, and by the 1970s, when it was already competing in elections for collective bargaining units, its behavior did not differ much from that of unions. In short, college and university teachers had learned that in matters of economic well-being and in maintaining academic freedom, there was no substitute for vigorous organization allied with kindred forces in the community. Teacher unions made use of the governmental machinery of the National Labor Relations Board; they took part in elections for representation, and when they won, carried on public campaigns in the interests of their members and their profession. Affiliation with organized labor often rallied public support more vigorously than a general appeal to the general public. But as far as policies and strategies were concerned, the differences became minimal between teacher unions affiliated with labor and those functioning as purely professional organizations acting on behalf of economic and professional interests. The old isolated professionalism that had made of professors what Harold Laski had called "the shabby genteel" had come to an end.

Three questions have played an important part in thinking about the relation of unions and governance. One is whether a union is in some sense an "outside organization"—a favorite formulation of administrators appealing to professors not to join. A second, once a union has been recognized, is the relation between being a worker or employee and being part of management; this becomes accentuated as a problem when some measure of democracy is granted, as when faculties are assigned an area of decision. The third is how far unions, and labor in general, constitute a "special interest" to be assessed in light of the general interest.

The inside–outside issue makes it necessary to draw fine

lines, but they may be quite principled ones. A teacher formally advocating a given policy may be asked whether he is doing so as a union spokesperson, as a department representative, or as a private citizen. In the same way a member of Congress might be asked whether she is speaking for her district, for her party, or for Americans generally. In short, a human being has many functional roles whose relevance varies with different contexts. Of course there may be critical situations in which a choice has to be made between "allegiances." In most such cases, even where there is strong tension, existing principles of decision may be definite enough; a standard example is a Catholic judge granting a divorce, contrary to his religious beliefs, because he is sworn to uphold the law. To make an absolute out of the inside–outside argument in the case of teacher unions is usually demagogic; the serious content it sometimes embraces is the general problem of conflict in ethical decision, not only in loyalties.

The worker–manager issue has assumed more serious proportions as a consequence of the Supreme Court decision in the Yeshiva University case (1980), which denied certification to the union under the Labor Relations Act on the ground that the faculty, in virtue of its powers of decision, is part of management.[5] Presumably, then, full democratization would mean the end of unionism, or perhaps the end of a need for it, or else its replacement by interuniversity faculty associations for pursuit of mutual interests. Technically, of course, this decision only deprives unions of a specific instrument of recognition; a union could still win it by its strike action or public pressure. It is not worth speculating here on what organizational possibilities and mechanisms might be developed even in the atmosphere of a spreading approach like that of the Yeshiva case; its actual role has been part of the battle against unionism in private colleges. Interestingly, the procedure of unions has sometimes faced comparable problems: For example, department heads or chairpersons are admissible to the union only if departments are democratized.

The Yeshiva case is only an extreme instance in which university administrations have attempted to oppose collective bargaining by setting unions against faculty governance. In the November–December 1987 issue of *Academe* (the bulletin of the American Association of University Professors) the possible conflict of collective bargaining and university governance is explored in a number of institutions. Most clarifying is the survey by Professor Irwin Yellowitz, treasurer of the Professional Staff Congress, the bargaining union for the City University of New York itself.[6] He shows how the union tried (and in significant cases succeeded) to protect the existing forms of academic governance through contract and campaigning; it did not seek to replace them. For example, on the question of peer review in appointment, probation, and promotion, some union members stressed the dangers of arbitrary faculty judgment; but the union safeguarded individuals against injustice by a strict grievance procedure, rather than attempting to supplant peer review by strict seniority and automatic promotion. And when the university attempted to establish tenure quotas, the union joined with the staffs in successfully opposing this as an illegitimate inroad on the peer-review process. It had to use its resources for broad public campaigning, since the New York State Public Relations Board had ruled that governance was not a mandatory subject for collective bargaining.

Such historical evidence suggests that there is no inherent conflict between democratic governance and collective bargaining by unions. Where general staff agreement exists on a specific policy, unity and mutual support are almost automatic. If there is disagreement, it is not on the principle of governance mechanisms, but on specific policy, just as there may be disagreement between different points of view within a governing senate.

Finally, there is the question whether labor unions constitute a "special interest." Of course any particular interest—an organization of senior citizens, of women to secure equality, of parents to secure preschool child care—is a special interest, and can be examined for its effect on the whole body of interests of humankind. Is the interest in an unpolluted environment a special interest? It will be so regarded by manufacturers whose disposal of waste will be regulated as a result. It is surprising how seldom in a free-enterprise milieu the interest of business is felt as a special interest—probably because it is claimed as common knowledge that what is good for business (or for General Motors) is good for the country. In general, if the charge of special interest has any definite meaning, it is in alleging not particularity of interest but unfairness to other interests.

There may at times be specific contexts in which a meaningful differentiation of policies arises, somewhat akin to the distinction that is being drawn. Debates within the New York Teachers Union in the 1930s sometimes involved a general split between those who urged pursuing teacher economic interests directly and those who argued that economic aims should be pursued only in those ways that had a broader approach to the problems of students and parents. The reticence to engage in a strike came not only from the insufficient strength of the union at that period, but also from the view that the children would be hurt; methods of political organization, of getting parent support while working for student needs (smaller classes, school lunches, etc.), might bring sufficient strength to secure teacher economic gains as well, and in any case would be better policy. The other side tended to regard these further efforts as ancillary or even fads and frills: A union, it was said, is an organization for the advancement of the economic well-being of the members, and that should be sought directly. In the long run, of course, when teacher unionism grew sufficiently strong, the strike was employed to win recognition.

Doubtless, what policy to follow depends on the particular context of forces, degree of development of unionism, and so on. There does remain a sense in which whether a movement fits the description of a "special interest" depends more on its policies than on its organizational functions. Selfishness is possible in organizational as well as individual affairs; however, if poverty is deep and intense, it would be callous to regard any concern for the impoverished as a special interest. This type of inquiry thus has deep roots in the morality of common purposes.

As for unionism in governance, many of the questions of the past are over, unless there is a general social regression in the country. As noted earlier in the case of the New York teacher unions, they have come to have a place in the orderly procedure of the social and political life of education. Thus there remains little of the older questions about the general place of unions. What unions ask for is recognition as a bargaining agent for the staffs. What precise place they win is not for the union, but for the staffs on whose behalf they bargain. Hence unions may add to the powers of the staffs in governance, but what they exercise is not governance but political–social influence. In this way, we shall see, it is comparable to influence exercised through monetary grants by the federal government. Such cases of habitual and regularized influence—more structured than a lobby—might raise the question of adding influence as a category in the study of governance, whether or not it is seen as a constituent part of a governance pattern.

Graduates

Alumni are often given some share in governance, particularly in private universities, where it may take the form of alumni representatives or alumni seats on the board of trustees. Chosen (often by alumni vote) from the more successful, and usually wealthy, graduates, or else from outstanding professional fields, they may both add lustre and keep open a smoother path for alumni contributions. Children of alumni also constitute an important source for future students of the university. In public colleges, too, alumni through chance or design may find their way on the board of trustees.

The part that alumni play in governance is not very different from that of other friends of the institution, even where a formal procedure of election of alumni to the board is followed. They are not seen as having a special alumni interest to safeguard or express beyond their concern with the general wellbeing of the college. Perhaps on many campuses it becomes specialized toward competitive sports or fraternities, but even this is linked in sentiment to the reputation of the institution. Alumni often too, especially in private institutions, play an active part in recruiting students for the college.

The bonds that tie alumni to their institution are multiple and complex. They continue to be interested in the value of their college certification: If the institution goes downhill, their degree may be depreciated. Perhaps the greater part of the sentiment is disinterested. It is bonded by the mingled recollections of youth, of going out on one's own into the world, of new and lasting friendships, often of broadening interests and self-discovery, of setting firm steps on major work and career.

How far do such grounds justify a claim to continued participation in the governance of the institution? One basis is the existence of a body of solid and continued goodwill. This can and often is exercised through friends-of-the-university organizations; it does not of itself require a share in governance. More important is the distinctive role of graduates in being able to assess through extended experience the effects of their higher education. The opportunity for this is manifest in professional training, but it is also important in looking back to general atmosphere and cultural influence. Such a function too could be expressed without participation, and utilized formally in commissions of review set up by the institution itself. The multiplication of justifying grounds would seem, however, to warrant some share in governance rather than ad hoc utilization, in the case of so stable and continuous a benevolent source of interest. The one possibly negative argument might be that alumni are bound to the image of the past, and might stand in the way of change—for example, widening opportunities of women and minorities, regulating or abolishing fraternities. Traditionalism, however, and resistance to change can be a mark of any social group that has had the advantage of society's instruments. It should not be charged distinctively against alumni.

It would seem then that graduates might well have some share in governance, though not as focused as that of faculties on educational decision. Giving alumni seats on boards of trustees seems therefore to be a serviceable way of securing their general participation. Whether this gives them too much power is not a function of their special seating, but of the role of trustees as such.

Parents and Families

Children going off to college—even where college is a local institution and they live at home, but certainly more so when they go away—is a trying time for parents. They know that there will be fresh influences on their children, who may embark on new paths leading away from not only strong familial desires but even deeply held familial standards. (This refers, of course, to the usual case, not the young who came to college in the late 1940s after having fought in World War II.) Yet on the whole, in spite of the strength of parental will for the good of the young, parents as such should have no direct hand in the governance of higher education. College is a time when the young learn to stand on their own feet, should learn to think for themselves, to begin evaluating traditional ways and be open to the possibility of change in a changing world. Parents have had the greater part of two decades to impart their standards and outlook to their children; they have to take their chance on the children growing up.

What critical relationships parents may have with respect to the ways of the institution can, of course, be expressed to individuals—teachers and administrators if necessary. This sort of relation takes more organized forms for younger children in primary education, usually through parent–teacher associations, which themselves have more or less official status— voice without vote at public board meetings. Such channels are imperative, both for general policy and for immediate problems of one's own children. Some organized form may be desirable for parents on the college level too, to deal with general concerns of present students, such as residential provisions or campus safety: for example, the proposal, which became law in Pennsylvania, that every college have a publicly available record of crimes on the campus. Of course, parental interest need not be limited to matters of immediate health and welfare.

On the whole, parental influences, if they seek to be efficacious through the route of legislation or public pressure, have to operate as part of a broader community effort. This is likely to have a salutary effect. In general, what influence parents may want to exercise on the policies of higher education requires a filtering to ensure it is oriented to general welfare, not particular bias. At least for a start this is done through community and its instruments. It is the community group, not the family as such, that thus has generally made a claim to some share in governance.

Communities and Community Groups

Communities, as in some sense the ultimate matrix for which education and its consequences are intended, present a serious claim to influence of a strong sort. It is helpful in this case to discuss the question first for elementary and high school and then compare—and in an important sense contrast—higher education. Our concern here is with the pressure that is non-governmental; the role of government in educational governance is a separate, subsequent matter.

Community pressure on the lower schools often has a bad reputation. It achieves notoriety in cases where prejudice attempts to constrain the school, for example, to censor books in school libraries or to curb the teaching of evolution in science classes, or to campaign in a broadside manner against "secular humanism." Comparably, racist attitudes prevalent in the community may operate in students as well. Where such attitudes are limited to a narrow community, they may be checked by higher court action. But where they are widespread, as in the McCarthy period, or in the history of race prejudice in the United States, they may bring the country, not merely education, to the brink of social disaster.

On the other hand, a pattern of community control of the lower schools may be tried out as a mode of governance. Such an experiment roused strong passions in New York City when it was introduced some decades ago. It meant setting up local boards, to be elected by the local community, with certain appointive and control powers in the various school districts. This was a reaction against a fairly impersonal centralization of school controls in central headquarters that had proved insensitive to the problems of ethnic and racial groups in the neighborhoods. No attempt is made here to evaluate this experiment; apparently it helped further its major purpose of greater attentiveness, though it sometimes added other problems of local irregular operations.[7]

The situation takes different shape where the community is split in social outlook, say with one side advocating progressive methods in the schools and the other the older virtues of discipline and homework. (These are the headline designations, not intended here as descriptions of essence.) Where the community elects the board of education, which then determines the character of the curriculum and the kind of schooling, a large minority may be left in a serious predicament. (They might have preferred to take their chance on teacher control of the schools.) Some dissident parents send their children to private experimental schools of different sorts, but then they are paying twice since they are continuing to be taxed for public schools. An experiment in California was started with alternative kinds of schooling within the public schools. In this community there had been a seesaw of election victories between so-called traditionalists and progressive factions, with unsettling effect on the schools. Instead of changing the character of the schools whenever there was a change of victor, the "progressive" victor proposed that there be schools of different kinds, with the parents sending their children to schools of their choice. The schools differed in the features about which there had been dispute: formality, strictness, homework, discipline, and so forth, the features that are generally ascribed to the older educational methods—as against the informal, "permissive" individual emphasis generally attributed to progressive methods. The proposal was carried out, to the apparent satisfaction of all parties.

Up to a point such a solution, democratic in providing for minority will as well for majority, would seem workable. But it does not prevent the emergence of fresh controversies in the community. For one thing, the child might demand the right of choice, and differ from the choice of the parents. Where the teachers preponderantly agreed with the child, there would be a conflict of social values. Even more, there could be demands for different schools on other bases: for example, dictating different teaching of science, as in the creationism—evolution controversy; or different teaching on religion and politics. Here the importance of other factors in governance stands out: the expertise of scientists in determining the content of science to be taught, and the traditional liberties of American constitutionalism that are needed to equip the individual for decision rather than having an answer imposed. At such a point emphasis in governance falls on the procedures that guarantee educational standards rather than the will of community groups.

Community groups in the sense discussed are too complex and too varied to have a general claim to direct participation in governance. The special conditions of special communities and special problems have to be assessed. For the most part the channels of influence open to them are through political action and through the general advocacy that is open to all citizenry. A special governance role, as in the New York case cited above, has more the character of an elective political role.

If these are the conclusions about community participation in governance for the lower schools, then they are even stronger for higher education. Colleges and universities have markedly different features that argue for their independence. For one thing, selection of college is voluntary; the types of institutions are many, with ample scope for student choice guided by interest. One college may teach through the "great books," another through organized life experiences. There are religious colleges, and universities with different excellences in professional schools. Nevertheless, there are notable instances where community pressure reoriented a college in the light of pressing social demands. The introduction of open admissions into the New York city colleges, considered above, was of this sort. It was not doing much more with respect to openness than had been done by many of the state colleges throughout the country. Its occurrence in the midst of the Black liberation movement, and with the overt application of massive public pressure, gave it a special significance.

What most differentiates the situation in higher education from that in the lower schools is, of course, not merely a role in the transmission of knowledge but an assigned role in the extension of knowledge. This, however, does not free the university, even with respect to that function, from obligation to the wider community. Here the experience of contemporary science in relation to the public is illuminating. The driving interest of science is in research, and in the educational preparation of future researchers. It has increasingly come to recognize that its own support and welfare depend highly on its character being widely understood. This means not only that it should be appreciated enough to be supported, but that the attitude to it be a realistic one. Some scientists have undertaken the task of rendering intelligible what they are doing; education about the character of science has grown alongside of preparing scientists; journalism has developed science reporting as one of its specialties, and so on through the rest of the media. In applied science this has had important consequences, as in medicine, where the public now raises questions of the rights of the patient (e.g., "informed consent") and there is increased responsibility of specialists. So too in the important field of nuclear energy, organizations of scientists have borne the weight of informing the public about dangers in its use for war and in peace, and so added to the possibilities of realistic public policy. Now higher education has tended more or less to coast on the general assumption of its utility. In times of prosperity it tolerated the argument that college education resulted in higher-salary jobs and greater chances of employment, while in times of depression it shifted gears and talked of the intrinsic values of education.

Even a fair understanding by the community of the importance of higher education may not touch the practical problems of university–community relations within a given city. A college town may be economically dependent on the college. In a city too, a large university affects the economic well-being of the community by its tax exemption, by growth that often encroaches on the living space of its neighborhood, by its labor relations to its manifold types of workers, by its services or lack of services to the community, by its regard or disregard of problems of minorities and the impoverished. In these and other various areas, community needs, desires, requests, pressures, will be a graded response to the extent of university sensitivity to problems.

In the long run higher education has to recognize the community as a source of both support and criticism. A democratic conception of governance will see the community and its groups as a proper matrix of its policies; this involves responsibility for education about higher education and welcoming rather than shutting off criticism. Although ancient battles of town and gown have long gone (except for occasions of irresponsible student behavior on the town), advertisements of students in caps and gowns with shining faces will scarcely do the educational job. What Plato said about his absolute rulers in a setting of autocracy holds today for the community as "We the people" in an atmosphere of growing democracy—it can do the greatest good, but it can also do the greatest harm. The difference lies in enlightenment—of both public and university.

Agencies of Supervision and Evaluation

As noted earlier, there exist modes and agencies of supervision and evaluation. The most important on the American scene are the state board of education and accrediting bodies. The state government issues charters or gives formal authority to institutions to award an academic degree, and its standards have to be met. This is the equivalent of having a license to operate, and the standards employed by the state are in this respect foundational. Periodic evaluation is done by accrediting agencies of two sorts: regional, which assess the performance of institutions as a whole; and national special boards, which evaluate specific programs. A negative verdict, if serious enough to remove accreditation, is in effect like the loss of a license to continue operation. The college will not be forced to close down, as the loss of a liquor or driver's license will make selling liquor or driving illegal. But the effect on the reception of graduates in the professional milieu, the loss of entries and opportunities, the removal of recognition in various contexts, and perhaps most of all the loss of federal funds to both institution and students will act as the strongest of sanctions.

Accrediting would be acting as governance insofar as it set down goals to be adopted or followed and definite means to be employed to achieve them, under the threat of sanctions. The agencies do not follow this path. They seek rather to be the voice of the general professional standards, both in the way they are constituted and the criteria of excellence they enunciate. The association responsible for setting up particular evaluation committees is, in the first place, itself a more or less democratically organized assembly of institutions that have come to satisfy the standards. It is thus, a growing body through which the approved ways of the profession are filtered. Again, the specific committees consist of volunteers, educators and practitioners, including outsiders from the public. The institution is asked first to engage in a self-study, setting forth its goals and objectives, its means and methods, and the outcomes. The evaluating committee will thus avoid imposing goals, and a wide range of differing institutions can then be evaluated in their own terms. The criteria of excellence in performance are likely more specifically to embody the general lessons of the profession about the ways of doing things.

Evaluative criticism is, of course, a complex matter, for standards themselves may be undergoing change, developing, or even be subject to conflict. In general today there is much concern about the relation of criticism to reconstruction. We find the complaint on the part of writers, architects, musicians, that critics and reviewers are ceasing to be engaged in reflections after the fact of creation or production, and becoming rather advisors on how to create or produce. Indeed there is a general ferment in the theory of criticism. Perhaps the lines between production, appreciation, and criticism are breaking down in an age so marked with value change. It becomes desirable therefore to pinpoint the values invoked at every step in assessing the institution or program. For example, if the laboratory resources of a college are criticized, there may be underlying judgments about the desirable role of laboratory work in the teaching of science or it may be a concern with the health and safety of the students, and similarly for laboratory work in psychology or practical work in sociology. If a college is criticized for failing to submit questions of educational policy to faculty deliberation, it may be reshaping the internal pattern of governance. Doubtless some demands will be made as traditional or habitual and hardly felt as value assumptions. For example, a statement of standards for accreditation lists the requirement that an institution "have employed a chief administrative officer";[8] this is probably felt as obviously necessary for efficiency and responsibility, not as imposing a preferred mode of governing. We may expect also—on the side of change rather than tradition—to find openings for value growth, as experience with concrete cases leads to interpretation and extension of rules. For example, the requirement of "humane and non-discriminatory policies in dealing with students, staff, and faculty"[9] could conceivably lead, after comparative experience, to some demand for an independent channel for complaints and their investigation, such as an ombudsman. The convergence of problems of this sort may lead eventually to standards about governance.

An interesting example of the way in which the specification of criteria can have implications for governance is found in the proposal of the secretary of education in 1987 that accrediting agencies for higher education include student achievement as a criterion, in short, that failure of students to make academic gains be a measure of deficiency in the institution.[10] This raised serious issues about both the criterion itself and the implications of a power on the part of the federal government to require specific criteria. Discussion about the criterion of achievement followed familiar paths: for example, that success admits of no ready measure without reckoning the problems of particular student bodies and the character of supporting extraacademic conditions; or that the use of the criterion as central would lead teachers to stress examination preparation rather than intellectual development, and so lower the quality of education. The issue of government power to specify criteria raised less familiar but very subtle questions. Government does indeed have a proper interest in accrediting agencies, since it gives grants to institutions and makes loans to students only for properly accredited schools and colleges. Since accreditation agencies were not set up by government, but could arise in a variety of professional and vocational fields, government can properly list those it recognizes. But to specify the criteria to be employed in accrediting judgments, rather than leave them to the professional resources of the field, opens the way to dictating the character of the education itself. Might it not mean, it was asked, that the federal government would be free to specify required elements in the curriculum? In effect, in this indirect way, the federal government would be engaged in active governance of higher education. Such controversy shows the potential of evaluation for control, unless careful distinctions are made between what is legitimate and what is illegitimate federal regulation.

Apart from the major modes of evaluation by the state and by accrediting agencies, many special modes and influences are to be found in American education. Lines of influence radiate on particular fields of higher education from professional societies directly, and where professional education is concerned with some industry and organized practice, standard expectations of the field often have a strong effect on procedures and employment. Thus a particular path of learning may be entrenched because it is counted on in engineering, or a standardized way of doing things taught because it will open the door to medical practice anywhere throughout the country. Professional societies may sometimes specify requirements that individual institutions cannot but follow; often the regularities of practice are definite enough to need no specification. Accumulated or systematized expectations play an important part when a visiting committee of outsiders comes to inspect the working of a department, invited by the administration either because questions of performance have arisen, or because expansion is planned, say into graduate work, or just in accordance with some periodic schedule.

Boards of visitors or overseers may be part of the general plan of operation for a university or college, set up in the governance pattern to engage in periodic review of successes or failures. Where they address the broader aims and functioning of the institution as a whole, they may prompt a general self-evaluation.

Organized Government

Since the business of government is governing, one might have thought that educational governance would be one province of its business. But ours is a limited government, which has to justify where it enters and on what grounds and to what extent. Whole provinces of life and society stay out of its reach, except where they become entangled with its admitted functions; for example, it is normally expected to stay out of religion, morality, family life, associations of people.

Several features of education today invite government participation. First, there is the importance of education in the contemporary world; it is now necessary for the citizenry to be literate, and this has passed beyond just reading ability to so-called functional literacy. Education in some degree becomes essential to employability, and advanced training is needed for our complex technical civilization. That government is implicated is well indicated in the preamble to the Constitution, with its call for a more perfect union to, among other objectives, "promote the general Welfare and secure the Blessings of Liberty to ourselves and our Posterity." Again, the point has long been passed where private support is sufficient for education. It makes no sense to wield a general slogan that government should stay out of education when we have public schooling with public support (developed in the late nineteenth century) and public higher education has taken giant steps in the second half of the twentieth century. In the United States such public higher education has for the most part become a state function, with a few municipal exceptions, though even those now rest to a large extent on state support.

Standards for education have consequently been tied to determination by the states, through designated educational agencies as well as through state legislation. This has become the admitted vehicle for determining educational policy on a popular basis, and its broad character has often served to overcome the partial biases of local communities. Insofar as the many pathways of pressure, influence, voting, are exercised through state political channels, the overall character of state participation in education may be conceived as democratic, though it may often suffer from the passivity and inattention of the voters.

Federal influence has been exercised largely by attaching conditions to financial grants. During the 1960s its funding for research projects and development projects encouraged a vast expansion of higher education and practically determined the direction (largely in the sciences) that that development took. Now there was no suggestion that a federal representative be put on faculty research committees, but there might as well have been—except that different federal agencies were involved! With the later drop in funding, colleges found themselves in financial trouble and also realized that they had been fashioning their educational direction in response to federal instigation. Much the same thing happens in any case on the individual level of scientific work in response to available grants for research from federal and corporate funds. The question is how planning for basic research can take place in such a way as to free scientists in the universities to follow ideas of their own devising, rather than the flow of funds. One suggestion, given the general realization of the importance of basic research, is government grants to universities for regranting within. (Other provision would be required to take care of

novel projects that might be thrust aside by traditionalist emphases in such channels.) Such a policy would neutralize the
federal influence in determining educational direction. In
other areas it might be desirable to strengthen this indirect
mode of federal governance—for example, in regulating minimum standards for medical or psychiatric training, or again, in
breaking the monopoly of a professional group in some important areas of health and welfare. An alternative would be to
separate research entirely from the university, as is done in Europe—in Germany, France, Yugoslavia, and the Soviet Union—
where much of the research is carried on in institutes or acade-
mies financed by the state. Again, salutary federal influence
through conditions attached to tax exemption is found in curb-
ing racial and other forms of discrimination. Of course the
same route is capable of playing a negative role in times of general political repression. Eventually, democratic battles are
waged on the broadest political front.

Since education has few ramparts of its own, it is wise policy
to pay careful attention to the different ways in which the
federal influence is exercised. Tax exemption is perhaps the
strongest way. Less strong, but often equally effective, is a financial grant for a special program. A parallel set of distinctions might concern whether the result alone is mandated, or
the methods of achieving it as well, or even further, whether
detailed regulations are specified for achieving the result. In
part, the acceptability of such federal measures depends on the
importance of the program; and it would probably be best to
use the least directly regulative method, only increasing
strength to the extent that the less strong one did not prove
successful. For example, on racial discrimination, stronger
methods have had to be employed where weaker ones were un-
successful or where they allowed too much scope for evasion.
On the treatment of the handicapped, stronger methods pro-

duced a revolution in what had been an area of less than benign neglect. On curricular matters, there has been occasional speculation on what the states would do if the federal government offered large educational improvement grants (this for high schools) but attached a set of curricular requirements for them. An obviously wiser procedure, which would tread less on the educational prerogatives of the schools, would be to offer curricular objectives and leave the rest to an institution selected as educationally reliable.

Direct governmental influence on education comes, of course, through the action of the courts, both state and federal. They have acted on probationer rights and on many questions of student civil rights (such as permissible dress or freedom of student press, as well as the well-known cases of racial discrimination). An interesting case was the right of a pregnant, unmarried high-school student to continue attending classes. On problems directly concerned with university governance, there have been cases of faculty appeal against trustee trespass on faculty governance rights, such as to judge qualifications for tenure or other measures that rest on specific educational judgments.

In general, there are fine lines to be drawn and correlated with the importance of specific policies and the effects of governmental action and procedures. It is clear that federal action is not only a habitual and regularized influence in governance, as unions are, but a legitimate democratic guardian of and instrument for educational aims, as part of the broader governance pattern of higher education.

CHAPTER 10

The Nature of Democratic Governance

NOWADAYS, ALMOST EVERYONE is directly or indirectly affected by the kind and quality of education—by literacy, by the extent of knowledge and skills, by the moral and social attitudes cultivated or neglected in the schools. In principle then, everyone should *count* in the reckonings of governing. But counting is not participating. Participation concerns who decides what, where, when, and what responsibility this carries—from whom, to whom, and about whom—and who carries out the decisions in the operation of the enterprise.

At the outset the idea of governance seemed clear enough with its functions of policy decision, power or control, and administrative authority set on one side, and the workaday functions of teaching and learning on the other. Concessions to claimants seemed to spread the center of decision, disperse authority, and obscure the line between the managerial or administrative role and the active work of the enterprise. The outcome seemed more like cooperative decision and mutual adjustment than governance. At least there was a change of meaning in response to modern social development, even perhaps to a changing conception of learning in the contemporary world.

The tasks of this chapter are several. Its general aim is to explore changes in the nature of governance under democratic restructuring. It examines, in particular, a number of models or paradigms that have been offered for governance: a business managerial one; an assortment of more or less political ones built around ideas of authority and command, of group conflict, and of deliberation about means permeated by common educational ends. Exploration in terms of models is found to be at best suggestive, leaving the resolution of critical issues to detailed problems of the educational enterprise. Finally, there is an assessment of the changed categories in democratic restructuring, and some of the next steps likely to be taken.

Admittedly, democratic reorganization stretches the notion of governance by spreading participation. Of course not all claimants gained full recognition. Some were allotted permissible processes less than governing: for example, recommending or advising (before decision) or evaluating (afterwards). (Traditionally, faculties may recommend, whereas students petition or request, although in crises students have sometimes demanded.) Evaluation, we saw, may involve specialized agencies with powerful influence. Faculties may possess delegated powers, say to decide whether students have fulfilled the requirements for a degree; but delegated power is always subject to the appeal to the source of original power and is responsible to it. Finally, some groups were left with only opportunities for regular pressure, habitual or regularized influence, a chance to work through political channels.

Despite efforts to preserve an undivided notion of governance, the idea has been shaken in the process. In every phase there are continuities rather than strict separations. If governance is marked by the power of ultimate decision, then decision is too pervasive, and ultimacy (even if judged by the possibility of appeal) too tenuous. A full map of decision making in education is complex, and what we think of as governance usually fastens on a particular range of action that has important consequences.

Where, for example, does the ultimate power lie to terminate a student's presence in the institution? He or she may be expelled by decision of a discipline committee, or dropped automatically by an official for failing to meet educational qualifications. Or the student might simply drop out on his or her own volition. In high school, on the other hand, neither the student nor the school authorities may be permitted to override the school-leaving age set by state law. In some cases where the student is expelled, the ultimate decision, even against the college authorities, might be by the courts. If we include "delegated authority" as governance, then all these have a share. If we insist on ultimate decision on appeal from delegated authority as the mark of strict governance, then the courts are part of the governance pattern.

The sharp distinction between governing administrator and nonadministrative professor also becomes tenuous. It is only disguised by labeling some happenings as educational consequences of administration. In the days before the ready tape recorder, to have the use of a record player during class hour was in some places a complicated procedure, particularly if the administrative ruling was that a special assistant had to bring, use, and remove it. The very use of the fifty-minute hour or the fifty-three-minute hour is an administrative shaping of teaching. The calendar for the school year is much improved when faculty and students have a part in deciding how holidays will fit with a period for writing term papers or reading or studying for examinations. Conversely, class assignments should appreciate the problems of administrative procedures, for example, in preparing graduation lists. Such matters, trivial as they may sound, are not simply a question of mutual courtesy or mutual checking, but of active cooperation made necessary because problems constantly arise in different and unexpected contexts and have to be seen from fresh angles. Only after the fact may it seem a simple matter of communication. For example, the administration wishes to introduce photocopying, and decides to withdraw all departmental mimeographing machines; departments will have allotted quotas, and the photocopying will be done centrally. But meanwhile (an actual case), in a graduate philosophy class, teacher and students decide that time for discussion could be increased by a third if students prepared, mimeographed, and distributed their reports to be read in advance. To their surprise, the machines they expected to use in the department office are gone. And the quota for photocopying will not allow so much additional material beyond departmental administrative needs. If there had been an opportunity for thinking it through together, it might have been possible merely to leave the old machines.

Professors tend to think of the cases where administration, operating separately, may have impeded the free flow of teaching. Doubtless, administrators can list cases where professorial insensitivity to administrative problems produces its own blockages. Perhaps occasionally there ought to be commissions of each to survey the procedures of the other and make suggestions after cooperative discussion. After all, much of the theory of administration—as diverse as accounting methods and the development of computers—has come in the first place from the professorial wing. In practice, habits seem different for teaching and administration: One may demand rapid and definitive decision, the other allow more extended deliberation and change of answer. If so, the community of values might be preserved by common experience—say, by rotation in office. Department chairpersons nowadays, when elected, generally serve for a limited time, and often cannot succeed themselves.

Perhaps administrators ought also to rotate, or else have a period of teaching to keep in touch.

Experiment alone, suited to the conditions of the particular institution, can decide what form of cooperation can lessen the gap between administration and teaching. It may be that in very large institutions with constant multiplication of administrative functions, increasing specialization in some areas calls for distinct administrative careers. Thus the problem of hazardous waste disposal now requires educating research personnel, and this becomes a specialized administrative task. Fresh administrative tasks of considerable complexity are demanded by increased specialized forms of federal or state support, by conditions affecting student health and residence, by community relations, and particularly by financial support of the institution. Hence there can be no set formula for the mode of cooperation and mutual understanding between administrators and professors. Indeed, it resembles in many ways the gap within scholarship itself between the alleged "two cultures" of science and the humanities, and will doubtless require as much effort to overcome.

Concepts and distinctions used for analyzing governance play an important part in shaping the separateness of the administration. Yet they do not offer a fixed vocabulary that political specialists can tap. Their making is an ongoing process geared to the needs and functions of the state of development and complexity of the situation. Concepts are instruments, and there is always room for a new distinction to help untie a practical knot. A brilliant legal example of such innovation was Louis Brandeis's distinction between a "closed" shop and a "union" shop. Agreement could not be secured on a closed shop, because it meant only union members could be hired. The owners wanted to do their own hiring, whereas the union would not consent to nonunion workers. The idea of a union shop made possible the hiring by the owners of whomever they wished, but the person employed had then to join the union. Practical compromise went hand in hand with conceptual distinction. The conceptual has to be understood in relation to the practical; otherwise there is the danger that an entrenched vocabulary will structure the situation toward one special outcome.

The vocabulary of a managerial model entrenches a distinction between those who manage and those who are managed. The latter (the teachers) may be thought of as the workers, and the students who graduate as the products. At bottom this is the distinction of the business–industrial world between the managers and the workers, or—if the paradigm be given a political turn—between the authorities (rulers) and the subjects. This business model (in its management structure often seen as a bureaucratic paradigm) has been most persistently used in analyzing educational governance. For a time it seemed to be giving ground, but recent complaints are found in educational circles that it is in use again, in a form that business itself would now reject.[1] When strictly applied, the business analogy regards the trustees as a board of directors, the president as chief executive officer, administrative officials down the line as a hierarchy of managers and submanagers, and (as noted) the teachers and other staff members as workers, with students passing examinations and getting degrees as products. A bureaucratic rationality in the operations calls for a hierarchical order, distinct division of labor or function, specific enumerable tasks with discernible steps of progress (compare the three-month profit statements of business corporations), and an ideal of increasing efficiency understood in cost–benefit terms of greater achievement at lesser cost. For example, a single lecture given to five hundred students is more efficient than one given to three hundred students. The system of course credits, large lectures, examinations (preferably objective and electronically marked, such as true/false or multiple choice), graduate assistants for discussion sections, and markers where necessary for examinations, all make greater measurable efficiency possible.

Perhaps the most instructive lessons for this model come from the actual history of the broadening inquiries into management itself in the business world.[2] These show a growing concern with the workers, with their needs and motives and values, insofar as these affect actual work and insofar as that population can be reconciled to its position within the structure as a whole. The one thing that these studies do not propose is that workers have a share in management; the dividing line between worker and management remains sharp and generally uncrossable. Workers may be given a part in advising about production and organization of work; they are tempted with merit bonuses and perhaps investing in shares. But the line is not crossed into participation in running the business. (When the term "participation" is used, it refers to determining such matters as pace of work, specific goals of the workday, and the like.) In effect, the line between the managers and the managed becomes a Maginot Line with full-scale theoretical fortifications. This is the dividing line that the New York city colleges crossed in 1938, the separation that current arguments for increased power of boards and presidents today want to guarantee. To cross that line is to shake the usual management model.

Business itself, in this century, has developed a more sophisticated understanding of management structures. The science of management has grown, drawing on psychology and social science for its theoretical bases and producing a multitude of observational–statistical studies and experiments. The history of this development suggests that there is in fact no one model. There is rather a developing set undergoing change in response to changing aspects of business and labor over the century, as well as growing theoretical input. At the beginning of the century the prevalent business model corresponded to the situation that largely existed—autocratic control by owners, with workers unorganized and assumed to be motivated solely by the economic interest of higher pay. This was the period in which Social Darwinism was at its height, with its slogan of "survival of the fittest" and its view of the owners as the fittest, having no special obligation to those who (in Spencer's language) have been "shouldered aside." (Sometimes, however, paternalism supervened on the Darwinism.) There followed a concentration on efficiency in a scientific spirit, whether in the theories of Taylorism or in the practices of Henry Ford. These, while still assuming the dominant economic interest of the workers (Ford raised pay dramatically), were facing the problems of rapid growth of large-scale industry. Succeeding steps in management theory lay in recognizing the many aspects of worker motivation; organizational efficiency would find the right keys to press or the right notes to strike. (This began with the Hawthorne studies of the work scene.) Theory and research went into comfort and attractiveness of the workplace, motivation of the workers, interpersonal relations, short-range or long-range goals, participation in setting goals and pace of work, types of reward, and so on. The treatment of personnel grew into an elaborate division of management, especially as corporate organization became more complex.

These developments were intertwined with the relation of business to the growth of labor unionism, and much of the concern with the treatment of personnel was directed to heading off worker interest in joining unions. As unions won bargaining elections and put forward their own demands, they contributed by the character of those demands—not only higher pay, but security, retirement benefits, health insurance, conditions in the workshop, limits on authority exercised against workers—to an understanding of what workers felt necessary or desirable for their labor to be effective. Still, none of this crossed the line into management. Contemporary views of capital–labor relations may think of possible collaboration on specific points, but not of rights following from the nature of a common enterprise. Countries other than the United States have experimented more in reconstructed governance patterns, as in Scandinavia or the pattern of worker self-management in Yugoslavia. In the present relative weakness of the labor movement, and the problems of American industry arising from competition with Japan and other countries, it is unlikely that there will be much novel experiment in the United States in the near future.

Another aspect of managerial science was the study of management itself. As the body of managers grew, and with the separation of ownership and management,[3] and especially with the dispersal of ownership through shareholding, the inner organization of management itself—for example, bureaucratic, hierarchical, collegial—attracted study. Psychological and cultural studies in corporate life now abound. The relations and frictions of functional areas (such as finance, production, personnel) are aggravated with the changing character of corporate structure. Doubtless, further varied lessons about the effects of different modes of management can be learned from the experiences of the 1980s in the era of large-scale consolidations and corporate takeovers.

A serious use of a managerial model for educational governance cannot rest with merely general features of management and the allocation of authority to those who manage over those who are managed. It requires some reference to the ends of the enterprise, both general and particular, in terms of which the pattern of governance is justified. The general ends of an industrial economy were posed traditionally as profit for the owners, work and fair livelihood for the workers, and safe products of good quality for the consumers. As the managerial responsibility narrowed mainly to showing a profit for the shareholders, the responsibility for the welfare of the workers was taken over largely by union organizations, and that for the safety and quality of the product by government regulation, with the support of the courts. Thus business itself has a dispersed governance in the same sense as we have seen the dispersal proposed for higher education. Moreover, the character of particular business enterprises and other specific ends affect the pattern of their governance. The production of steel, the launching of new kinds of materials or products (as in research-oriented business like Du Pont or Apple or the frontier of biotechnological enterprises or pharmaceutical businesses), the publication of books, the running of nuclear installations, may be so different as to require quite different arrangements for personnel in production and quite different participation in decisions and their carrying out. A large oil company may very well, in the light of major oil spills, give superior decision and veto power to a technical branch to serve as guardian—or else let this fall to government. These same general lessons follow for higher education: No satisfactory structure of governance can be derived from features worked out from either the general or the specific character of management in business enterprises without considering how they compare to the ends of education itself and the means that those ends require.

From these considerations we may suggest that the management model on the analogy of business should have run its course in the theory of university governance. It should be clear in any case that a model in which tasks can be broken down into single operations more or less automatically performed, where hierarchical organization produces no interfering problems, and where efficiency is defined in cost–benefit terms of maximum output for minimum input, would have serious disadvantages. The chief residual function of this model would appear to be the claim of separate, superior authority for administration.

To cross over from a business managerial model to one or another kind of political paradigm is not difficult. If the Maginot Line is at least half the point in a managerial model (efficiency being the other large part), political rule keeps it even more secure in its sharp distinction of rulers and subjects. The use of political models was encouraged by the conflicts of the 1960s in higher education, when in the popular view the field became highly "politicized." In some respects the transition was mediated by describing business management—in terms of its general features of hierarchy, distinct subdivision of tasks, regulation by explicit rules, and so forth—as a "bureaucratic model." It could then be applied indifferently to business, politics, and education.

As we move into considering an assembly of models of different kinds, it is well to remind ourselves not to be too impressed by the trim shape that a model can give to the materials of a field.[4] Models come in all sorts of shapes and sizes. Sometimes they are closer to metaphors and analogies than to scientific structures. They may function like dresses, which, as designers point out, can either reveal the lines of the body they cover or the lines of the fabric that obscures the bodily shape. In normative inquiries models often stamp in one rather than another set of social values. Everywhere they should be treated as suggestive, to be tried out in theory or practice for their utility in advancing the aims of the inquiry, and not be deemed legislative nor entrenched in one field because it or something like it has been successful in another field. Indeed, since a model is an aid to experimenting, it is best to start with a variety. Moreover, a good model is not one that shuts us off from the detail of the inquiry and furnishes quick answers, but one that compels us to look further for detail in fresh directions, for that is how reliable answers are more likely to be found. Model building is a useful tool when its limits are understood and observed.

The three models to be examined vary in the extent to which they move away from the traditional political idea of governing, that is, a ruler commanding with authority, whether on particular matters or through rules or laws, and a subject obeying or suffering a sanction. (The subject obeys because of force, fear of force, or through habit.) The first model accepts and modernizes this major traditional approach through the concept of sovereign authority. The second model calls on us to look to the realities of the social situation in which governing takes place and to recognize the conflicts of groups and interests, the methods and outcomes of their battles. The third goes even further to understand what is going on. We have to look beyond the commanding, beyond the power struggles, to the permeating ends of the field, in this case higher education, which hold the structure together and determine its desirable shape. Because of the different disciplines from which these models have come, we shall refer to them briefly as the *strictly political*, the *sociological*, and the *socioethical*. While the strictly political model treats governance as a distinctive activity with authority as a central quality, the other two present it rather as the structure of a field in which complex activities are taking place. The question thus arises what has happened to authority.

The central feature of the strictly political form is that it lodges full and ultimate power in one place. Governing is a very special kind of activity. It cannot be handled in a cooperative way by some particular division of labor. It is of the nature of authority to have a definite locus and so be unified, to have an acknowledged ultimate status, and to possess full independence.[5] These three features of authority require careful examination, for they involve the basic assumptions on which this view of governance has rested. Authoritarian governance, of course, involves this whole complex conception of authority, or some variant adjusted to the rise of political democracy in general. Democratic reorganization of governance in higher education has to reckon with the form that authority may take in its scheme or what may replace it.

That authority has a fixed locus can be seen in the traditional notion of sovereignty. Either the king is sovereign or parliament is, and when it is not decided there is a civil war. When the people as a whole are taken to be the locus of sovereignty, it is only to select their rulers, not themselves to engage in ruling. So too, the argument would go in higher educational governance. The various other claimants, apart from the one properly possessing authority, should be regarded rather as groups affected by authoritative decision. They enter not into governance, but either into instruments of governance (for example, delegated tasks) or into the success or failure of the acts or plans decided upon. If, for example, students do not elect a particular program in which a great deal has been invested by the governing board, if a new project does not win alumni or federal support, if a salary scale is met with a strike, these are all to be regarded as disagreement with or rebellion against a governing decision. Wise steering on the part of the administration might have tested the waters before charting a course. Or regular channels for advice might, if necessary, be developed. But all such disagreements are not "participation in governing."

How basic the assumption of the inherent unity of authority

has been can be seen from its strength in political and legal theory and (more covertly) in moral theory. Politics, as noted above, has tried to trace the sovereignty lost by the absolute monarch through the theory of the state, even when it grows democratic. It rarely suggests that the idea of sovereignty itself is a residue of monarchy, and the search for its location a search to replace the missing king. Jurisprudence maintains comparable assumptions even in opposing theories. In natural-law theory, the law expresses divine command, while in legal positivism law is the command of the sovereign. Because they are opposed on this and because they differ on whether morality lies within the law or is a wholly outside concern, one may easily miss the fact that both are theories of unified sovereignty. For an alternative in which the assumption of unified sovereignty is shed, one has to go to pragmatic conceptions with a strong sense of the complexity and pluralism of human affairs, the intimate place of human purposes in experience itself, and a sense of the historical and functional in human institutions. In such a view, the Common Law is the story of exploratory practice in adjusting legal mechanisms to changing social needs and circumstances and developing innovative ideas for coping with such changes.

The most surprising thing is that morality itself, at least in its modern individualistic approaches, has kept the unity of sovereignty and only transferred it to the individual. Appeals to the rational self as ultimate legislator, theories of the state as a contract between individuals, conceptions of moral autonomy and individual conscience that make the individual into ultimate moral judge, and comparable views of individualistic moral relativism all presuppose authority as an undivided whole.[6]

With such a strong tradition, it is naturally taken for granted that the first question in any situation—educational, familial, business, military, governmental—is not "What's going on here?" but "Who is in command here?" Now this takes for granted the whole host of conditions of existence whose control by leadership is so blithely assumed in the idea of unified sovereignty: the supporting system of needs, aims, objectives, opportunities or their lack, standards of living, degrees of aspiration or resignation, institutional forms that channel or frustrate pressure. In sum, the spotlight falls wholly on the activity of the ruler, not on the whole scene as a dynamic interaction in which the acceptance of rule and its quality play a constitutive part. This is equivalent to looking at the master, not the servant, the father rather than the mother and children, the priest rather than the flock, the teacher rather than the student, the president rather than the representative legislators. Only when the institution begins to change may we become aware of the conditions that support the previous stability.

Perhaps the role of conditions of existence, so neglected in the theory of unified sovereignty, can be best conveyed in those striking cases where there is scarcely a revolution, but simply a rapid crumbling of what appeared to be overwhelming power. Examples in our time are the communist takeover of China, the fall of the Shah in Iran, the collapse of the Marcos regime in the Philippines. Take the following account of the Chinese episode:

> The broad picture is that after the war, Chiang Kai-shek emerged as the undisputed leader of the Chinese people. Only one faction, the Communists, up in the hills, ill-equipped, ragged, in very small military force, was determinedly opposed to his position. He had overwhelming military power, greater military power than any ruler had ever had in the entire history of China. He had tremendous economic–military support and backing from the U.S. He had the acceptance of all other foreign countries, whether sincerely or insincerely in the case of the Soviet Union is

not really material to this matter. Here he was in this position, and four years later what do we find? We find that his armies have melted away. His support in the country has melted away. His support largely outside the country has melted away, and he is a refugee on a small island off the coast of China with the remnants of his forces.

As I said, no one says that vast armies moved out of the hills and defeated him. To attribute this to the inadequacy of American aid is only to point out the depth and power of the forces that were miscalculated or ignored. What has happened in my judgment is that the almost inexhaustible patience of the Chinese people in their misery ended. They did not bother to overthrow this government. There was really nothing to overthrow. They simply ignored it throughout the country. They took the solution of their immediate village problems into their own hands. If there was any trouble or interference with the representatives of the government, they simply brushed them aside. They completely withdrew their support from this government, and when that support was withdrawn, the whole military establishment disintegrated.

Now one might think that this is a communist account, in the light of the clamor during the McCarthy period on who in America gave China to the communists. But the speech is by a secretary of state—Dean Acheson, before the National Press Club, January 12, 1950.[7] In any case, one could hardly find a more striking picture of the neglected base of the conception of sovereign power and the unreality of the idea of its unitary character.

It is the long march of democracy in the political life of society that has increasingly brought the realization in politics, and to some extent in law and moral theory, that the concept of authority has waned.[8]

We move now from the assumption that authority has a unified locus to the assumption that it has an ultimate status. By this is usually meant that it acts from knowledge, not just ordinary opinion or prejudice. In classical times the sharp distinction between knowledge and opinion or impressions would have rested on distinguishing the absolute truth that the intellect grasps (for example, in logic or mathematics) from the merely tentative judgments resting on the senses. But such foundational views in the philosophy of science are long superseded. The dynamic force in changing our conception has been the growth of science as a body of knowledge making no claim to absoluteness, open to correction at every point in its theory and in the refinement of its observations, hoping to become more comprehensive and more refined, but not even with a guarantee of this. Knowledge becomes thus more of a collective product, far in its character from the lone insight of the wise ruler into the absolute good.[9] Indeed, within the university, the collective character of knowledge is mirrored in the spread and interplay of faculty learning and research rather than in concentrated executive wisdom. At this point too, a shift is often found, therefore, from the claim of superior knowledge to the possession of a broader point of view. But perhaps the contemporary shift is even more far-reaching, in the light of the explosion of knowledge in almost every important field today, in the development of information theory, and in the significance of securing the appropriate information for complex decisions. Important decisions in higher education require adequate knowledge of the institution, its strengths and weaknesses, its past experiences and their outcomes, what has been attempted and what has succeeded or failed and why, as well as new directions proposed and new ideas or instruments.

Too often each generation or each administration starts afresh, and too often a new broom may repeat old mistakes. The relative ultimacy within a democratic organization lies accordingly not in a given officeholder, but in the systematically accumulated knowledge built up in experience, though open to correction and expansion.

There remains the assumption that authority involves rational control by the ruler over the passions and dispersive interests of the subjects. This ancient thesis was early presented in Plato's *Republic:* The human psyche consists of a ruling reason; an executive, administrative, or effective will; and a mass of conflicting desires—acquisitive, sexual, aggressive. In a well-ordered society, the rulers have the appropriate authority, a supporting military–executive class carries out their bidding, and the mass of the people carry on the work of society without a share in ruling. Democracy is the revolt of the third part of the psyche and invariably yields autocracy, with a deterioration of standards and chaos.[10]

In the earlier theory of democracy, there are residues and analogies of this aristocratic psychology. The variety of particular interests in the groups of society inherits the blindness and conflict of the passions and desires, while the rulers—usually the executive rather than the legislature—are assumed to have the overall view of the general well-being. Such a pattern of argument persists as long as the separation of reason from the passions or of the general will from the plethora of interests is maintained. Gradually over the centuries, however, the psychological assumption of a separate reason as an independent force is abandoned. Reason comes to be understood as a functional balance of impulse and desires. The passions are not without a certain reasonableness in their striving, and so too for the varying interests in different groups in the community. The task is not one of an outside reason but of a common and cooperative learning, to distinguish those components that are worthwhile from the momentary, the misleading, the grasping, the hostile. At the same time, the growth of sociological theory of ideology, as well as political experience, teaches the lesson that the supposed impartiality of rulers may reflect the taken-for-granted entrenchment of particular class or sectional interests. A cooperative community is to be *built*—with effort, compromise, mutual learning and sympathy, and long-run trial and error—not to be assumed as preexistent. In this, rationality in the human being and common purpose and organization in the community are on the same footing.

Many of the criticisms of the assumptions of authority come, as we have seen, from a democratic perspective. Whether the notion of authority survives such criticism is not a simple matter to decide. We could say that a democratic organization moves authority from one to another set of governors. But the dispersal of authority in democracy runs against authority's underlying assumptions. We could continue to speak of "authority" but say that its meaning has undergone change; we might then have to trace changes in the meaning of "governing" as well. (Indeed, we shall have to ask later what governing becomes if it ceases to be a distinctive activity vested in a single agent.) If we want to continue using the term "authority," perhaps we have a "family resemblance" rather than a different species of a single genus.

That the critique of authority opens the way to a democratic reorganization is clear enough. Yet it is not decisive against an authoritarian structure as such. While the latter is no longer entrenched as unavoidable or "in the nature of things," it can still be argued that experience has shown it is likely to work better than any alternative scheme. This argument can be general, for all fields, or for any one or another particular field, as we saw in the case of the military given earlier. Other schemes can now, however, ask to be tried out, particularly in light of the troubles the authoritarian structure, which has permeated most of our life hitherto, has been running into in one field after another. As our lives have become more complex, and various areas of the world more interrelated, people at large are less ready to remain quiet subjects and have no voice in their fate. If rulers were really as wise and disinterested as Plato hoped his guardians would be, if businessmen who nowadays learn that "greed runs the world" produced by their pursuit of profit a satisfactory level of life for all the people, if dictatorial parties in visionary and reformist movements when in power markedly advanced the interests of the people as a whole rather than their own interests, perhaps the questioning of authoritarian structures might be an abstract, theoretical rather than an urgent, practical matter. The cost of stupidities among rulers is today as great or greater than that of short-sightedness among subjects, especially given the risks of our technological world. The lesson would seem to be that whatever the picture of human nature and whatever the variety and spread of abilities among humans, collective or communal action in any field requires the designed cooperation of all involved in it and the counterpoise and checks and balances of genuine powers in each.

This is, of course, the language of the American Constitution, and the framers clearly had such a design in mind for political life. Unlike those who saw the alternatives to be only absolute rule or chaos, because of the assumed nature of the mass of men, they accepted human nature on its own terms, whether good or bad, and even were ready to build on its being bad. In short, they sought a third way as a great experiment. They counted on division of powers and on checks and balances to prevent tyranny, and on the variety of interests given representation to promote interchange and deliberation. Many of the founders feared most the tyranny of the ruler, while many others feared most the consolidation of a majority faction of the propertyless. Some looked to the rural life of the agricultural community, others to urban commerce. Like the Constitution they framed, this third way is not to be interpreted wholly in terms of their wishes, fears, and intentions, for its meaning has broadened with the changes of the years and the insights these in turn brought. The new circumstances are the immeasurably increased complication of the life of the society, multiplication of diversities of interest and occupation, and the vast expansion of knowledge and its technology, with vast new opportunities and critical new dangers. Accordingly, just as the constitution could over two centuries accommodate the growth of federal controls under the commerce clause, and more hesitantly the growth of measures of social welfare under the statement of intention to promote the public welfare, so the experiment as a whole can act increasingly as a model to provide direction in many other areas of community activity.

The stability of this mode of government and its long-run educative effect on its people have compared well with the more drastic experiments of other parts of the globe. It has admitted of adjustment, sometimes indeed belated and much of it carried through in the twentieth century itself. The pivot for such readjustment has varied. In the 1930s the Supreme Court was a barrier to necessary change, and change came through the executive and the legislature. After World II, the legislature lagged in carrying out the obvious social lessons of equality, and equality was advanced by the Supreme Court in its business of interpretation. For a time, it looked as if a concentration of power was taking place in the executive, the "imperial presidency," but the Watergate and Iran–Contra episodes have shown it important to be wary of such a concentration as well as to maintain openness. It is not too much to say that the division of powers and checks and balances emerged as the heroic ideas of the theory of political governance. It is clear that they cannot be applied mechanically, that there are hard tasks of specific mechanisms and the devising of fresh ones. They indicate rather a direction for the detailed theory, experience, and experiment of governance.

The sociological model, to which we turn next, often takes an almost adversarial stance toward the strictly political discussion of the activities that enter into governing. It calls our attention to the social conflicts of different interests and groups, to their methods and the outcomes of their battles. Here, it contends, lies the reality of what is going on. This approach has a long and spirited history in twentieth-century America. It was signaled by A. F. Bentley's *Process of Government* (1908), which called for realism in getting behind slogans and ideals to the specific conflicting interests involved. Lasswell's work (noted in Chapter 2, above) directed inquiry toward the psychology of power, which was central also to the twentieth-century Machiavellian political tradition. After the mid-century, sociologists turned to middle-sized problems and small and middle-sized groups—as against the already trite contrasts of society, state, and individual. They explored, for example, family and street-corner society, hospitals and social-work institutions. Among complex organizations they included the university. With an eye on complexity, plurality, and conflict, they mapped carefully the variety of groups and interests involved in the different organizations, and the detailed modes of their interaction and conflict. Often, however, goals and social policies were pushed so far into the background that the account was largely of modes of organization and the tactics of power plays, with the interests characterized generically rather than by their detailed content and differences. For example, the distinction was between administrators and professionals, not in terms of the particular differences between different fields of professionals and different areas of administration.

J. Victor Baldridge's *Power and Conflict in the University* (1971) is an interesting example of this kind of sociological approach.[11] He selects his paradigm explicitly, uses it to study New York University, and is self-conscious throughout about the methods employed. New York University at the time of his study was a very large private university with two campuses (one in the Bronx and one, the main center, at Washington Square in Manhattan). It had had neither the financial stability nor the status of an elite Ivy League university like Columbia, nor the municipal (and eventual state) support as well as the popular appeal of the city colleges. Hence it furnished more than its share of crises for sociological analysis.

Baldridge distinguishes three organizational paradigms. *Bureaucracy*, formulated in the tradition standardized by Max Weber, corresponds to the managerial model considered above rendered in terms of its formal features. A second sees the university as a *collegium*, a community of scholars (in the words of Paul Goodman's well-known work urging the abandonment of most of the trappings of the contemporary university).[12] The third Baldridge calls the political model, corresponding to what we have called the sociological. He rejects the bureaucratic paradigm because it is purely formal and does not correspond to what is actually going on in the university. He rejects the collegium paradigm as unrealistic in the contemporary world. He accepts the political paradigm because he sees politics as dealing with a multitude of conflicting interests.

Baldridge is well aware of the fact that issues of fundamental educational policy lie back of the shaping of interests and internal struggles. He examines carefully a case in which the president got control of the entrance requirements and upgraded the quality of students admitted. Behind this lay the social changes in New York City; the expansion of the city colleges, which made it possible for larger numbers with lower entrance grades to attend the municipal system, and so make inroads on New York University's traditional clientele; a Ford Foundation report on the desirable path for New York University to raise its standing; and the president's own conclusion that the shift in the student base would be manageable. Baldridge thus has available a paradigm in which values and goals determine program, which in turn guides means, which in its turn compels attention to the pattern of governance and to bending it or changing it—what we shall examine as the socioethical model. Yet in the rest of the book he does not follow this pattern. Instead he describes organization and modes of struggle: central administration with local administration, deans with higherups, deans with departments, departments with one another, students with administration, and so on. When the fight is over the budget, we learn little about how deans or departments would spend the money if they controlled it. Educational issues are apparently bunched under the category of "curriculum" for the purpose of interviews and statistics, and the question investigated is who controls it and in what degree. Even within governance itself, significant items are missing. For example, academic freedom is not investigated, although it is historically a fundamental measure of degree of repression. The lower ranks receive proportionally much less attention in the surveys: For example, of faculty interviewed, sixty-one are professors; nine, associate professors; and only two, assistant professors. On the whole, the view is from above, not from below, and the higher structures tend to occupy more of the landscape. When the AAUP presents an argument for broader faculty participation in governance, Baldridge is led to discuss not the educational merits of their claim, but the differences in the habits and the ways of thought between bureaucrats and professionals.

This comparatively wholesale treatment of group interest is found in sociological studies of complex organizations even where special attention is given to the contrast of professional and administrative. For example, Amitai Etzioni, in his *Modern Organizations* (1964), carefully considers the relation of administrative and professional authority, construing the problem as the use made of knowledge and expertise in determining the locus of decision. Professional authority is examined in nonprofessional organizations (e.g., business), in professional organizations (e.g., universities, hospitals), and in semiprofessional systems (e.g., primary schools, social-work agencies). On the whole, it is administrative authority that decides where professional authority will be decisive.[13]

This general conclusion, which of course corresponds to the still largely nondemocratic structure of governance, invites inquiry as to how democratic organization would construe the situation. This inquiry is much helped by the effort of the sociological approach in rendering explicit as many as possible of the groups and their interests involved. If we continue to seek help from the analogy of the Constitution, we have to render explicit the governance role of any group that is latent or obscure.[14] The Constitution sets forth a pattern of governance with three branches—legislative, executive, judicial. Now some of the rights in the Bill of Rights, particularly the First Amendment, could readily be construed as setting forth a fourth branch of government—the individual—and indicating some of the areas in which the individual's decision can count on the protection and support of the state. Controversies over the nature of rights—natural and prior to society or positive with a strong social backing—would be unaffected by this reading. In any case, the centrality of persons in the scheme of life in the modern world would make this view of the individual in governance readily intelligible. Correspondingly, in university governance, academic freedom or professional autonomy in the classroom becomes viewed not as a right granted by the administration, but as part of the desirable pattern of governance itself. Its profoundly individual character is seen in the fact that academic freedom protects the individual's inquiry and expression even against the majority view of the faculty, not just against administrative coercion.

What is entrenched and what is not entrenched in this view of the individual in governance? Take the familiar example often expressed as that the doctor in the hospital, not the administrator or the patient, decides whether to operate. This has to be refined somewhat. The doctor (if there is no medical disagreement about the type of case) decides whether an operation is desirable and how immediately necessary from the point of view of improving health. But nowadays the patient has to give "informed consent" and may even prefer dying to major suffering. The administrator too may intervene on legal grounds to which he or she is bound—for example, where the law forbids abortion in a public hospital or some other procedure affecting the fetus. Behind all this is the financial question: whether there is insurance or other resources to assure the hospital sufficiently to let the operation take place! What seemed at the beginning to be a simple assignment of jurisdiction to the professional becomes in many cases a cooperative deliberation in which democratic decision will involve making clear the ends and values at stake and providing the means. All parts of this may be open to evaluative reconsideration.

The last of the models, the socioethical, is most at home with such complex considerations of ends and means in determining the pattern of governance. It holds that the ends of the enterprise or those bearing upon some particular part of it should always come into play to shape the pattern of governance. Appeal to a distinctive activity of governing or to a general end of power will not do. We tend to ignore the ends partly because we take them for granted, and partly because recognizing their role will usually complicate the inquiry. Moreover, we have not simply to invoke them but to show how they affect the particular kind of situation. Reference to the Constitution here again proves helpful. The preamble establishes the Constitution to secure certain ends— "a more perfect Union, establish justice, insure domestic tranquility, provide for the common defence, promote the general Welfare, and secure the blessings of liberty to ourselves and our posterity." These ends are not referred to constantly in the body of the document. This does not mean that they cannot guide the interpretation of the Constitution as conditions change in the decades and centuries that follow. The least controversial example is the interpretation of the commerce clause, which, after all, was written before the invention of the steamship, and now supports a complex network of regulation throughout the land and beyond. So too, in the governance of higher education, the pattern of democratic governance would require a constant reference to the ends as conceived for the enterprise and the conditions that make it possible to attain those ends. This means that the pattern of governance is not independent of the ethical and social values envisaged in the philosophy of education and the major instrumentalities that the university can utilize.

The story of educational ends is complicated. Indeed, the tracing of ends in higher education has moved slowly in the twentieth century; apparent ends became revealed as means, and the horizon of ends moved on. Earlier emphasis was particularly on teaching as the goal, with learning as an effect. This was congenial to a period of behavioristic psychology in which teaching was regarded as a kind of conditioning, the student as raw material to be conditioned, and the learned lesson as a product. In the philosophy of education of the mid-century, major analytic effort went into providing an analysis of "teaching." Even in analytic terms, however, it was argued that teaching could not take place—successful teaching at least—unless learning had taken place. Attention was gradually refocused on learning, particularly as the importance of nourishing and eliciting creative and innovative participation by the learner was recognized.[15] In fact, John Stuart Mill had more than a century before pointed to the sense in which learning on the part of the individual, even where it is of something well known to others, shares the character of discovery that is found in novel research and the revelation of the hitherto unknown. As behavioristic psychology yielded to views of the more active character of learning (from the "insight" of the Gestaltists to studies of infant awareness and exploration), teaching became more clearly instrumental, learning more endlike. In higher education the consequences of the shift are evident: Given a creative character to learning, tutorials or discussion sections rather than lectures, and essays rather than true/false examinations, the participation of teachers and students in governance becomes desirable, and a continuous learning experience itself.

The shift from teaching to learning—associated in the lower schools with the ideals of "progressive education"—has taken a long time to win acceptance. Much of what passed for it was, for a long time, simply a relaxation of guidance and discipline. Perhaps it is the growing impasse of traditional education in the welter of contemporary problems that has brought an emphasis on the creative and the innovative as a necessity rather than a luxury. In any case, the important consequence for governance is that the character of learning as now understood and its improvement should be constant criteria entering into every judgment of efficiency, that there should be a full realization of how the structure of governance itself, and not merely the particular decisions in governing, affects learning.

The question remains what the learning itself is directed toward. Different further goals are to be found in the arena of our common life: the advancement of knowledge, preparation for cultural understanding and appreciation, preparation for profitable careers or jobs, preparation for or initiation into the sociopolitical relations of citizenship and the moral ties of a community. Certainly higher education has some part to play with respect to all of those; indeed, an objective reviewer of the American scene may be appalled by the extent to which the one aim of profitable career has become dominant, even in much of the self-consciousness of higher education. The point here is not to offer a peremptory settlement of controversies about the ends of higher education, but to recognize that they play a part in determining the desirable type of governance pattern, and that democratic governance is related at least to a common life with a basically moral cooperative outlook on social tasks. It assumes also some lessons of the history of what is required in social organization for the advancement of knowledge and the maintenance of culture. An honest treatment of governance has to put all the cards on the table.

The fundamental point that is here being stressed—the extent of dependence of the pattern of governance on the scheme of ends involved—could be shown readily by comparison with an institution now even more troubled than higher education: the family. In this institution the patriarchal model began to crumble when women got the vote, only a short seventy years ago in the United States. Older patterns of authority in which all property belonged to the husband, his authority over the children was near absolute, and the familiar rest of the story are almost ancient history. State action imposed some demands and lessened some burdens: for example, compulsory schooling of children, diminution of support beyond the nuclear family with the extension of welfare institutions. Within the family, changes do not lie in granting women and children the opportunity to offer advice. They have definite rights— even, increasingly, children—so that familiar decisions of many sorts represent balance of interests, as in, for example, changed laws covering divorce. As a consequence, fresh paths become evident in several directions. Government intervenes to forbid child abuse and is appealed to more directly against wife abuse. With a large part of the women of the family at work, institutions of child care have (still) to be developed on a broader scale. The area of controversy bearing on governance of family life is large today. Feminist theory shows conflicting strands about ends in male–female relations. Some outside control is sought in family planning, as, for example, in the attempts to outlaw abortion and in attacks on contraception. New paths of control are opened up in occasional court decisions, such as holding a woman responsible for the ills of a newborn child due to her taking drugs while pregnant. Marginal procedures of child entry into families—adoption, surrogate motherhood—raise social and legal problems. Many of this large budget of problems in the family today focus on who is to have the power of decision, that is, on the pattern of governance. But this in turn cannot be effectively answered because of the uncertainty and present conflict over the ends to be achieved through the institution of the family. Attempted answers to particular problems have therefore to be looked at by what effect they would have on what is desirable in a family structure.

Given an intimate relation of specific ends to how governance is shaped, it is clearly unfruitful to think of governing as an essentially distinct activity. Perhaps this was congenial to an authoritarian structure that focused on commanding, controlling, authorizing, sanctioning. Since democratization disperses governance, it focuses instead on the distribution of decision making through deliberation about the achievement of ends. A pattern of democratic governance in higher education is a map of decision making in its contextual distribution. The structure may have been set down at one time—like the Constitution—but, again like the Constitution, it may be constantly transformed in the process of pursuing goals. Some governance changes may be made self-consciously—for example, to give nontenured assistant professors place and vote in the faculty to secure the influence of a younger professional group. Some may be collateral effects: for example, where American studies is created as a new department on important educational grounds and so is entitled to the governance prerogatives of departments in the university. Or again, suppose the range of student electives is enlarged, as against previously required courses, because the alternative subjects in a field have now grown—say, the host of social sciences, where once stood history alone. The student is now empowered to decide—the individual as fourth branch of government that we unearthed from the Constitution.

Perhaps the best examples of the interrelation of ends and governance are the large-scale ones evident in the history of the last half century. The most dramatic comes from the controversies over the general role of the university in the 1960s. In the early part of that decade it became evident that the universities were being transformed as the demand for higher education grew. Industrial and technological advance particularly depended on a stream of university graduates. Under these pressures, college presidents tried to articulate the new directions. For example, lectures by James A. Perkins, president of Cornell (*The University in Transition*, 1965), trace the rapid growth, call attention to the fears generated—uncontrolled growth, loss of direction, loss of principle, too great a rigidity—and project coherence in a triple mission: teaching, research, and public service.[16] The element of coherence is essential: "The real integrity of the university is violated when large decisions in one area do not consider the impact on the other two. I would state it even more strongly: university integrity is compromised when decisions about any one of our three aspects of university activity fail to *strengthen* the others" (33–34). Consequently he calls for wider participation at all levels of the system: "The old pitting of faculty against administration must be recognized as a quaint reflection of an outmoded idea of the university. The lines between teacher and administrator will be increasingly blurred" (88–89). But he goes no further than to call for new leadership.

In *The Uses of the University* (1963), Clark Kerr, president of California's sprawling university system, calls on the university to produce new knowledge, as the most important factor in economic and social growth, and to transmit it more extensively to the population.[17] The "multi-university" is to have a vital role in national policy as well as economic development. Intellect itself, he says in an unfortunate remark, has become "a component part of the 'military–industrial complex'" (124). Steeped in the history of governance in European and American universities, he assigns the president the role of mediator between the multitude of interests. This view of a knowledge industry in the service of a military–industrial complex as the goal of higher education enraged the Berkeley students. Their desire to change the educational character of the university found immediate expression in a demand for student participation in governance.

Take, as a perennial and recurrent problem of ends, the relation of research and teaching in the university. If the advancement of knowledge is a central objective, how should governance be shaped if research is primary? A "research model" for governance would call for maximum participation in determining the character and conditions of work by those closest to research. (It might come close to the collegial model, the community of scholars, which Paul Goodman advocated and which Baldridge judged unrealistic.) Insofar as creativity and innovation, the core of the research spirit, enter into the character of the learning aimed at generally in the university, the model might apply to the whole university, not merely to a research division. (Indeed, even in business, the most successful enterprises, where their operations impinge on research, go as far as they can to let the researchers decide.) If the research spirit characterizes all learning, it should shape teaching in general, or at least a frontier segment of it. If graduate teaching is closely related to research, in that it is training researchers, then here too the model would have application.

In the present situation of research, some constraints are evident, and others may still be needed. The direction of research may not at times be determined by the pure spirit of research, but by the source of funding—federal or corporate. Governance provisions, whether administered by the university or by government departments, may then be needed to restore a wider moral perspective. For example, universities have sometimes opposed research on poison gas within their institutional limits. Research on human subjects is monitored, or the research treatment of animals. Where the products of research will be put to public use, tests may be demanded for health and safety—for example, in the case of drugs, or sprays to be used in agriculture. It is only a step from this to consider other social effects. For example, the development of a tomato with a hardened skin enables it to be picked by machine rather than by hand, thereby putting a large group of people out of work, as well as bringing some deterioration in taste.

To maintain the traditional morality of scientific research

may also call for governance mechanisms. Falsification of results and plagiarism are well enough punished generally. But with great financial gain now at stake in patenting inventions, elements of secrecy quite out of tune with the traditional openness of science are coming to the fore. There is even the beginning of university contracts with private corporations for research in given areas, with agreement to preserve secrecy in the process. In the past many scientists have refused to work on state projects because of the secrecy involved. A moral conflict is looming within the scientific community, and it is conceivable that scientific organizations may be enlisted in the public defense of the traditional openness of science.

Conflicts between teaching and research in the university are often serious. Research has the greater prestige and usually brings greater rewards in appointment, promotion, reduced teaching schedule, and so forth. Even colleges that affirm a primary interest in teaching may not give it parity. To solve this problem by separate research institutes would deprive the colleges of the beneficial influence of research in the academic community; indeed, colleges with graduate schools have a marked advantage over those without them, except for very special small colleges. Perhaps specialized representation for the teaching interest within the scheme of governance would be effective in keeping the problem of parity more consciously before the institution. (Much earlier in the century it might have seemed that a School of Education with a Department of Higher Educational Teaching could have had a salutary effect, but this is no longer a realistic possibility.)

Balancing the liberal and the professional is another of the familiar general problems that calls for help through the patterning of governance. It tries to cope with the competition of different schools—medicine, law, business, liberal arts, and so on—and with the pressures of departments within liberal arts.

The development of a senate among the organs of governance, with school representation, was obviously a device to achieve a balance of educational ends. Comparable problems arise in liberal arts itself, where students are allowed to devote themselves wholly to advanced work in their specialities at the expense of general education or cultural education. On the whole, the balance of departmental representation within the faculty and its curriculum committee will help toward resolving such problems. But most important is agreement on the canon of desirable cultural development of the student. Where this end is clear, it may be embodied in curricular requirements. In an extreme situation, the neglected area may be given explicit place in the governing committee to safeguard the end.

As a final example of how educational ends may become intertwined with governance, take the concern in the Law School of the City University of New York over the use of a clinical approach in teaching law. The school, located at Queens College, has the students assist community groups and disadvantaged individuals in legal matters. It aims particularly to train public-interest lawyers. The claim was made that two professors had been denied tenure after being approved by three university committees and the law school dean, allegedly because the novel direction of the school's work was being held responsible for only 30 percent of the school's graduates passing the bar examination. The faculty claimed that the president of Queens and the chancellor of the CUNY system were trespassing on faculty governance prerogatives with respect to educational decisions by overruling the tenure recommendation. The lower court and then the New York State appeals court ordered the two professors returned to their teaching jobs while the trustees consider their application for tenure. The decision was that the chancellor did not have authority to deny tenure to the professors at that point, but had to submit his recommendation with his reasons to the trustees for their decision. Interestingly, the trustees had meanwhile approved a revised governance plan for the law school that included creation of an external review committee from other law schools to make recommendations to the dean on tenure and promotion.[18]

The same educational issue seems to be arising at Columbia Law School, where the disagreement about the value of a legal clinic is to be found within the faculty between "advocates of such practical studies in the education of a lawyer and traditionalists, who believe the clinics detract from the school's academic image." Students supporting the clinic are protesting its possible closing. The tenure of the director–professor seems also involved.[19] This issue, whether of educational method or of tenure, has not so far taken shape as a conflict of governance. If it did, the difficulty of appeal to the courts would be much greater than at CUNY, where governance bylaws provide a legal foothold.

Although the relation of the educational issue to governance in the CUNY Law School case seems a matter of historical accident, yet it is significant not merely that the school and the professors appealed to existing governance rules, but that the trustees in looking for a solution did not pass on the educational issue but introduced a fresh governance device, that of the external committee, as a solution. Presumably it would be passing any questions involved to the standard of the profession at large.

The examples we have considered make it possible to sharpen the relation of educational ends or goals to forms or patterns of governance in the socioethical model. A difficulty arises from the fact that we may think of governance in the narrow sense derived from the older, authoritarian approach—namely, the governing group within the institution. Or we may think of governance in the broader, democratic sense in which it is the contextual pattern of decision making. In the narrow sense, of course, the less we need to appeal to "government" to achieve educational aims the better; if ways to achieve them can be agreed on in the deliberation of the parties concerned, there is no need to move into matters of government. If, however, conflicting interests do not permit agreement or compromise on policy, then it is better that the representation in government be wider and not one-sided, so that its deliberation and decision may be more reasonable as well as fairer and not repressive. Now in the broader sense of democratic governance, any serious change in educational goals and consequently policy will make changes in the pattern of who decides what, and so of governance. The socioethical model is simply calling attention here to the need for explicitness about the powers and functions of decision, and to the conscious decision about decision in areas of conflict.

In any case, it is clear today that governance need not take a single permanent shape in all of higher education. Higher education is a complicated and vital social system. Many a university is now larger than a Greek city–state was when it dealt with problems of authority reflectively and worked out the idea of face-to-face democratic participation. In a changing world, higher education today has therefore to work out and rework its modes of governance. It has many advantages as a setting for such experimentation. For one thing, its major body of workers are skilled possessors of special expertise, in general highly educated themselves. They are capable, where competition does not become excessive, of a high degree of cooperation. In many areas they are on the frontiers of knowledge and investigation. Even its students are selected in terms of certain qualifications. In its exploratory practice with patterns of governance, higher education therefore has a good start, if it will only take sensible advantage of it.

A further advantage is that higher education in the United States can draw on the lessons of political democracy. No general or wholesale choice has to be made between direct democracy, representative democracy, participatory democracy. Each can be seen as a reservoir of mechanisms, to be tried out in special contexts: for example, where an all-inclusive assembly should have the power to elect a representative body, where it should be able to overrule the latter's decision (whether by simple majority, two-thirds, three-quarters), or where the representative group or committee should have full powers during its period of office for the domain it covers; where and how far to make use of appeal mechanisms, either judgmental or mediating (as in the institution of the ombudsman); how the functions of decision and supervision and evaluation should be separated; what should be advisory and what decisive; and countless other matters, many of which will be discovered in practice.

The diversity of colleges and universities, with their varied traditions and interests, reinforces the conviction that the move toward democratic governance need not proceed from a single blueprint. It can fruitfully try out different shapes in different places, with their strengths and weaknesses. From an overall view, the result might well be that of multiple experiments, with innovation in a great variety of mechanisms. Such diversity is found in the political realm among states and municipalities—initiative and referendum in California, city managers rather than mayors in many places. So too a small or middle-sized college with a stable program and with a firm tradition and financial base might well consider a European pattern of limited-term rectors elected by the faculty in place of presidents. Or a large university with strong professional schools might well pattern itself on a looser federation rather than have a unity in which the schools jostle for primacy.

A view of governance as open-textured imparts to it a continuously experimental character, an attitude of exploratory practice. This is particularly fitting for an age of rapid and complex transformation in which, as we have seen, higher education has grown in vast proportions, in which its tasks and underlying aims have multiplied and raised problems of integration, and in which the whole articulation of goals and their relation to means has become a continual institutional task rather than a completely preassigned set of definitive objectives. Under these conditions the critique of past ways and the shaping of future ways become a comprehensive intellectual task, distinguishing what is relative and temporary from what is of perennial worth in human growth.

The wisdom for such tasks is not located in only one segment of higher education or of its matrix in social life. It is an essentially cooperative enterprise, which the idea of governing has to express. This gives a more positive character to a democratic division of labor, the division of powers, the existence of checks and balances, than the theory of the Constitution possibly had at its outset. The negative effect of preventing the consolidation of tyranny, whether of the few or the many, ceases to be the sole gain. The division of labor involved in broadening governance enlarges the sense of community. The division of powers brings a variety of perspectives into policy deliberation and determination. Even checks and balances become tests of proposed policy from divergent standpoints—putting varying interests through the strainer of common welfare. Democratic structure assumes more and more the character of common learning. It is fitting that governing in higher education should be in significant respects itself a process of learning.

We turn in conclusion to two issues of importance in understanding the fundamental change that has been going on from an authoritarian toward a democratic perspective in governance. One is the basic shift in categories that epitomizes the change and can help guide its direction. The second is to suggest the likely next steps as the drama of democratization unfolds.

If the unifying concepts of an authoritarian structure were *ruling* (or *authority*) and *loyal obedience,* the emerging concepts of a democratic structure are *participation* and *responsibility* with a sense of *community purpose.*[20] The older concepts do not disappear from ordinary use; some people may still be authorities in the sense that their learning inspires the acceptance of their assertions, and loyalty as a personal tie to person or ideal remains an important human relation. They cease simply to be the major organizing principles of social order and take their place in the rank and file of virtues and moral relations.

Why the concept of participation has moved into a prime place in the scheme of social order has by now been amply explored. It was in some ways overdetermined: by the magnitude and complexity of tasks in modern life; by the necessary scope of division of labor; by the growing impossibility of one person or even a small group holding with competence all the threads of a national (much less a global) society. Indeed, we can read the history of the growth of democracy as successive experiments in the failure of one after another of limitations to fuller participation.

With the concept of responsibility the picture is far less clear; its importance as the correlate of participation is evident enough. Indeed one of the most powerful of arguments against the extension of participation has been that it will scatter responsibility to a vanishing point. So too, one of the common complaints against faculties is that they never get things done until some administrator pulls them up sharply. In a system of broad participation, it is argued, it is always possible to feel that someone else—or the group as such—has the responsibility for the outcome.

The theory of responsibility is indeed one of the most difficult problems in moral philosophy. Three important points about it will suffice, however, for its relation to our present topic. First, its conceptual difficulties arise from the way in which it reacted to the authoritarian conception of reason. Second, whatever dispersion of responsibility may be feared under broader participation, the picture cannot be worse than the actual dissolution of responsibility that has taken place in contemporary authoritarian culture. Third, there is growing evidence that increased participation may restore responsibility rather than dissolve it.

The conceptual difficulties go back to the early history of popular movements against absolute sovereignty. Since, as we have seen, the authoritarian view had captured the idea of reason as against the dispersive passions and interests of the multitude, popular theory pitted the idea of will against that of reason, and set up the general will as the source of social policy. With the growth of individualism and the fragmentation of will, each individual became regarded as responsible only for what he or she willed. The picture of struggles with this narrowing are found in the detailed history of case law on problems of fault and liability. In the long run, as the notion of reason became less monarchical and was interpreted more in relation to the lessons of human experience and learning, it became possible to think in terms of an educated will, particularly with the acceptance of education as a public necessity, and an increasingly refined distinction between teaching/learning and dogmatic indoctrination. Hence the shedding of responsibility by retreat to a relativistic individual assertion of will or preference is transcended.

That the present picture of the dissolution of responsibility under authoritarian schemes of rule is as bad as or worse than what is feared for participatory forms is being widely documented today for varied social systems and for the moral atmosphere at large. For socialist authoritarian forms the most startling evidence came from the Soviet Union in the 1980s in the revelations under *glasnost*. For corporate capitalism, there has been a stream of revelations—ample in the United States—of irresponsibility in the scramble for profit: pollution, neglect of nuclear dangers, adulteration of products and collusive control of prices, manipulation of government contracts and government regulatory agencies. It is not, however, merely a matter of underhand operations. The dominance of the competitive, profit-guided economy is accompanied by large-scale phenomena of poverty, most visible in recent years in the plight of the homeless, and in the Third World by the export of food to pay interest on indebtedness while starvation grows at home. Occasionally the rent in the moral atmosphere—like the hole in the ozone layer that humankind has created—is seen dramatically, as when a young woman is murdered in the streets of a city in the night and in spite of her screams no one calls the police. Although there are notable bursts of compassion, and stalwart moral groups devoting their lives to assisting the impoverished and the struggling, these are clearly patterns of participation, not authority.

The hypothesis that participation will increase responsibility rather than further dilute it rests in part on the belief that the irresponsibility of groups often comes from their lack of participation. It was suggested earlier that the character of faculty proceedings complained about may be due to their lack of power, to their feeling that they have no effective contribution in the current scheme of governance. If so, then we might expect a change in behavior and a sense of responsibility with a fuller participatory share in governance. Hopeful hypotheses about the change in attitude of working groups in industry find some degree of confirmation: Experiments in having workers decide on and manage their productive processes, instead of simply following orders on what to do after what, have yielded a higher degree of quality control. In general, the position with respect to responsibility is that there is little to lose and much to gain in turning to greater participation.

Finally, the longing for community is evident enough today, as a clear reaction to the culture of isolated individualism. Care must be taken in the search for community purpose not to jeopardize the moral gains of individualism—the freedoms and rights that had to be so vigorously fought for. Nor should the search for community be sidetracked into cults with charismatic leaders or even in crises into inroads on civil liberties or worthy communal purposes. Community springs up naturally in common undertakings. In many respects the university provides a congenial home for it in its many smaller communities. In its larger groupings, democratic, cooperative deliberation with respect to the purposes that bring people together in such an institution can readily give shape to community purpose and strengthen common allegiances and ideals.

The significance of change in basic categories is that it reverberates through the whole field and calls for reconstruction in many of the central ideas. Now the treatment of democratization in governance, both by opponents and supporters, has been chiefly in terms of an opposition of administration and faculty. The growing shift has been seen as faculty empowerment, first to a limited degree but now spreading. Battles were fought and still are fought at vital points in the fortifications of the dividing line, for example, at the control of budget and its allocation.

Even in the 1980s, books about the management of the university still take sides with administration or faculty as separate units facing one another.[21] In our account, both historical and descriptive of the present situation, emphasis has accordingly fallen on showing the artificiality of the dividing line for governance, and how the concerns of each side enter intimately into those of the other. Such a formulation, accurate as it is for the situation that still exists, does not analyze the character of the basic units—administration and faculty—and their appropriateness for examining democratization in governance. If we think now about next steps in democratization, this question becomes central. For as long as we conceive of democratization as the dispersal of governance among the existing units, we are likely to limit the inquiry to questions of proportion and degree of control. That is, we still remain trapped in the older categories of authority.

If, on the other hand, we think in terms of the revised concept of governance and the changing ends and conditions of contemporary higher education, the next step in democratization is to recognize the artificiality of the existing units themselves. The complexity of tasks that are today embraced in administration makes it a very strange whole, and the shift in end from teaching to learning has played havoc with the image of the faculty as a naturally unified body of teachers. It follows that these are not the terms in which allocation of decision making is fruitfully to be considered.

Of course it is easy to fortify the distinctions by tracing conflicts of interest, particularly with the proliferation of the administrative apparatus in many universities so that it takes a surprisingly large proportion of the total budget. Specific conflicts too may easily be cited—for example, whether a given amount of money should be used for a new post of a specialized vice-presidency or for buying more books for the library. Conflicts may equally be found within the faculty bloc—for example, whether to add a distinguished professor who will bring chiefly a new area of research or several young instructors who would relieve the pressure of numbers in the classes.

How then shall we conceive of what is now called the administration? In an authoritarian system of governance it contained the hierarchy leading up to the pinnacle of authority. If that unity is diminished, it is difficult to replace it with a unity in the vast variety of work that it embraces. In fact, its general character seems to be much less one of *administration* than of *service*. We would have a clearer functional picture of the university if we saw it as a mélange of service functions as diverse as plant and health, financing and recording, student housing and various forms of advising, a variety of external relations to community and government and alumni, and so on. Of course decisions are made in all these areas, but there is a great deal of arbitrariness about where decisions are located. Take, for example, protection against fire. It is administrative to make sure that the electrical system throughout the university works properly according to the code of the municipal fire department. But the chemistry department must ensure that its chemicals are properly stored to avoid an explosion. The university may establish international exchanges through its relations with administrations in foreign countries; but professors in different disciplines will belong to international professional associations. There is no need to multiply examples. Once the unifying thread of authoritarian rule is gone, we have the diversity of service functions and the new question: Which of them are best carried on in an independent way, and which should bring in for their handling other branches and departments of the university that work in areas of knowledge and that could usefully contribute to decisions for that function? Some precedents for such collaboration already exist: for example, the faculty of medicine and its hospital for student health, branches of the school of business for the financial and accounting aspects of the university, architects for maintaining coherence of building styles on the campus, and so forth. (It would be interesting to know how far anthropology and sociology and social psychology have been consulted for the study of problems of race relations or of fraternity life and student community.) Now if administration is seen in this broad service sense, it might very well be reorganized in a more pluralistic way within the university as a whole.

Similar questions may be raised about the faculty. At present, its governance structure is generally departmental. The justifying basis for such a scheme is what is sometimes called the architecture of knowledge. Different fields of knowledge operate with a relative independence and should continue self-governing. Up to fairly recently the scheme was regarded as fixed by the nature of things—the physical, the biological, the psychological, the sociocultural, the historical. But complexity has broken through all neat classifications, and hyphenated disciplines (biophysics, biochemistry, neurological psychology, comparative literature, etc.) come on apace. Moreover, for university purposes, relatively artificial classifications come to be used—the *humanities* is one of the most conglomerate. Still, there are sound educational reasons for not abrogating the relative autonomy of traditional disciplines. The reasons are largely historically grounded: The disciplines have accumulated a rich substance of problems and methods and organized knowledge that should not be jettisoned too hastily. Yet on the other hand, the interdisciplinary, which is often the seedbed of innovative trends, still is treated as a kind of second-class citizen within departmental frameworks. Scientific projects during World War II compelled scientists from different fields to work together, and practical projects since—from space travel to nuclear energy—have made multidisciplinary demands. In many fields an isolating conception of "autonomy" still reigns. Interdisciplinary interests are often forced into separate "institutes," frequently on grant money. Changes in the governance pattern of the knowledge branches of the university should therefore be geared more consciously to the goal of advancing knowledge. In some places this has been done by grouping—for example, the social sciences as a division to be represented, the humanities another. Perhaps institutes, where well established, should have representation in wider bodies, consonant with their role in the particular university. Sometimes programs, particularly those attuned to the cultural aim of general education, will have departmental or quasi-departmental status. (Columbia's Contemporary Civilization or the successive Harvard programs of general education set standards for a great deal of course integration.) The general problem may be stated as how to preserve the benefit of departmental differences without the feudal-like character of interdepartmental relations in the governance pattern, while making adjustments to a changing picture of the architecture of knowledge.

This changing picture of knowledge is only one side of the forces impinging on the character of the faculty. The shift of educational orientation from teaching to learning is equally serious, especially when linked to technological developments. It is now commonplace that learning is spread out today—with libraries, television, videocassettes, tape recorders, computers, and rapidly growing information banks that can be tapped fairly readily—far beyond the teaching and lecturing that were once the bulk of education. (Yet lectures, introduced in the eighteenth-century Scottish and American universities, then marked a notable gain: Professors who hitherto had been obliged to carry a class through all its subjects now could cultivate special fields, advancing both research and teaching.) If the faculty has had problems of self-identity with respect to the relation of research and teaching, it will soon have more momentous problems about its place as it becomes dissolved in the much broader grouping of educational workers. Such a conglomerate new group will not have the identity that gives it a unified role in governance. What part its various segments should play in decision making is likely to be variable, depending on the specific nature of the tasks and the work involved.

"Students" as a unit is also breaking down. Graduate students who handle discussion sections are in that respect teachers. In fact, legal problems have arisen about whether their compensation is taxable as income or is exempt as scholarships; also whether they can unionize under regulations of the National Labor Relations Board. Some universities have given separate representation to graduate students and to undergraduate students. Again, with the growth of "lifelong learning," increasing numbers of more mature students, senior citizens, and people with varieties of developed interests and experience come to the university. They require a distinct voice. Even "undergraduates" may prove too omnibus a grouping when we compare the incoming first-year student with the mature senior.

With the dissolution of the "en bloc" character of administration and faculty and students, from the point of view of pattern of governance, the formulations of democratization in terms of their sharing power, or the arguments over which should determine the scope of the other in the university as a whole, or which should have the last word about budget, and numerous other questions become pointless, if not wholly meaningless. They are recollections of past unified authority, or dreams of its recapture, or fears about a new feudalism. Instead, democratic governance offers the prospect of increased learning and refinement of the pattern of decision to the needs of different contexts, each of which will make the best use of the state of knowledge, the resources of the university, and the goals of higher education.

We have come a long way from the revolution of 1938. But when we see the present state of the argument, the timidity of programs for participation, and the continuing controversy as to whether the administration or the faculty is better fit to rule, it becomes clear that the revolution of 1938 in New York's city colleges was a far-reaching pioneer effort. It tried to substitute rich participation for autocratic governance of higher education, to bring into a major institution the lessons of American political life in the unfolding of democracy. Its constructive attitude was evident both in its concern with developing and testing detailed mechanisms and procedures and in its relating them to releasing potentials for contributions to the life of education. Its experiences have still much to teach us in facing the issues of educational governance today.

Joint Program on Faculty and Administrative Organization

[*Author's note:* The Joint Program on Faculty and Administrative Organization, which follows, was drawn up on December 4, 1937, at a meeting of representatives of the New York College Teachers Union and the several instructional associations and AAUP chapters of the New York city colleges. The meeting was the last of three that were held to frame a coordinated program.]

Faculties

1. Each Faculty shall consist of all Professors, Associate Professors, Assistant Professors, Instructors, holding full-time positions on annual salary; and such other officers as the Faculty judges should be added because of their educational responsibilities.

2. Subject to law and the authority of the Board of Higher Education, each Faculty shall be the supreme governing authority of its college. The general charge of the college is entrusted to the Faculty, and the Faculty may make such investigations, and by by-laws, regulations or resolution adopt such administrative measures as it may deem in the best interests of the college or of any department thereof. The Faculty shall be re-

sponsible for: matters concerning course of study; standards for admission and degrees; graduate, vocational and guidance work; new departments; principles of organization and administration in and between departments and the assignment of work therein; general rules governing teaching and working load; standards of discipline and control of students and student activities, to be carried out by deans, faculty committees and joint faculty–student committees; measures to facilitate and promote research by members of the staff; the extension and utilization of college facilities in the service of the community; and any other matters it may deem necessary.

3. Departmental recommendations and appeals by individual members of the staff regarding appointment, salary, promotion, increments, shall be subject to review by the appropriate committee of the Faculty, augmented by representatives of non-teaching staffs when questions concerning the latter are dealt with.

4. There shall be a committee of the Faculty, augmented by representatives of non-teaching staffs when questions concerning the latter are dealt with, to hear and investigate charges brought against a member of the staff where tenure rights are involved.

5. The Faculty shall have a general committee or special committee to safeguard any educational interests involved in matters of plant, equipment, maintenance, plant personnel, and in planning for future developments.

6. The Faculty of each college shall elect a committee which in conjunction with the President shall have prepared under its supervision a tentative annual budget based upon recommendations of the departments. Upon the approval of the Faculty, this shall be submitted to the appropriate committees of the Board.

7. Each Faculty shall organize itself in any way it deems suit-

able. It shall elect a vice-chairman, secretary, and any other officers it may desire. It shall establish its own by-laws and rules of procedure. Each Faculty shall meet at least once each term, or oftener upon call by its executive officers or by petition of ten percent of the members. In colleges which have constituent faculties, a general Faculty shall regulate their relationships, subject to appeal to the Board.

8. Each Faculty shall elect a Committee on Committees and any other standing or special committees it may deem necessary. All committees within the college shall be responsible to the Faculty. The Committee on Committees shall receive suggestions from members of the Faculty. It shall report to the Faculty its nominations of members for positions on committees to be elected by the Faculty. Nomination and election by the Faculty of any officer or standing committee shall be conducted as follows: At least one month before the date of the election the secretary shall give notice of the coming election, with the names of the incumbents at the time. The Committee on Committees shall, through the Secretary of the Faculty, report its nominations to each member of the Faculty at least one week before the meeting of the Faculty. Nominations may also be made from the floor. The voting shall be by secret preferential ballot. A Committee on elections consisting of the secretary and two members of the Faculty appointed by the presiding officer shall supervise elections.

9. The Faculty shall have the power, through representatives elected by it, to communicate with or appear before the Board of Higher Education on any matter pertaining to the college.

10. There shall be a committee from each college, consisting of one professor, one associate professor, one assistant professor, and one instructor, elected by the members of their respective ranks, which shall attend meetings of the Board of Higher Education and of the administrative committee of their

college, with the privilege of being heard but not the right to vote.

Presidents, Deans and Directors

Presidents

The Presidents shall be the chief executive agents of the Board, and, subject to the jurisdiction and interpretation of the Faculty, shall be entrusted with the following:

They shall have immediate supervision in carrying into effect the by-laws, resolutions and policies of the Board, and lawful resolutions of any of its committees or of the several faculties, and they shall exercise superintendence over matters of plant, equipment, maintenance and plant personnel of the educational establishments maintained by the Board. They shall preside at all meetings of the respective general faculties and shall attend all meetings of the Board. Between the meetings of the Board they are authorized on the recommendation of the department concerned, in an emergency, to fill temporary vacancies in the instructional staff below the rank of Assistant Professor, and to make such temporary administrative appointments and arrangements on the recommendation of the department or administrative office concerned, as cannot well await the action of the Board or its appropriate committee; and in conjunction with the appropriate committee of the Faculty they shall cause to be prepared under their supervision tentative annual budgets for submission, upon ratification by the appropriate Faculty, to the appropriate committees of the Board. They shall have the duty of fostering and encouraging public and private support for their colleges, and of recommending to the Faculty plans for the advancement of research and publication, the extension and utilization of college facilities in the service of the community, and any other activities to further the purposes of higher education.

Candidates for the office of President shall be nominated by a joint committee composed of at least three members elected by the Faculty of the college concerned, and an equal number appointed by the Board. No candidate shall be made president without the approval of the Faculty and the Board.

Deans and Directors

Recommendations to the Board concerning appointment to the office of dean or director shall be made by the Faculty of the particular college or school concerned, on the basis of a secret preferential vote on a list of nominees presented to it by a special committee consisting of the President and four elected members of the Faculty concerned. Information concerning the candidates shall be provided in advance by the committee. The Board shall select the dean or director from the first three preferred candidates. The dean or director shall discharge such administrative and executive duties as the Faculty may delegate to him.

This program was immediately adopted by the union as a common basis for wide staff agreement. In the months that followed it was approved by the instructional staff organizations at the three colleges. The bylaw proposals made by the City College Chapter of the AAUP early in April 1938 showed substantial agreement with the program.

Union Program for Departmental Democracy

I. Departmental Assemblies

1. Composition: For purposes of decision on matters of personnel (including salary and promotion) the departmental assembly should consist of all permanent members. (Permanent, as defined in the Union program of tenure: i.e., all who have completed three years of satisfactory service or have been made members of the permanent staff in less than three years.) For all other matters it should consist of all members of the department.

2. Organization: Non-teaching members of the staff (Clerical, Laboratory, Library, Research and Secretarial Assistants) who are allied with the various academic departments should be included in the assemblies of their respective departments. The departmental assembly should decide on which matters the non-teaching members shall have voting privileges. (a) Minutes of meetings should be taken and should be available to any member of the department. (b) The agenda of the meeting should be announced in advance and should always be open to any additions by department members. (c) A department may set up any committee it finds necessary and should spec-

ify a term of office. All committees should be responsible to the assembly. (d) All decisions involving questions of policy should be arrived at by the assembly vote. (e) On all important matters the department should vote by secret ballot. (f) The departmental assemblies of two or more departments should be free to vote to conduct part or all of their business jointly and to act therein as a single department.

II. Departmental Chairman

1. The department chairman* should be elected by the departmental assembly, subject to approval by the faculty.

2. The period of office should be from one to three years.

3. The department chairman should preside at department meetings, transmit departmental recommendations to administrative officers of the college, be a member ex officio of committees, and perform the requisite executive duties for the department.

4. The chairman should receive applications from members of the department for sabbatical leave or leave of absence and make recommendations thereon to the departmental assembly.

III. Department Committees

There should be a committee on Committees, and in addition, committees on Appointment, Probationers, Salary and Promotion, Curriculum, Research Facilities, Supplies, Library Purchases, Grievances and, for the non-instructional departments, in addition, a committee on Distribution of Work, and wherever necessary on any special matters. The following principles should be observed concerning committees:

---

*This position involves no additional remuneration, but smaller teaching schedule and adequate clerical help.

1. The Committee on Committees and the Grievance Committee should be elective. The other Committees should be selected by the Committee on Committees after members of the department have been given an opportunity to indicate preference as to the committees on which they would like to serve. All committees should then be passed on by the assembly.

2. Committees should be chosen annually.

3. On Committees on Curriculum, Supplies, Research Facilities and Library Purchases it is important various major divisions of the department be adequately represented, whereas on committees on Salary and Promotion it is important that the various ranks be represented adequately. On the Committee on Committees and on Appointments both ranks and divisions should be represented. The Grievance Committee should consist of about three members elected without regard to rank or division.

4. Committees should keep minutes of their proceedings.

5. Each committee should have the further duty, when its recommendations upon adoption by the departmental assembly become matters concerning the faculty or committee thereof, of transmitting the department's recommendations to the faculty or its committee and appearing in justification of its recommendations.

6. Each committee should have the right to cooperate with any similar committee of any other department.

IV. Appointments

1. When a vacancy occurs, there should be a meeting of the departmental assembly to discuss the particular qualifications desirable in the light of the work the appointee is to do, and the

role he is to play in the department, e.g., whether an experienced person or a beginner is wanted.

2. In order that the best available candidates may be considered, the committee should see to it that the fact of the vacancy becomes known in educational circles in sufficient time for any who desire to apply. For example, notice should be sent to all institutions of higher learning maintaining an employment service, or notification given through scholarly publications that provide such facilities.

3. The committee should investigate the applicant's qualifications (including scholarship and the character and validity of his degrees) and rights arising from previous service in the institution. It should interview the most promising of the candidates and where practicable observe them in the actual conduct of a class or in practical performance of duties similar to those to which he will be assigned.

4. The committee should report on the several leading candidates to the assembly of the permanent members of the department, and make recommendations on appointment. After discussion of the report, the final decision on the department's recommendations should be made by majority vote of the assembly of permanent members.

5. No person should be appointed to any post who has not been approved by the department concerned.

6. In case of an emergency that cannot be covered by this procedure, a temporary appointment may be made for a period of time not to exceed the current academic year.

7. Recommendations to appointment should be subject to review by a college staff committee on appointments elected by the whole college staff, to which the relevant evidence should be presented and records of relevant department meetings be made available.

V. *Probationers*

(For the sake of simplicity, the following procedure is outlined specifically for the teaching staff. The same principles, however, with appropriate modifications, should apply for the non-teaching staff as well.)

1. A person who has been selected to a staff position after approval of his scholarship, prior experience, and recommendations, and after a personal interview, is presumed to be capable of developing into a good teacher (i.e., meeting the standards democratically set by the department), and of correcting any faults which may be due to insufficient experience. If charges of insufficient competence are brought against a probationer, they should be judged democratically within the department as outlined below. Dismissal on the charges of insufficient competence should follow only if it is decided that his faults have not been removed by the corrective procedure hereinafter described. In cases where no charges of insufficient competence are brought, the probationer should automatically, on the expiration of his probationary period, become a member of the permanent staff.

2. The function of the committee on Probationers should be to welcome and assist probationers. If there are any complaints against a probationer they should be referred to the committee. The Committee should decide whether the complaints merit consideration. If they do, the probationer should be informed and his classes thereafter visited for at least one full period by each member of the committee. Any other relevant sources of evidence should also be examined. If the committee finds serious faults in the probationer's qualifications as a college teacher, (i.e., in his teaching or research and publication of graduate work) it should then give him "due warning." This warning should be accompanied by a state-

ment in writing of what specific defects the committee has found in the probationer's qualifications together with a notice that one year shall be allowed for remedying the specified faults.

3. The aim of the committee's procedure should be primarily the remedying of faults in the probationer's work. At the end of the year after "due warning" was given, the classes of the probationer should be visited separately by each member of the committee and by the chairman of the department for the purpose of recording in writing any improvement or lack of improvement in the probationer's teaching, and any other previously specified shortcomings should again be investigated.

4. Discussion of these reports should take place openly at a meeting of the permanent members of the department, of which a permanent and open record should be kept. The probationer should be heard and allowed to present any evidence in his favor.

5. If at least two-thirds of the total number of permanent members of the department vote by secret ballot in favor of dismissing the probationer, the department chairman should then and only then proceed to recommend dismissal on the basis of specified charges of insufficient competence, and he should present all the evidence in writing to support such charges. A copy of this should be presented to the probationer.

6. A recommendation of dismissal should be subject to review by a staff committee on review democratically elected by the whole college staff, to which all the evidence presented and the records of department meetings should be made available (this committee might be identical with one charged with reviewing appointments).

VI. *Salary and Promotion*

1. Recommendations for increments and promotions should be made by the Committee on Salary and Promotions in conjunction with the department chairman. The recommendations should be open for department inspection before transmittal. Any special increments and special promotions should be ratified by the assembly of permanent members before transmittal as departmental recommendations to the appropriate elected college staff committee.

VII. *Charges of Incompetence*

1. A person who has served beyond the initial three years or who has been made a member of the permanent staff in less than three years is presumed to be competent. This places the burden of proof on those who may claim insufficient competence.

2. Charges of incompetence should not be made unless there have been serious complaints concerning the work of a person. Whether the complaints are of a serious enough nature to warrant investigation is a question best decided by the department of which the person concerned is a member, that is by the assembly of the permanent members. Such a decision and the discussion leading up to it, should take place openly at a departmental assembly.

3. If and only if the assembly of the permanent members of the department decides democratically that the charges of incompetence are serious enough and have some basis in fact should the case go to the college staff committee (IV-7 and V-6). This committee should have the power to investigate the case fully.

4. Nothing in the above procedure should prejudice a per-

son's right to an open hearing by the trustees or the Board of Higher Education.

5. If the individual concerned desires to avoid the publicity involved in the above procedure, he may at any point stop further action by resigning his post. If the person concerned resigns, all steps in connection with his case should cease.

VIII. Curriculum

1. The curriculum committee should have the task of making suggestions on curricular revisions and additions, and of receiving such suggestions from individual members, students, and from other departments.

2. This committee should be responsible for examining wherever necessary the relations of the content of courses within the department; also of examining wherever necessary the relation of department courses to other departments.

3. This committee should also make recommendations on which elective or required courses should properly be rotated, in virtue of their content, and which offer opportunities for cumulative specialization. It should recommend assignment of the latter to members of the department according to interest and special preparation.

4. The committee should formulate its results for the departmental assembly's discussion and action.

IX. Standards

In the interests of good teaching, there should be a minimum of restraint placed upon the teacher. Members of the permanent staff are presumed to be competent teachers who can be trusted faithfully to perform their duties without the aid of a guiding hand. However, in considering the questions of standards, it is necessary to distinguish between elective and required courses.

1. Elective courses: Here complete freedom should be allowed within the limits provided by the section on curriculum (VIII-2). The teacher entrusted with an elective course should be considered competent to determine his own objectives and to set up his own standards.

2. Required courses: Here certain standards to ensure equivalence are essential, since these courses are usually divided into two or more sections. Those who teach such courses, including permanent and non-permanent members, should constitute a committee to determine objectives and establish standards, subject to approval by the department assembly. Provided these requirements are met, the teacher should be free to emphasize whatever aspect of the subject he sees fit. The requirements should not be so rigid nor so extensive as to exclude this freedom.

3. Methods: There should be no prescription of methods of teaching. This should be a matter for consultation and suggestion, rather than prescription.

4. In general, the best method for securing uniformity where desired, and for maintaining minimum standards, will be found in cooperative discussion of problems of objectives, methods, etc., as they may arise.

X. *Teaching Schedules and Distribution of Work*

Teaching load and schedule arrangements should be an executive function of the department chairman, except that in the non-instructional departments this should be a function of the committee on distribution of work. (It should be the function of this committee to draw up a work plan, make assignments to the various members of the department, arrange time schedules and vacation schedules after individual members of the department have had an opportunity to indicate preferences, give aid to probationers and warning when a probationer's work is not satisfactory. It should render its report to the assembly which should have the opportunity to discuss and criticize it. The final report should be adopted by vote of the assembly and should be carried out by the committee.)

XI. Supplies and Library Purchases

Planning, control and distribution of supplies and the determination of library purchases should be handled by departmental committees. All recommendations for the allocation of funds should be approved by the assembly.

XII. Research Facilities

The research committee should make recommendations to the department for the allocation of funds, supplies and space, or other facilities for research.

XIII. Grievances

Grievances should be investigated by the Grievance Committee.

Arguments Advanced During the Campaign

[*Author's note:* the following is a summary of the arguments advanced during the campaign for democratic governance, relating to both the evils of the autocratic system and questions raised about the functioning of a democratic system. The material is taken from the campaign literature of the time.]

Primary Evils

The major evils of this "dictatorial" type of organization are consequences of structure rather than of particular personalities. Department heads are themselves victims of the organization and are sometimes profoundly dissatisfied with it. Resentment in department members grows from the realization that they have and will have little or no share in the formulation of departmental policies, that their role is to perform an assigned task rather than to have a creative share in the institution's welfare. Apathy arises from the same realization; the teacher comes to regard his college duties as ended when he leaves the classroom. There is a depressing sense of futility in probing for fundamental educational directions when one's curriculum and teaching methods are prescribed by one's superiors. Thus a system of control, modelled on the business world, and decked with the rationalization that the teacher has an "academic" mind and should not be burdened with the cares of administration, ends in the devitalization of the teaching staff. It is now almost a commonplace for administrators to say that faculties are conservative and are the chief obstacles to much-needed change and curricular revision. The department head who would like to have his subordinates cooperate in determining policy and practice may meet with the sullen insinuation that he is seeking others to bear his burden. The kindly trustee, surveying the situation, may begin to feel that there is a lot of "dead-wood" in the college, and that only a ruthless series of dismissals will produce a well-functioning system. But cathartics do not cure systemic diseases. What is needed is reorganization and the opportunity for development.

Such strong statements are not intended to disparage the genuinely scholarly work—both in research and in the classroom—that is done by many members of the college staffs. They are intended to suggest that the potentialities of teachers are capable of greater and richer development if they are granted fuller democratic scope. Individual teachers should not be deprived of that sustained collaboration which makes the college not a congeries of classrooms but a unified educational realm. Nor on the other hand should discussion be construed as ignoring other causes that may operate in producing inadequacies in teaching. Certainly there are important questions to be considered concerning teacher-training, present ideals of research, the social forces affecting college teachers, and the role of the college in the life of the community. But before they can be fruitfully resolved teachers must achieve conditions under which their thinking may be more than aimless reflection.

Absence of Standards

Specific evils follow from the organization of departments as power systems. One very common feature where control is centered in a single administrative officer is the absence of explicit standards in the treatment of personnel and frequently, too, in the allocation of work. The worth of the individual is said to be best estimated by the unexplained insight of skilled administrators. Experience does not support this theory. On the whole it is the best judges who are best able to articulate their judgments. The judgment of competence and merit is no simple one. It involves at least implicit goals or objectives, with the teacher's competence determined by success in approximating these goals. Cooperative consideration will help to guarantee explicitness as well as to allow scope for the representation of differing viewpoints with respect to goals.

In Dismissals
In practice, the absence of explicit standards means more than accidental error and confusion. It has encouraged arbitrary prejudice. The records of the Grievance Committee of the New York College Teachers Union contain many cases of attempted dismissal for reasons other than competence and merit. Some cases involve principles of academic freedom: the attempt to remove teachers who were active in organizing their fellow-teachers and who were sympathetic to liberal student movements. Most numerous were dismissals which involved money-saving because the dismissed could be replaced by teachers at a lower salary. In still other cases, factors of race and religion, prejudice against foreigners, and personal dislike were operative. In many cases the unfairness became so apparent that the trustees of the colleges in question refused to act on the recommendations for dismissal.

Similar problems have arisen in connection with promotion.

There is a wide-spread feeling at many colleges that promotion is to a great extent a function of favor, or at least the avoidance of disfavor. Grounds of antagonism may be irrelevant to the judgment of teaching ability and even to the estimation of "personality." Teachers have sometimes been discouraged as well as mystified by sudden unexplained promotions of apparently unworthy colleagues. In one case of this sort the head of the department justified the action by saying "At least X doesn't give us any trouble." But more important than specific partiality towards individuals is the feeling engendered by such action that there is no relation between effective service and reward. If there were discoverable standards which were normally applied, occasional errors would not cause such harm.

It may, of course, be suggested that no "objective" standards of competence can be formulated. If the situation is indeed so desperate, there is, at least, less danger of error in having many, rather than one, "subjective" judgment. Numerous problems concerning standards have yet to be solved. But there is hope for their solution, especially if we rely upon cooperative discussion rather than impressionistic choice.

In Appointments
The situation with regard to appointments is still more serious. Except where pressure may be applied from above, these originate in departments, and are one of the chief responsibilities of the department head. Often he consults a few members of the department informally, but this is by no means universal; nor need advice be accepted. (In one flagrant case a department head asked members to grade candidates, and then chose one who had been placed in the lowest category.) On the whole no attempt is made to publicize a vacancy. Appointment frequently depends upon being available at the right time or being in the good graces of the department officer. The biases

mentioned above as arising in cases of attempted dismissal thus operate with equal force in appointments.

In Curriculum Matters

Although there is a greater readiness on the part of department heads to discuss problems of curriculum with their subordinates, these are nevertheless often decided on the basis of personal inclination. Introduction of new courses, the character of required courses, allotment of supplies, allocation of courses within the department, are in varying degrees decided without the participation of department members. Department heads have been known to bar the addition of courses regarded by the department as imperative (even when budgetary issues were not involved), and to allocate courses to favored individuals without regard to qualifications. Many teachers, especially the younger ones, are deprived of opportunities to teach elective courses, even when they are especially fitted to do so. Such malpractices as interrupting a teacher in class with trifling criticisms or insisting that every teacher move through the syllabus at the same pace, are fortunately infrequent. Their occasional occurrence does however indicate the extent to which autocratic organization places members of a department at the mercy of the personal idiosyncrasies of the head.

In Non-teaching Departments

Members of non-teaching departments, such as libraries and the various offices, in addition to being excluded from any part in decisions affecting the welfare of the entire department, are subject to numerous special abuses. Among these are speed-up and overtime when the necessity is not satisfactorily established; inequitable distribution of work and responsibilities; purchase of equipment without consultation of those who will use it; inadequate arrangements for the physical comfort of the staff; favoritism; and the appointment of personnel which may be unsatisfactory to the rest of the staff. Grievances of such a type rapidly affect morale and impair the assistance rendered to students and faculty.

Friction Between Departments

The relations *between* departments as well as relations *within* a department are affected by undemocratic organization. Unsound conditions result whether departments are split and multiplied, or unified.

Where there is a multiplicity of departments, each one represents a vested interest in a share of the budget and the curriculum. Under autocratic organization, the fate of the department is intimately bound up with such educationally irrelevant matters as the department head's "aggressiveness" or his "weakness," and whether he "stands in well" with the higher administrators. The cooperation of two departments, though educationally necessary, may be at the mercy of conflicting department heads. Sometimes there is a struggle of principalities in a fashion reminiscent of political history. Often precisely those departments which should be nearly merged for educational purposes manifest the most competitive relations. If one acquires additional laboratory space, the other is offended and determines to fight harder. The acquisition of a brilliant scholar by one is regarded as a slight by the other. The introduction of a course in one may be fought by the other as an encroachment; and when a genuinely common course is to be offered there may be a struggle to determine under whose aegis it shall be given. The elimination of such difficulties would require not merely the removal of autocracy from departments, but a complete democratization of the faculty and college administration.

Where a department combines several subjects, autocratic

organization frequently spoils the fruits of cooperation. The members of the staff representing different subject-matter are not empowered to discuss cooperatively their various interests, nor to plan a unified curriculum. Instead the particular enthusiasms of a single administrator often operate to destroy breadth of interest. In investigating departments combining several subjects, the Educational Policies Committee was struck by the tremendous dissatisfaction of the teachers with the arrangement. There were cases in which persons employed to teach one subject were assigned to programs in different fields; cases in which the department head, being necessarily ill-informed on some of the fields of knowledge that his department encompassed, made random decisions; cases in which the development of courses in some fields was retarded by the department head's lack of interest; and so forth.

The consequences of autocratic organization extend to every corner of our colleges and universities. In seeking to remedy the situation we are concerned not merely with the question of fair treatment for employees, but with the profoundly educational problem of the tone and the very content of our professional work.

[Discussion centered with equal force on the analysis of the following objections that were offered to democratic educational administration:]

1. Will Democratic Organization Be Empty Formalism?

Democracy does not mean a mere counting of heads; it means joint decision on the basis of evidence cooperatively considered. Such procedure has many advantages. It minimizes individual error. It spreads the work within the department. It gives all members some responsibility. It yields a more thorough understanding of policies adopted. It makes available for the department the best that each individual has to contribute. Above all it reduces prejudice and arbitrariness since reasons for actions are required. Merely to consult the members of the staff separately is not democracy; it is only a collection of opinions. For example, a department head thinking a particular person unsatisfactory, seeks the individual opinions separately of a number of his staff. Each has some criticism to offer of the person in question and cumulatively there is an imposing case against him. But it may happen (and has happened) that each has something different against him, and would be ready to defend the person on the other charges. A fair and complete picture will appear only after interchange of opinion and careful discussion by the people concerned.

Democracy therefore requires a certain degree of organization. The degree will vary, of course, according to the size of the department or faculty. Democracy requires general meetings of the group including everyone connected with it. It requires decision by the assembly, after careful discussion, as to what groups shall have voting privileges on particular questions. For example, discussion privileges may be granted to all; voting on matters of personnel allowed only to those who have achieved tenure or served satisfactorily for one or two or at most three years; curricular decisions limited to teachers, or for special courses to separate divisions of the body, and so forth. Many of these questions will have to be settled differently for different kinds of departments or faculties. There need be little worry about preserving the authority of specialists in their own fields. In an academic community (especially since the pattern of graduate study so frequently involves discipleship), there will be sufficient recognition and respect for the man of specialized knowledge. It is but fair to expect him to make his point articulately.

2. *Will Democratic Organization Overburden Teachers?*

It is said that democratization will overburden teachers with administrative work. It is true that the democratic plan aims to broaden the source of initiative and assent, to make the direction of departments and faculties more sensitive to the desire and needs of all members, and to secure wider recognition of student needs. This should not be understood to mean that college government will consist in a great series of general meetings in which all manner of trivial questions are decided. It is rather in autocratic bodies that meetings sometimes involve serious deliberation over trifles, to convey the suggestion of staff participation. Though a period of experience and experiment may be necessary in democratizing departmental and faculty procedures, it will generally be feasible to delegate a large proportion of business to proper committees or individuals, or to elected executive officers. For example, while the addition of new courses or relation of existent courses is a subject for department discussion, formulation of syllabus will be done in committee. However, under democratic organization committees and individuals are responsible to the group as a whole, deriving their powers from it and answerable to it.

Furthermore, it is important not to overlook the significance of what may at first sight seem mere technical questions. For instance, the departmental plan involves a committee for the distribution of supplies. In many departments, such as physical science or psychology, this item determines eventually which aspects of the subject shall be stressed and what kinds of research and experimentation will be possible. Thus, the handling of "purely material" problems, such as space or equipment, may determine the cultural or vocational, scientific or literary, experimental or theoretical, content of the curriculum.

3. Are Teachers Not Interested?

It is also objected that teachers do not wish to participate in controlling department and faculty policies. Where this aversion does exist it is to the kind of tasks that autocratic organization imposes upon the staffs. Their share in administration is barren of vital issues of educational policy; even worse, they may be consulted only to be saddled with the responsibility for the dismissal of a colleague or the penalizing of a student. Such phenomena are not purely departmental; they account likewise for the dislike of faculty meetings on the part of many teachers. The democratic plan provides that teachers shall be given an opportunity to concern themselves with the matters of broad policy which influence their teaching at every point. To any one really interested in broadening the education offered by the college, such a concern should be neither burdensome nor dull.

4. Is Discussion of Salary, etc. Unprofessional?

Again it is sometimes said that to open to staff discussion such intimate matters as the salary, the tenure, or the promotion of individuals, would violate a certain sense of modesty. But any virtues this modesty may possess are destroyed by the air of intrigue, suspicion, fear and personal ambition which a system of autocratic decision engenders. Where all decisions in these matters are made by a small group within the department or faculty, morale is undermined by favor-currying, resentment, and uncertainty. It may be expected that the rational discussion involved in the democratic process will make deliberation on salary and promotion increasingly an occasion for the elaboration of concrete standards and diminishingly a question of personal relationships.

5. Are Younger Members Mature Enough?

Again, it is doubted by some that the younger members of departments are mature enough to exercise the judgment required in administration. But the democratic proposal does not center control in any single age-group. Indeed, the maturity so admired in a good administrator can develop only in contact with actual administrative problems. Where younger teachers are permitted to join in group decisions, not only will their enthusiasms be tempered by the longer experience of others, but it can be expected that they will develop into wiser officers than do those who, inexperienced in self-government, are suddenly placed in administrative positions. Furthermore, the younger person is likely to bring a fresh point of view into departmental deliberations, since he is more likely to be in touch with the needs and problems of the students.

6. Would Democracy Lead to Anarchy?

It is also sometimes urged that democratic procedures would so scatter responsibility and diminish the role of the departmental administrative officer that no one would exercise initiative, but each expect it of his colleagues. This objective, where it is not sophistical, rests on a misunderstanding. From the standpoint of the faculty and higher administrative officers, the departmental executive officer would continue to be responsible for the functioning of his department, even though he is elected and expresses a departmental rather than a personal will. His task would continue to be a tremendously important one—the exercise of initiative and foresight in suggesting policies, and of efficiency in carrying them out. The difference would be that plans would come from him as proposals to the department, and also that they might issue from other members as well.

7. *Will Departments Stagnate?*

There remains the serious objection that a whole department might possibly be "stagnant" or even "corrupt" and that democracy would only perpetuate this situation. It must be remembered that under the autocratic system, the "stagnation" or "corruption" of a single person is sufficient to secure the dreaded results. It is true that occasionally a new head overturns the state of affairs in a department, sometimes for the better—but it may also be for the worse. In a democratic department bad conditions may occur. However, this is not an argument against departmental democracy; rather it points towards the extension of democracy beyond the department, and into the faculty. For example, appointments within a department should be subject to review by an elected committee of the whole college staff (or where the faculty is sufficiently inclusive, it may be of the faculty); so should the dismissal of probationers, to avoid the likelihood of discrimination. Charges of incompetence against permanent members of the staff, while given a first examination within the department, ought to be largely investigated by a general college committee. Recommendations for special or multiple increments, or special promotions, ought likewise be subject to review. Thus there would be checks placed upon the possible abuse of power by a whole department.

Summary of the Revised (1938) Bylaws of the Board of Higher Education on Tenure and Governance

[*Author's note:* The following summary of the bylaws on tenure and governance was issued by the union to the staffs after the bylaws were adopted. Some central union comments and criticisms made during the consideration of the bylaws are added.]

Tenure

1. Permanent Staff

The Tenure By-law defines a *permanent instructional staff* of the colleges and other schools under the jurisdiction of the Board of Higher Education. This permanent staff consists of all persons employed on an annual salary basis, from Tutor to full Professor, who have served three full years and who have been appointed for a full fourth year. Permanent status may be granted by the Board to persons appointed initially to the professorial ranks after one year of service.

2. *Meaning of Tenure*

All persons on the permanent staff shall have *tenure* of office, meaning "that those persons entitled to it shall hold their positions during good behavior and efficient and competent service and shall not be removed save by an affirmative vote of a majority of the members of the Board, for cause, after due notice and hearing as hereinafter provided."

3. *Handling of Temporary Staff Members*

Where persons on the *temporary staff* are not to be reappointed, notice shall be given them in writing by March 15 preceding expiration of the term of appointment, except that notice shall be given by March 1 if reappointment is not to be granted after three years of service.

If before the expiration of the third full year of service, the appropriate departmental authority (the elected committee on appointments) is satisfied that such person is competent to be appointed to the permanent staff, and the Board approves, the decision of the Board shall be communicated to the person not later than March 1 preceding the expiration of the third full year of service.

It is explicitly provided that although the Board may assign any person having permanent tenure to any appropriate position on the staff, "no such assignment shall carry with it a reduction in rank or a reduction in salary other than the elimination of any additional emolument provided for administrative positions." If the Board finds it desirable to discontinue any position occupied by a person enjoying permanent tenure and can find no assignment which can be efficiently and capably filled by said member, his name shall be placed on an eligible list of candidates for appointment to a vacancy that then exists or may thereafter exist in his college or school, in a position similar to the one which such person filled or in any other position which can be capably and efficiently filled by such person. Such reappointment shall be at the last salary received by such person.

4. *Causes for Removal of Permanent Staff Members*

Persons having tenure may be *removed or suspended* for one or more of the following reasons: a) incompetent or inefficient service; b) neglect of duty; c) physical or mental incapacity; d) conduct unbecoming a member of the staff. Here the by-law adds: "This provision shall not be so interpreted as to constitute interference with academic freedom."

5. *Form of Trial, Etc.*

Charges against a member of permanent staff may be brought by a department head, dean, president, or Board member. Such charges shall be submitted first to the President, who in turn submits them with all supporting evidence to a faculty committee on personnel. This committee shall make such investigation as it deems warranted and file its report with the president who shall forward formal charges and specifications to the Board together with his own and the Committee's recommendations. If the Committee or the President shall recommend a trial by the Board then the Board shall proceed in the following manner.

The Board shall make service upon the person accused in the charges. Such service shall not be made between June 1 and September 1. The accused shall have ten days from such service of charges to file an answer in writing with the Board. The Board shall then fix a date for the trial and the accused shall be given at least ten days notice of such trial. A Committee of not less than three members of the Board shall be elected to conduct a trial. The accused shall be entitled to representation during his trial by any person of his choice, shall be confronted with the witnesses against him, shall have the right to examine and cross-examine witnesses and to produce witnesses and relevant documents. The trial committee shall then report to the Board, and submit to all members a transcript of the testimony. Not later than two months after the presentation of this report the Board shall render its judgment.

Organization of the Instructional Staff

Faculty Organization and Powers
The *Faculty* of each college shall consist of the President, Deans, Directors, all members of the professorial ranks, and such instructors as have become members of the permanent staff. Instructors shall have the right to vote only after they have served two years on the permanent instructional staff. (All present instructors who now become members of permanent staff shall have the right to vote if they have served five years as members of the instructional staff.) The Faculty may add to itself other members of the staff because of their educational responsibilities.

In every college or school of a college in which the Faculty shall exceed 100 members there shall be a *Faculty Council*, consisting of the President, Deans, Directors, and three delegates from each department, where available. The three delegates shall be the department chairman, one from the professorial ranks, and one instructor, the two latter to be elected by the voting members of their respective ranks in each department.

"The Council shall assume all the responsibilities of the Faculty, subject only to the right of the Faculty upon its own motion to review such action. A two-thirds vote of the Faculty shall be required to overrule action of the Faculty Council."

Where the Faculty is less than 100, its voting members shall consist of the President, Deans, all members of the professorial ranks and a number of instructors equal to 50% of the latter, to be elected for a term of three years by secret preferential ballot by the instructors who have been members of the permanent instructional staff for two years.

Each College shall have a *Committee on Faculty Personnel and Budget*, consisting of the President, as Chairman, the Deans and all the department chairmen. All recommendations from the several departments for appointment, reappointment, promotion, compensation or dismissal, shall be transmitted to this committee and it will recommend action to the President. The President shall transmit its recommendations, together with his own, to the Board. The Committee shall receive from the President his tentative annual budget and make its recommendations upon it. The Committee shall also receive and consider petitions and appeals from members of the instructional staff with respect to matters of status and salary.

Where a College contains more than one school there shall be a Faculty Conference composed of the President, the Deans, and three members of each of the several school faculties elected by the respective faculties or their councils. It shall be the responsibility of the Conference to act as a coordinating body with respect to problems of administration, budget and educational policy as those affect the inter-relation of the several schools.

As no specific reference is made to the mode of *Appointment of Presidents*, the presumption is that they will be appointed by the Board as heretofore. Deans, specifically, shall be appointed by the Board, though in making such appointments the Board "shall have the advice of the Presidents and the Committee on Faculty Personnel and Budget."

Department Organization

Each *Department,* subject to the approval of the Faculty or Faculty Council, "shall have control of the educational policies of the Department through the vote of all of its members who are members of the Faculty. The executive officer of the department is the Chairman, who shall be a person of professorial rank, elected by secret ballot for a three year term, by the members of the department who are members of the faculty."

Each department shall also elect a *Committee on Appointments* every three years, consisting of the Chairman and equal representation from each available instructional rank included in the faculty. All recommendations for appointments (with exception of special cases in which the President with certain restrictions shall have the right), for reappointments, etc., shall be recommended to the Faculty Committee on Personnel and Budget by the Department Chairman after a majority vote of the Department Committee. Department Chairmen shall be responsible for assuring careful observation and guidance of probationers.

"Each department may name such *other Committees* as it chooses and shall have the fullest measure of autonomy consistent with the maintenance of general college educational policy."

Promotions to the instructorship shall be recommended by the Committee on Appointments; promotions from the rank of instructor to that of assistant professor shall be recommended to the Committee on Faculty Personnel and Budget by the Department chairman only after a majority vote of all the members of professorial rank in the department. Promotions to the rank of Associate Professor shall be recommended only after a majority vote of all associate and full professors in the department. Promotion to the rank of Professor shall be recommended by the Faculty Committee itself.

[During the period in which the bylaws were framed and accepted, the union made numerous criticisms and suggestions as various proposals came up for consideration. The following principles guiding these criticisms were set forth in a letter to John T. Flynn after the first open hearing.]

1. The need for flexibility: That the function of by-laws is not to set out a detailed organization which while freeing one department may constrict another, but to provide the framework within which and the freedom by which different divisions in the colleges may work out (possibly experimentally) an organization to suit their educational needs. Hence,

2. The need for self-determination: Those actively engaged in the educational work of the various departments, sub- or constituent faculties, and faculties, should be given full authority within their domain to legislate on questions of policy and to instruct and review the acts of their administrators, work out their own, often varied, organization while preserving fundamental democratic responsibility, and in general solve their educational problems by cooperative inquiry and rational deliberation.

3. The need for developing the sense of responsibility and the critical awareness of the teachers themselves: Hence proposed modes of organization are to be judged not merely by the question "Will they reduce grievances?" or "Will there be fewer irritations?" but by their probable effect upon the members of the staff. Will they encourage the formulation of more objective standards of competence? Will teachers by developing a greater sense of participation and responsibility begin to reflect more on the purposes of the college and the needs of the students? Will there be curricular revision, and increased cooperative discussion of teaching aims and methods?

[From the union's point of view the chief shortcomings of the bylaws as finally passed (apart from omission of groups such as the noninstructional staffs) were the following:]

1. Lack of provision for protection of probationers. The board insisted on an affirmative act by college authorities in placing a person on the permanent staff. No statement of reasons was required in failing to recommend probationers for reappointment conferring tenure. The union urged as a very minimum that there should be review of an appeal where a probationer believes that there has been some special discrimination against him on grounds of race, religion or political belief.

2. The omission of tutors having permanent status from the faculty. This entailed as a consequence that they would have no vote in their department. Some departments had a large number of teachers in this position after as much as eight and ten years' service.

3. The constitution and character of the Personnel and Budget Committee. Composed of departmental chairmen it would tend to strengthen departmental divisions; its members would be reticent in hearing appeals to go counter to a chairman fellow-member; not being responsible to the Council there would be insufficient incentive for it to develop standards consciously in its judgments about personnel.

4. The method of promotion. This would tend to intensify rank distinctions, broadening them into divisions of interest. It would not be conducive to the development of explicit standards.

Notes

Preface

1. Abraham Edel, *Interpreting Education: Science, Ideology, and Value*, vol. 3 (New Brunswick, N.J.: Transaction Books, 1985).

Chapter 2

1. For example, Harold Laski's *Rise of European Liberalism* (New York: Barnes and Noble, Unwin Books, 1962; originally published, 1936). Cf. Guido de Ruggiero, *The History of European Liberalism*, trans. R. G. Collingwood (London: Oxford University Press, 1927).

2. Even a Catholic philosopher like Jacques Maritain, in spite of the strong opposition of Catholicism to communism, could still regard the latter in the tradition, seeing it as the last of the heresies. See his *The Person and the Common Good* (New York: Scribner, 1947).

3. James Burnham, *The Machiavellians: Defenders of Freedom* (New York: John Day, 1943), pp. 26, 177.

4. For example, Russell Kirk, *A Program for Conservatives* (Chicago: Henry Regnery, 1954).

5. Herbert Hoover, *The Challenge to Liberty* (New York: Scribner's, 1934), p. 1.

6. Herbert Hoover and Hugh Gibson, *The Problems of Lasting Peace* (Garden City, N.Y.: Doubleday, Doran, 1942), pp. 131ff. (on the fifth freedom and the managed economy); 201–3 (on the war as a crusade

for liberty); 208–11 (on the contents of liberty, as against the managed economy).

7. The sharp separation of liberty as free enterprise from all other positions is also found in the libertarian movement, which, however, accentuates personal liberties alongside economic ones in a more permeating individualism.

8. For a central manifesto of this type of liberalism, see Arthur M. Schlesinger, Jr., *The Vital Center: The Politics of Freedom* (Boston: Houghton Mifflin, 1949).

Chapter 3

1. A good general account of the early history of the colleges is to be found in Sherry Gorelick, *City College and the Jewish Poor: Education in New York 1880–1924* (New Brunswick, N.J.: Rutgers University Press, 1981).

2. The controversy regarding the founding of Cornell as a nonsectarian college stimulated Andrew White's notable book *A History of the Warfare of Science with Theology in Christendom* (New York: George Braziller, 1955; originally published, 1895). White cooperated with Ezra Cornell in the founding of Cornell University.

3. *AAUP bulletin*, vol. 24, no. 1, January 1938.

Chapter 4

1. *College Newsletter* of the New York College Teachers Union, April 26, 1938, p. 4, reporting the meeting.

2. Ibid.

Chapter 5

1. *College Newsletter* of the New York College Teachers Union, October 14, 1938.

2. *Bulletin* of the American Association of University Professors, April 1939.

3. *College Newsletter* of the New York College Teachers Union, November 11, 1938.

4. *New York Times*, February 16, 1941, p. 44.

5. *New York Times*, February 23, 1941.

6. For a study of the Russell episode, see the various essays in *The Bertrand Russell Case*, ed. John Dewey and Horace M. Kallen (New York: Viking Press, 1941). Appendix I reprints the decision of Justice McGeehan.

Chapter 7

1. For example, Mark Alan Siegel, a major participant in the legislative front of the events that in 1979 resolved CUNY's financial status, has written an interesting article recounting the episode ("1979: Saving the City University," in *PSCcuny Clarion*, the publication of the Professional Staff Congress at CUNY, vol. 18, no. 4, December 1988). Even within its brief compass, the roles of traditional feeling, legislative initiative, basic city interests, balance of forces, emerge clearly. It points, in effect, to a rich study in the formation of social policy.

2. The *Chronicle of Higher Education* reports faithfully both incidents of importance and studies pertinent to problems of governance. *Academe*, the bulletin of the American Association of University Professors, publishes both case reports and topical articles. Many of these, particularly since 1987, have dealt with themes and aspects of governance. The *New York Times* is a good initial source for incidents when they are striking enough to become "news."

3. The article is reprinted from the July 11 and 20, 1987, issues of the *New Republic*, which in turn has its own paradox, for Kirkpatrick's book in 1926, asking for a restoration of faculty power in place of the power of outside boards, was published by New Republic, Inc.

4. *New York Times*, Sunday, October 11, 1987.

5. *Chronicle of Higher Education*, October 13, 1982, p. 10.

Chapter 8

1. *New York Times*, September 13, 1987, News-of-the-week section, p. 9.

2. *New York Times*, January 10, 1988, p. 6.

3. *New York Times*, May 29, 1949, p. 24. Copyright © 1949 by the New York Times Company. Used by permission.

4. For a historical treatment of the growth of a cult of efficiency in elementary and high-school education in America, modelled on the growing corporate character of American industry, see David Tyack and Elisabeth Hansot, *Managers of Virtue: Public School Leadership in America, 1820–1980* (New York: Basic Books, 1982), part 2.

5. Cf. Paul Lazarsfeld and Wagner Thielens, Jr., *The Academic Mind* (Glencoe, Ill.: Free Press, 1958); Ellen Schrecker, *No Ivory Tower: McCarthyism and the Universities* (New York: Oxford University Press, 1986).

Chapter 9

1. Exceptions are, of course, to be found. See the article "Crusader on the Charles," by Helen Epstein (*New York Times Magazine*, April 23, 1989, section 6), on John Silber, president of Boston University. Epstein reports that in the eighteen years of his presidency, Silber appointed nearly 90 percent of the current faculty: "He reads most tenure and promotion files himself, often grilling candidates for hours on everything from their private lives to their political beliefs." She quotes also from S. M. Miller, a sociologist who served at Boston University from 1973 to his retirement in 1988, that he had never seen an institution so poorly administered, "B.U. feels like a royal court of an absolute monarch. He has his favorites, his loves and his hates. One's fate seems to depend on the monarch's moods and prejudices. The monarch does not delegate; I felt that I lived in Kafka's castle as played by the Marx brothers." Copyright © 1989 by the New York Times Company. Used by permission.

2. *New York Times*, Sunday, October 11, 1987, p. 64. Material

quoted from article copyright © 1987 by the New York Times Company. Used by permission.

3. As reported in *PSCcuny Clarion* (the publication of the Professional Staff Congress at CUNY), vol. 17, no. 7, April 1988, p. 1.

4. For an interesting case that shows how special context may determine a decision between bicameralism and unicameralism, see the University of Pennsylvania's *Almanac* of April 4, 1989. A professorial member of the Faculty Senate (which includes all schools) advocates withdrawal from the University Council (which contains representatives of faculty, students, administration, etc.). A central point in his argument is that the council purports to speak for the entire university community, but "despite the fact that the Faculty constitute a majority of the Council membership, their low attendance rate has the consequence that the opinions of the Faculty do not weigh heavily in either the discussions or votes in the Council." Apparently students attend in sizeable numbers. The lack of faculty attendance is attributed to the character of the meetings themselves. Another proposal offered has been to have a smaller, more directly representative body, but to keep the unified council of various groups as the voice of the university.

5. 444 U.S. 672 (1980).

6. Irwin Yellowitz, "Academic Governance and Collective Bargaining in the City University of New York," in *Academe, Bulletin of the American Association of University Professors*, November–December 1987, pp. 8–11.

7. Interestingly, the New York City Board of Education has attempted to turn the election of the thirty-two community school boards (with 288 nonsalaried seats) into an educational experience by preparing lesson materials on how decentralization works, with a social-studies curriculum guide (*New York Times*, Sunday, April 16, 1989, p. 35).

8. *Characteristics of Excellence in Higher Education: Standards for Accreditation*, Commission on Higher Education, Middle States Association of Colleges and Schools, 1982, p. i.

9. Ibid., p. 1.

10. For a critical analysis of the proposal, see Thurston E. Manning,

"Are the Secretary's Intentions Honorable?" *Academe*, July–August 1988, pp. 12–15. This whole issue of *Academe* is devoted to an examination of accreditation.

Chapter 10

1. See, for example, Laurie J. Bilik and Mark C. Blum, " 'Déjà Vu All Over Again': Initiatives in Academic Management," in *Academe, Bulletin of the American Association of University Professors*, vol. 75, no. 1, January–February 1989, pp. 10–13. The editor's introduction, "The Corporate University," p. 10, says: "By substituting 'management' from above for consensus-building 'leadership,' this ethic proposes a radical narrowing of our professional activity."

2. See, for example, W. H. Holley and K. M. Jennings, *Personnel Human Resource Management* (Hinsdale, Ill.: Dryden Press, 1983); R. W. Griffin and Gregory Moorhead, *Organizational Behavior* (Boston: Houghton Mifflin, 1986).

3. The separation of ownership and management was discussed as long ago as the early 1930s. See A. A. Berle and G. C. Means, *The Modern Corporation and Private Property* (originally published, 1932; revised edition, New York: Harcourt Brace and World, 1968). The separation was expanded into a whole social philosophy in James Burnham's *Managerial Revolution* (New York: John Day, 1941).

4. Cf. Abraham Edel, "Metaphors, Analogies, Models, and All That, in Ethical Theory," chapter 4 in *Exploring Fact and Value: Science, Ideology, and Value*, vol. 2 (New Brunswick, N.J.: Transaction Books, 1980).

5. For a general analysis of authority, see Richard T. De George, *The Nature and Limits of Authority* (Lawrence: University Press of Kansas, 1985).

6. This dominance has continued in the major twentieth-century schools of ethical theory. Utilitarianism rested ultimately on the preferences of the individual as hard basic data. Emotivist theory did not move beyond the individual's emotive or prescriptive utterance in an effort to win over others, and rights theory was content simply to af-

firm protections and opportunities for the otherwise unanalyzed individual. At the beginning of the century there had still been idealist philosophies that sought to understand the formation of individual character and aspiration in terms of the shape of material life and institutional functions within the history of the given society. During the century there remained a current of pragmatism to demand an understanding of the problems to which the preferences and emotive utterances and demand of rights were responsive answers. For the most part, however, these questions were relegated by the dominant schools to the sciences as causal matters or to genetic accounts, irrelevant to present *autonomous* moral decision. Thus authority was perceived as the content of autonomy. Only in recent decades has the pressure of social change made that autonomous decision itself so complex and so dependent on a fuller grasp of the context of decision itself—as evidenced in the spectacular growth of "applied ethics"—as to highlight ambiguity, uncertainty, tentativeness, and the need for a fuller reach of experience and innovation. In such a situation, the stress on authority becomes empty, and its waning brings a demand for an altered meaning to moral autonomy.

7. Quoted in Hans Morgenthau, *In Defense of the National Interest: A Critical Examination of American Foreign Policy* (New York: Knopf, 1957), pp. 257–58.

8. For an interesting sign of the waning of the concept of authority, compare its treatment in *Nomos I, Authority,* ed. Carl J. Friedrich (Cambridge: Harvard University Press, 1958), and in *Nomos XXIX, Authority Revisited,* ed. J. Roland Pennock and John W. Chapman (New York: New York University Press, 1987). In the earlier, authority is still a substantial concept whose role is being investigated. In the later, vagueness and pluralism have taken over. But even in the earlier, Hannah Arendt already entitles her essay "What Was Authority?", claiming explicitly that "authority has vanished from the modern scene."

9. The philosophical story of the way in which knowledge becomes understood as a collective product is of course long and complex. Among its major episodes are: the development of non-Euclidean geometry, which altered the interpretation of mathematical insight

from a grasp of absolute truth to the construction of alternative possible schemes; the dethroning of elementary sensory data as a fixed foundation for knowledge; the analysis of experience as involving purposive–selective aspects throughout; and in the long run, the realization from the study of the history of science of the complex interrelation of theory, observation, and logic in the production of knowledge, and how the body of knowledge can be self-corrective in further experience without any part of it being sacrosanct. The vast scope of the body of knowledge today itself underscores its collective social character.

10. In the history of political psychology, the Platonic scheme in which reason is an outside master over the passions was challenged by Hume's thesis that reason is the slave of the passions, that it has a purely instrumental character with no intrinsic ends. In subsequent evolutionary theory the passions are themselves seen to have a kind of reasonableness of their own insofar as they become stabilized in the organism because of their survival advantages (e.g., fear, an intimation of danger; aggression, a quickness of defense; sexual attraction, a path to reproductive group survival; sympathy, an advantageous sense of group cohesion).

11. J. Victor Baldridge, *Power and Conflict in the University: Research in the Sociology of Complex Organizations* (New York: John Wiley and Sons, 1971).

12. Paul Goodman's view is that the anarchist principle of free association is the best arrangement, not top-down management. See his *Community of Scholars,* in the paperback *Compulsory Mis-education and the Community of Scholars* (New York: Vintage Books, 1964).

13. Amitai Etzioni, *Modern Organizations* (Englewood Cliffs, N.J.: Prentice-Hall, 1964), ch. 8. For a variety of relevant sociological studies, see Amitai Etzioni and Edward W. Lehman, *A Sociological Reader on Complex Organizations,* third ed. (New York: Holt, Rinehart and Winston, 1980). For example: Michael D. Cohen, James G. March, and Johan P. Olsen, "A Garbage Can Model of Organizational Choice," pp. 144–59 (a formalization of organized anarchy, based on seven studies of universities—not without an appreciation of some merits for unavoidable sets of conditions); J. Victor Baldridge and Robert A. Burn-

ham, "Organizational Innovation: Individual, Organizational, and Environmental Impacts," pp. 160–73 (organizational factors as explaining organizational change); Harold L. Wilensky, "Blockages to Organizational Intelligence," pp. 194–206 (problems arising in hierarchy, specialization, and centralization); John W. Meyer and Brian Rowan, "Institutionalized Organizations: Formal Structures as Myth and Ceremony," pp. 300–318 (how rationalized myths affect structures).

14. Appeal to the Constitution may take different forms. An interesting one is found in William M. Evan, *Organization Theory: Structures, Systems, and Environments* (New York: John Wiley and Sons, 1976), ch. 7. Evan advocates an "organizational constitutionalism" with a concept of "organizational citizenship" that at one blow gives all within the organization the rights of due process and imposes on management fiduciary responsibilities to the members of the organization as beneficiaries. He suggests that this fits the desirable picture better than a democracy of voting, and of course much better than the bureaucratic paradigm.

15. For a discussion of the shift in the philosophy of education from an emphasis on teaching to one on learning, see Abraham Edel, *Interpreting Education: Science, Ideology, and Value,* vol. 3 (New Brunswick, N.J.: Transaction Books, 1985), ch. 10.

16. James A. Perkins, *The University in Transition* (Princeton, N.J.: Princeton University Press, 1966).

17. Clark Kerr, *The Uses of the University* (New York: Harper Torchbooks, 1963).

18. The case at the CUNY School of Law is reported in *In These Times,* April 6–12, 1988, p. 3. The decision of the appeals court and the revised governance plan are reported in *PSCcuny Clarion* (the publication of the Professional Staff Congress at CUNY), vol. 18, no. 8, May 1989, p. 3.

19. The issue at the Columbia Law School is reported in the *New York Times,* Sunday, April 16, 1989, p. 34.

20. For a more comprehensive treatment of this categorial shift in political and social theory, see Abraham Edel, "The Good Citizen, the Good Person, and the Good Society," in *Citizenship and Education in*

Modern Society, Proceedings of the Symposium on Citizenship and Education in Modern Society, Mershon Center, Ohio State University, April 1980, pp. 3–55.

21. For a formulation that continues to think in terms of administration as against faculty and looks to new and better administration under current conditions, see, for example, George Keller, *Academic Strategy: The Management Revolution in Higher Education* (Baltimore: Johns Hopkins University Press, 1983). For a survey of "academic authority" today, with a strong sense of its "organized anarchy," see Burton R. Clark, *The Academic Life: Small Worlds, Different Worlds* (Princeton, N.J.: Carnegie Foundation for the Advancement of Teaching, a Carnegie Foundation Special Report, 1987), ch. 6.

Index